Contents

Left *Tobermory Hostel*, Mull (see p.238) **Previous page**
Sleeperzzz, Sutherland (see p.244)

Introduction

Everyone has heard that holiday story from a friend, relative or neighbour – about the marvellous Spanish mountain inn, Turkish beachfront pension, Moroccan boutique riad or Thai forest eco-shack – the story that ends, triumphantly, *and it was only thirty quid a night!* It struck us that it's not a tale you hear told about Britain too often, and we wondered why.

After all, Britain is brilliant, and our Rough Guides to England, Scotland, Wales and the regions celebrate its inspiring destinations and world-class attractions. What's more, there's been a real renaissance in domestic tourism in recent years, as country weekends, city breaks and "staycations" have become a big part of the holiday market. British accommodation providers have raised their game, from boutique makeovers for hotels and B&Bs to an entire "glamping" industry of yurts, pods and teepees that barely existed a decade ago.

True, it can be expensive to holiday in the UK, and there are understandable gripes when it comes to handing over £80 or more for what looks all right on the internet but turns out to be a character-free, chintz-filled B&B, or when the best you can do as a family is an undeniably cheap but charmless chain "inn" or "lodge", sited on a main road near a trading estate. Could it really be that there is nowhere decent in Britain on a budget; that there's no amazing accommodation that won't break the bank; that there's nowhere, in short, to show off about? Off went our indefatigable researchers, and this book is the result – showing that counting pennies doesn't mean cutting corners when it comes to finding a great place to sleep.

Clockwise from top left *Ann Tyson's*, Hawkshead (see p.182); *Willy Wallace Hostel*, Stirling (see p.221); *One Broad Street*, Brighton (see p.43); *The Fort*, York (see p.169) **Opposite from top** *Houseboat Hotels*, Sheffield (see p.166); *YHA Ambleside* (see p.174).

Our selection doesn't limit itself to B&Bs and youth hostels, those traditional mainstays of budget British accommodation, though we found plenty that we think are great value for money. We were also on the hunt for boutique farmhouses, hip city pads, historic inns, offbeat hikers' bunkhouses and anything else that caught our eye, and we've come up with over 250 novel and exciting places to stay, from a twelfth-century Welsh priory to a Cornish pilchard press, by way of a Sheffield canal boat, a York convent and

a Highland vintage trailer. Crucially, unlike other accommodation guides, none of these places has paid to be included – every review is based on the independent opinion of our writers.

Not all our choices will appeal to everyone – some people want a hostel up a mountain, while others are looking for a chic city break. To help you decide, we've highlighted our authors' favourite place in each region (see p.6), and also recommended top picks for those seeking somewhere to take the kids, to travel to by public transport or to spoil themselves (just a little).

While the guiding criterion has been price, it's not the only thing that matters. Most of our selections weigh in at under £70 for a double or twin room, or £20 and under for a dorm bed, though prices are obviously higher in the more touristed parts of the country. But all our choices, even if strictly budget at heart, are big on the things that make a stay special, from super-friendly hosts and fantastic breakfasts to dramatic decor and lovely locations. Here, on our home turf, from Scilly to Orkney, East Anglia to west Wales, we're delighted to show you that quality accommodation abounds, even on a budget.

Author picks

Our writers travelled the length and breadth of Britain to bring you the best places to stay on a budget. These are their favourites in each of our thirteen regions.

LONDON Hampstead Village Guesthouse
Why stay in a bland chain hotel when the capital has a budget beauty in a hip locale close to airy Hampstead Heath? See p.16

EAST ANGLIA Old Red Lion Chilled out place in a medieval Norfolk village that's part hostel, part B&B, and all alternative and arty. See p.28

SOUTHEAST ENGLAND arthouse b&b
Canterbury's quirky, funky *arthouse* – as much gallery as guesthouse – is one of a very distinct kind. See p.44

SOUTHWEST ENGLAND Old Chapel Backpackers A cool café and bunkhouse with an excellent adjacent pub makes for a great stay near St Ives on the rugged Cornish coast. See p.74

MIDLANDS The Porch House Historic England comes to life in this charming Shropshire B&B fashioned from a half-timbered Elizabethan house. See p.82

SOUTH WALES Mandinam Hidden away in rolling hills, this peaceful estate has a choice of rustic-chic overnight options. See p.106

NORTH WALES Pen y Gwyrd Snowdon-bound hikers love the period-piece inn where mountain-climbing history was made. See p.132

NORTHWEST ENGLAND YHA Manchester Explore northern England's hippest city from its big, bold, purpose-built, canal-side hostel. See p.146

YORKSHIRE YHA Haworth This Victorian mansion-turned-hostel provides extravagantly decorated digs in the Brontë sisters' backyard. See p.158

CUMBRIA AND THE LAKES Shepherd's Hut at Crake Trees Manor Romantic bolthole that offers real countryside glamour in an idyllic farm setting. See p.178

NORTHEAST ENGLAND Barrowburn B&B, bunkhouse or self-catering, it's back-to-basics at its best, deep in the heart of Northumberland National Park. See p.198

LOWLANDS Loch Lomond Hostel The best address on the famous loch – a glorious former hunting lodge with magnificent views. See p.208

HIGHLANDS AND ISLANDS Am Bothan
Remote but cosy Hebridean island bunkhouse with a nautical feel that's the perfect base for exciting sea trips. See p.232

Agree? Disagree? Let us know your favourites at ✉budgetstays@roughguides.com – the best suggestions will be included in the next edition.

How to use the guide

We've aimed to make the guide as easy to use as possible and have split Britain into thirteen regional chapters, with establishments arranged alphabetically by their location, often listing remoter places under the nearest village. As well as a review, each entry includes full pricing information, a list of facilities, opening times and instructions on how to get there.

Details may change, and we'd recommend that you confirm them when you book. Prices, quite apart from rising over time, will vary according to the time of year, day of week and when you book. Unless stated otherwise, we have quoted the cheapest price for a given kind of room or bed in high season, excluding any discounts for YHA members, longer stays, quiet times of year or single occupancy.

Each chapter begins with a map showing all the places we recommend and a chart detailing the best features of each:

Real bargain Even in the context of the book, these places offer decent beds at refreshingly low prices.

Treat yourself Whether you're after huge rooms, the plumpest of pillows or extravagant extras, these establishments stand apart in providing that extra degree of comfort.

Family-friendly They may have great rates for kids or child-friendly attractions nearby, but more than anything these places will make a family feel at home.

Great rural location The setting might be pretty countryside or a wind-blasted moor, but head to these spots for a splendid break from urban Britain.

Outdoor activities Accommodation that's near great hiking, biking, windsurfing or other natural adventures – and which won't mind you stowing your dirty kit somewhere.

Great food & drink Whether it's a brilliant local pub, a Michelin-starred restaurant down the road or cracking meals on site, you'll eat and drink well here.

Dorms Shared rooms with several beds, usually single-sex unless you're sharing them with friends or family. Hostels offering dorms will often have private rooms too – we've noted where this is the case.

Public transport Leave your car at home – you can realistically get to these places by bus, train or ferry.

Above from left *Coombe House* (see p.65); *The Falkland Arms* (see p.47) **Opposite from left** *Old Red Lion* (see p.28); *Barrowburn* (see p.198); *Shepherd's Hut* (see p.178); *Mandinam* (see p.106)

LONDON

London is one of the world's most exciting cities, and, for a visitor, can be one of its most tiring. There's so much to pack in: so many areas to explore, so many buses to hop on and off, so many museums to scour, so many restaurants, bars, shops and clubs. If you've had the kind of fun you deserve, you're likely to be weary and footsore by the end of the day.

The capital is also one of the most expensive places to stay in the world. It's unsurprising then, that many visitors turn to the identikit budget chains when planning a trip – an effortless approach that leaves all the more time to make sightseeing plans. The chains are worth considering, for sure, but anyone who wants to fully experience the character and appeal of staying in this captivating city would do well to branch out.

London is enormous. Travel cards and rentable street-side "Boris" bikes make getting around relatively simple, but it can take some time to cross from one side of the city to another. Staying centrally, while being more expensive, will not only allow you to pack more in, but also means you can stop off at your hotel for a

while each day – it's reassuring and restorative to have a bolthole for some down-time once you've "done" everything from Buckingham Palace to Tate Modern.

The closer you get to the West End, the higher prices become – but there are good deals to be had. Literary Bloomsbury, with the British Museum on your doorstep, is perennially popular, and its old-fashioned guesthouses in Georgian buildings can prove excellent value. London hostels are more expensive than in the rest of the country, but there are a couple of excellent options – par-ticularly appealing for young people out to enjoy the city's vibrant nightlife. If you're happy to stay further out, you've also got the option of staying in a B&B in a private home – a wonderful way to get to know neighbourhoods such as Hampstead, Islington, Greenwich or Hackney that could lure you away from the West End for days.

Wherever you stay, you'll find most budget accommodation in old, listed build-ings. Rooms are often small, and large bathrooms – not to mention lifts – as rare as hens' teeth.

LONDON

NAME	LOCATION	PAGE		REAL BARGAIN	TREAT YOURSELF	FAMILY-FRIENDLY	GREAT RURAL LOCATION	OUTDOOR ACTIVITIES	GREAT FOOD AND DRINK	DORMS	PUBLIC TRANSPORT
16 St Alfege's Passage	Greenwich	14	13		✓				✓		✓
Arlington Avenue Guest House	Islington	18	10	✓					✓		✓
Avo Hotel	Hackney	15	12		✓	✓			✓		✓
Caring Hotel	Bayswater	12	2						✓		✓
Clink78	Bloomsbury	13	8						✓	✓	✓
Hampstead Village Guesthouse	Hampstead	16	11			✓			✓		✓
Lincoln House Hotel	Marylebone	20	4						✓		✓
Morgan Guest House	Belgravia	12	5						✓		✓
The New Inn	St John's Wood	21	3						✓		✓
Portobello Gold	Notting Hill	21	1						✓		✓
Ridgemount Hotel	Bloomsbury	13	7			✓			✓		✓
Tune Westminster	Lambeth	19	9						✓		✓
YHA London Central	Fitzrovia	14	6						✓	✓	✓

Clockwise from top left Hyde Park; the Millennium Bridge runs between St. Paul's Cathedral and Tate Modern; Hackney's *Avo Hotel* (see p.15) **Previous page** Looking east along The Thames

Caring Hotel

From the outside, the *Caring* looks like a far more expensive place – the street is leafy and peaceful, and the hotel is in a pretty four-storey building with stout white columns and cast-iron balconies. Even the location feels exclusive, tucked away in one of the nicer corners of Paddington, away from the alienating roar of traffic in nearby Queensway and Lancaster Gate. And one of London's great royal parks, Hyde Park, is just moments away. Inside, however, you are firmly in respectable budget hotel territory: the decor really is nothing to write home about, with all the panache of a corporate chain or a university residence. That's not a problem though, as the *Caring* is spick and span throughout, with tea- and coffee-making facilities in all the rooms and spotless shared spaces. There's a good choice of rooms, from full en suites to those

Caring Hotel, 24 Craven Hill Gardens, London, W2 3EA ☎020 7262 8708, ⓦcaringhotel.com.
Price 15 en-suite doubles £92, 4 doubles with shared bathroom £76. Various other rooms with flexible pricing options depending on number of visitors. Breakfast included.
Facilities Internet. TVs in rooms.
Open Year-round. Check in: noon. Check out: 11am.
Getting there Paddington, Queensway, Bayswater and Lancaster Gate tube stations are a 5–10min walk away. Numerous buses stop on Bayswater Road. A Boris bike docking station is nearby, on the corner of Craven and Devonshire Terraces.

with showers only (a shared toilet is in the corridor) and basic shared options. These cheaper rooms tend to be on the higher floors and there's no lift, but there are plenty of showers and WCs between them. The continental breakfast is perfectly acceptable for the price, and staff are eager to please – there may be no frills at the *Caring*, but there is friendliness in spades.

Morgan Guest House

Just minutes away from the tourist hubbub and roaring traffic around Victoria station, this peaceful, listed Georgian town house transports you somewhere else. To Europe, perhaps – or at least to Belgravia, as it sits right on the edge of Chelsea and feels far closer to Sloane Square than Victoria coach station.

It is all rather peaceful. The welcoming rooms are light and airy, individually and tastefully decorated, with original features – including fireplaces – wicker chairs, scatter cushions and huge mirrors. Some have iron bedsteads. Those with shared facilities have basins, and one spotless bathroom between just three rooms,

Morgan Guest House, 120 Ebury St, London, SW1W 9QQ ☎020 7730 2384, ⓦmorganhouse.co.uk.
Price 2 singles £58, 2 twins and 2 doubles all £78, 1 triple £98; all with shared bathrooms. 1 twin and 2 doubles all £98, 1 triple/quadruple/family room from £138; all en suite. Breakfast included.
Facilities Internet. Garden. TVs in rooms.
Open Year-round. Check in: 1pm. Check out: 11am.
Getting there Victoria station is a 7min walk away; the #C1 bus stops very nearby.

which is something of a luxury in this price bracket. English breakfasts are served in a room that, despite being on the lower-ground floor, feels flooded with sunshine – all splashy Provencal colours, sunflowers and oil paintings, with a cosy brick fireplace at one end. The little paved courtyard at the back is cute but not spectacular, and smokers aren't permitted to light up out there. Above all, the location is supreme. You're cheek by jowl with a cute cupcake café, the famed *Ebury* wine bar and some great coffee shops, and just around the corner from pretty Elizabeth Street, lined with chichi independent designer stores.

Clink78

Occupying the old Clerkenwell Magistrates Court – where Charles Dickens was a scribe, and punk band The Clash were hauled up for shooting at pigeons – the *Clink* combines history with funky styling to fabulous effect. The internet room and TV lounge are in the old wood-panelled courtrooms, jazzed up with disco balls and leatherette sofas; that's Dickens' face screenprinted on the judge's chair, upholstered now in bright yellow. You can even stay in a cell, with their wooden bunks, heavy iron doors and old (unusable – and clean!) toilets – they're tiny, but atmospheric. Spray-paint graffiti art adds urban edge, from the scrappy little fellers by each of the cell doors to the faux dressing tables and cherry blossom in the "de luxe" girls dorms, which have hairdryers, hangers and mirrors. Other thoughtful extras include daily walking tours and a handy travel shop selling everything from tickets to toothbrushes. The shared spaces, including the toilets, are clean and though the dorms can be small, the pod beds, each with a light and tiny locker, have partitions that afford you some privacy. This is no place for wallflowers, anyhow – it's a party hostel, with a lively crowd enjoying the Clash Bar downstairs; if you want a quieter stay, check out the smaller *Clink261*, around the corner.

Clink78, 78 King's Rd, London, WC1X 9QG ☎020 7183 9400, ⓦclinkhostels. com.
Price 30 doubles/twins with shared bathroom from £50, 17 en-suite doubles/twins from £60. Dorms: 432 beds in 4- to 16-bed dorms with shared bathroom from £10; 54 beds in 4- to 10-bed en-suite dorms from £14; 96 female beds in 4- to 14-bed dorms with shared bathroom from £12; 10 female beds in 4- to 10-bed en-suite dorms from £15. Breakfast and bed linen included.
Facilities Internet. Kitchen. Bar. Shop. Games/common room. Tours. Lockers.
Open Year-round. Check in: 3pm. Check out: 10pm.
Getting there The hostel is about a 5min walk from King's Cross/St Pancras station.

Ridgemount Hotel

B&Bs are ten a penny in Bloomsbury's Georgian terraces, but the *Ridgemount* offers something special – the warmth of a family home. You'll get friendly greetings and heaps of help from the sweetnatured owners, who have run the place for more than thirty years – there's a decorated tree in the lounge at Christmas, and grandkids toddle about the back garden (separate from the peaceful guest garden).

Yes, the patterned hall carpet may be a little worn and the wallpaper a little tired, but the entire place is spotless – including the shared facilities. The guest lounge, which has two drinks machines (coffee and tea are free, cold drinks aren't), is a comfy place to hang out and chat with other guests – repeat visitors, visiting lecturers, small groups of students – browse the lending library, or check your email on the single PC (wi-fi is free). Rooms come in all shapes and sizes, some quite small, but even the tiniest have elegant high ceilings and windows, and the en-suite showers are spacious. Those without showers come with basins, while shared facilities include baths, perfect for a post-sightseeing soak.

Ridgemount Hotel, 65–67 Gower St, London, WC1E 6HJ ☎020 7636 1141, ⓦridgemounthotel.co.uk.
Price 4 singles £48, 4 twins and 2 doubles all £66, 3 quadruples £108, 2 quintuples £125; all with shared bathrooms. 5 singles £60, 2 twins and 3 doubles all £86, 2 triples £108, 3 quadruples £120, 1 quintuple £135; all en suite. Breakfast included.
Facilities Internet. Games/common room. Garden. TVs in rooms.
Open Year-round. Check in: noon. Check out: 11am.
Getting there Goodge Street, Warren Street and Euston Road tube stations are all about a 5min walk away; buses #10, 24, 29 and 73 stop nearby on Gower Street.

YHA London Central

FITZROVIA

This is the kind of hostel that even non-hostellers love. In a quiet location, central but tucked away from the craziness, it's bright, clean, safe and friendly, and in this part of town it just can't be beat for price. Walk into the bright, buzzy reception area, which doubles as a 24hr café/bar and lounge, and you'll instantly feel at home, given a warm welcome by the unerringly friendly and helpful young staff. They don't take groups here – and if you're after a quieter, family place, then the YHAs at Thameside or Holland Park might be more suitable – but neither is it over-noisy or boisterous. Seven floors of institutional corridors, only accessible by swipe card, lead to the simple dorms, all of which offer adequate space and storage, with an electric plug and a light for each bed. Nearly all are en suite; those that aren't have showers and toilets right next door. Note that you can't specify dorm sizes when booking online through the YHA, so if you prefer a smaller – or a larger – dorm it's best to go through a third-party site. Incidentally, they're very near Radio 1, so expect lots of excited sightings of celeb DJs on sneaky fag breaks and pop legends being ushered in for interviews.

YHA London Central, 104 Bolsover St, London, W1W 5NU ☎0845 371 9154, ⓦyha.org.uk, ⓔlondoncentral@yha .org.uk.
Price Rooms: 1 two-bunk room and 1 double/triple-bunk room (single bunk above and double below), both from £36, both with shared bathrooms. Dorms: 47 rooms sleeping 4–6, all from £16, all en suite; 13 rooms sleeping 4–8, all from £15, all with shared bathrooms. All 4- or 6-bed dorms can be booked for the sole use of families and small groups, from £49 per room.
Facilities Internet. Kitchen. Bar. Café. Games/common room. Tours. Lockers. Breakfast available.
Open Year-round. Check in: 2pm. Check out: 10am.
Getting there Great Portland Street and Oxford Street tube stations are both about a 5min walk away, and countless buses run along Oxford Street. The nearest mainline train station is Euston.

16 St Alfege's Passage

GREENWICH

Follow the passageway next to Hawksmoor's St Alfege's church to this dinky old cottage, once a grocery and now a fabulously quirky guesthouse. Step through the tiny terrace garden, with its tangle of foliage – make sure to dodge the grumpy house cat – and knock on the huge wooden door. Host Robert Gray will greet you warmly into his beautifully designed home, full of curiosities and delightful pieces of art. Gray ran a King's Road antiques store before he became an actor – and then a B&B owner, and then a minor TV star (ask him about how *The Hotel Inspector* changed his life) – and his guesthouse bears all the stamps of his charming and none-too-serious personality. The smallest room, a single that can be converted into a double (with no room to fit a cat, let alone to swing one) is fine at £90, but it's best to splash out, if you can, on one of the large doubles. These are more luxurious, one decorated in cool *toile de jouy*, the other in warm golds and reds; fun touches include a pair of antique boxing gloves hanging on the bathroom wall. Breakfast is served downstairs, in a modern, comfortable kitchen where you will feel right at home.

16 St Alfege's Passage, 16 St Alfege's Passage, London, SE10 9JS ☎020 8853 4337, ⓦst-alfeges.co.uk.
Price 2 en-suite doubles £125, 1 en-suite single/double £90. Breakfast included.
Facilities Internet. Kitchen. Garden. TVs in rooms.
Open Year-round. Check in: flexible. Check out: flexible.
Getting there Cutty Sark DLR station is a 5min walk away.

Avo Hotel

Avo is an intriguing little boutique hotel that has carved out a niche all of its own. Incongruously set on a flyblown stretch in Dalston – a scruffy but hip Hackney neighbourhood – the building was once a family-owned newsagents. When a chain supermarket opened up down the road, the family followed a long-cherished dream and transformed their business into a hotel. Today brothers and sisters, mum and dad all muck in – working on reception, cleaning the rooms, chatting to guests – imbuing the place with a warm, welcoming cheer. They keep neighbourhood links strong, too, with an ambitious schedule of events – chocolate-making workshops led by the in-house chocolatier, vintage fashion shows, foodie potluck suppers – that pull a regular crowd of Hackney hipsters.

Avo Hotel, 82 Dalston Lane, London, E8 3AH ☎020 3490 5061, ⓦavohotel.com.
Price 2 standard doubles from £79, 2 larger doubles from £89, 1 suite from £99, 1 studio from £119; all rooms en suite. Breakfast included.
Facilities Internet. Bar. TVs in rooms.
Open Year-round. Check in: 3pm. Check out: 11am.
Getting there Dalston Junction, on the East London Overground line, is a 5min walk away; Dalston Kingsland, on the North London Overground line, is 3min further. There are also good bus links from Dalston Lane into central London.

The bijou reception area, with its book and DVD lending library, leads up to the super-smart rooms. The decor is uniform, but cosy and stylish, with mango-wood furnishings and local art and photographs on the walls. Bathrooms, gleaming in sparkly black marble, are rather glamorous, with luxury Elemis toiletries, and DVD players and iPod docks are standard.

Breakfast, a continental buffet that includes organic fruits and cheese, is served at rough-hewn wooden tables in reception. Greeting the day here over a cup of good strong coffee, you'll feel delightfully cradled in *Avo*'s sociable extended family.

Clockwise from left *YHA London Central*; a room at the *Avo Hotel*; The Old Royal Naval College, Greenwich

Hampstead Village Guesthouse

HAMPSTEAD

A double-fronted Victorian in a peaceful residential street, the *Hampstead Village Guesthouse* has grown over the last 35 years from a family home into a charming place to stay. Host Annemarie van der Meer brought up her four children here, and it's extremely kid-friendly, with endless wonders to discover – from the antique sleigh bed in one room to the free-standing bathtub in another – and quirky knick-knacks in every corner. There's even a house cat. It's not for everyone, though. The type of traveller who runs their fingers over the skirting board to check for dust, or who wants big bathrooms and bedding changed daily, might want to look elsewhere – but bookworms, thrift-store bunnies and daydreamers who can while away hours in a quiet, overgrown garden will be in heaven.

> **Hampstead Village Guesthouse, 2 Kemplay Rd, London, NW3 1SY** ☎020 7435 8679, ⓦhampsteadguesthouse .com.
> **Price** 1 single £55, 1 double £80; both with shared bathrooms. 2 en-suite doubles £95, plus 1 apartment sleeping up to 5 from £100 for 1 person.
> **Facilities** Internet. On-site parking. Garden. TVs in rooms. Bike rental. Breakfast available.
> **Open** Year-round. Check in: 3pm. Check out: 11am.
> **Getting there** Hampstead Heath Overground station and Hampstead tube (Northern Line) are a 5min walk away.

Surprises reveal themselves at every turn. A little sink is hidden away in a train sleeper carriage closet; a sober wardrobe disguises a pull-down bed. And open those tongue-and-groove "cupboards" to discover pretty (and tiny) Edwardian-style showers dappled with dancing light from narrow windows.

The location is idyllic, just footsteps away from Hampstead Heath. It's a short stroll, ducking beneath overhanging fuchsias and nudging past lush jasmine, to the Regency villa where Keats fell in love with his neighbour Fanny Brawne; casually stylish Rosslyn Hill, with its upmarket delis, gastropubs and café-bars, is around the corner.

Each of the rooms is different. "Marc" has a small balcony leading onto a tiny roof terrace. "David" is a stunner, with dark green painted radiators and woodwork – including the old fireplace – bare floorboards and a French antique steel bathtub. Downstairs, the Music Room fits in a piano and a pine dresser crammed with colourful crockery; the original wooden shutters are painted sunny yellow. The biggest bargain, however, is the studio, a garage conversion with its own small kitchenette. This sleeps five – and welcomes dogs – and, with its simple, nautical decor and modern fittings, makes a wonderful sanctuary. The smallest room, a single with shared bath, is an economical £55, but lacks the wow factor of the others.

Some details: every room comes with kettle and mugs, TV, iron, hot-water bottle and mini-fridge, and most have their own phone number. A cooked breakfast costs £7; in the summer this can be served in the mature garden with its weatherbeaten wooden chairs. Laundry can be done for £10; parking costs £15 per day. Meanwhile, wi-fi is free, and they can loan you a pay-as-you-go phone and a laptop for use in your room. But really, a stay at the *Hampstead Village Guesthouse* is less about the nitty gritty and more about the big picture – quite simply, the perfect hideaway for free spirits and bargain-hunters alike.

Clockwise from top left Nearby Hampstead Heath has ponds, views and is a fine place for a walk; *Hampstead Village Guesthouse* – through these doors, a free-spirited urban idyll lies

Arlington Avenue Guest House

In a quiet, raffish corner of Islington, this stylish Georgian guesthouse offers a home from home, and rather a classy one at that. While the decor is elegant, all artfully presented antiques and old prints, the atmosphere is informal – books and magazines spill out from every corner. You are given space here, and there are few rules other than displaying good manners and mutual respect. Guests prepare their own breakfast, for example, whenever they wish, from a selection of cereals, breads and jams – but are not expected to wash dishes.

The double room is the jewel, large and sunny, with a huge, comfortable bed, but the single, with its view over the back garden, is sweet, and has ample room for one. Some may not like having to trek two flights of stairs down to the sleek, modern guest bathroom – but so far, in the fifteen years *Arlington Avenue* has been welcoming visitors, there have been no mishaps.

You can't sit in the pretty back garden, tangled with greenery, but you're just footsteps from leafy, tranquil Arlington Square; hard to believe the thundering traffic of New North Road, the hip nightlife of Shoreditch, and the buzz of Upper Street, with its restaurants, bars, shops and cinemas, are just minutes away.

Arlington Avenue Guest House, Arlington Ave, London, N1 7AX ☎07711 265183, Ⓦarlingtonavenue.co.uk.
Price 1 single £40, 1 double £50, both with shared bathroom. Breakfast included.
Facilities Internet. Kitchen.
Restrictions No children under 16.
Open Year-round. Check in: flexible. Check out: 11am.
Getting there Buses #38, 73, 341, 476 and 56 stop on Upper Street, a 7min walk away, and buses #141, 21, 271, 394, 76 and N76 stop around the corner on New North Road; the nearest tube stations are Angel and Old Street (both on the Northern Line).

Stylish *Arlington Avenue Guest House* wears its elegance lightly

From left Lambeth's other palace: *Tune Westminster*; *Tune's* rooms are as frill-free or feature-laden as you can afford

Tune Westminster

A big hit in its native Malaysia, the *Tune* chain has brought its add-on pricing concept and minimal, modern rooms to London. You get what you pay for here. Literally. You can pay for wi-fi. Or not. Or towels, or TV, or a hairdryer – or not. It's not one of the city's most beautiful buildings, converted from a postwar office block on a traffic-choked corner, but it's next to the tube, and just a hop away from the South Bank. Rooms are clean and simple, anonymous even, with crisp white bedding and storage areas, folding tables, safes and four hangers. The windowless options are generally smaller – but they cost the same as the others, so ask when booking if you care about such things. Guests get breakfast deals at the coffee chain next door, and half-price copies of *Time Out* at the desk. It's all brisk, breezy and reassuringly straightforward.

Though you do tailormake your stay, there will be unknowns – some rooms are larger than others, and are allocated depending on how many of you there are and how long you'll be staying. They're adding another thirty rooms in 2012, and further London branches are in the pipeline. Incidentally, the pub next door, *The Horse*, offers free wi-fi.

Tune Westminster, 118–120 Westminster Bridge Rd, London, SE1 7RW ☎020 7633 9317, ⊛tunehotels.com.
Price 79 en-suite doubles from £50.
Add-ons include: towels & toiletries £1.50; hairdryer £1; wi-fi £1.50/hr, £3/24hr, or up to £10/stay; TV £3/day, £7/3 days, £10/stay; in-room safe £2/day; daily room cleaning £7.50 (otherwise rooms cleaned prior to arrival, and every third night, for free).
Facilities Internet. Breakfast available. TVs in rooms.
Open Year-round. Check in: 3pm. Check out: 10am.
Getting there Lambeth North tube station is just across the road, or it's about a 6min walk to Waterloo train station. There's a rank of Boris bikes on Baylis Road outside Lambeth North tube station.

Lincoln House Hotel

MARYLEBONE

You'll spot the *Lincoln House* straight away on this street of stern Georgian terraces – it's the one with a profusion of greenery and flowers brightening up its town house exterior. Inside, porthole mirrors and nautical memorabilia line pine-panelled, tongue-and-groove walls, while Indian brass ornaments, urns, framed etchings and fresh flowers add even more character. This is no cookie-cutter hotel, then, but a well-run, friendly place imbued with the personality of its ebullient owner, Joseph Shariff. Most of the rooms are a good size (though there are a couple of smaller bargain singles), with the odd dash of style – decorative cushions, huge framed mirrors – and tea- and coffee-making facilities, thermos flasks and mini-fridges. The en-suite shower cubicles are – there's no two ways about it – tiny. Unusually, a couple of rooms have been set aside for smokers.

> **Lincoln House Hotel, 33 Gloucester Place, London, W1U 8HY ☎020 7486 7630, ⓦlincoln-house-hotel.co.uk.**
> **Price** 5 singles from £69, 4 twins from £125, 8 doubles from £109, 4 triples from £129, 3 family rooms from £135; all rooms en suite. Rates decrease for stays of more than 2 nights, and are between £15–20 less/night for a stay of 7 nights. Overseas visitors can request a further 5% discount if paying in cash.
> **Facilities** Internet. Kitchen. TVs in rooms. Breakfast and dinner available.
> **Open** Year-round. noon. Check out: 11am.
> **Getting there** Marble Arch and Baker Street stations are a 10–15min walk away, and buses #2, 13, 82, 74 and 274 stop nearby on Portman Street.

Rates can often be lower than those quoted here, and twins go for £90 or so. Prices drop the longer you stay, and go down considerably at quiet times. They also offer a number of other ways to save money: a simple three-course dinner (£7) is served in the kitschy dining room, which is a good way to fill up before (or after) a night out, and laundry and wi-fi are free. All in all a great deal in an unbeatable central location.

Clockwise from left The *Lincoln House Hotel*; take a load off in Regent's Park; shops along Portobello Road

Portobello Gold

In a prime location among Portobello Road's ice-cream-coloured antique shops, *Portobello Gold* is a popular neighbourhood pub – always busy, serving food and beer to a mixed crowd of eager tourists and boho locals. There's a funky tropical courtyard restaurant at the back, complete with caged songbirds, weeping figs and flagstone floor, its walls lined with the black-and-white retro photos taken by Mike Bell, the pub's owner. Oysters are the speciality, but they do decent modern European food, too, and dishes from around the world. The whole place is tatty, quirky, noisy and fun – brimming with Notting Hill atmosphere, and a little rough around the edges.

> **Portobello Gold, 95–97 Portobello Rd, London, W11 2QB** ☎020 7460 4910, Ⓦ portobellogold.com.
> **Price** 6 en-suite doubles £75–135, 1 en-suite twin £80. Roof terrace apartment sleeping 6 £180 for 2, plus £5/extra person. Continental breakfast included.
> **Facilities** Internet. Bar. Café. Restaurant. TVs in rooms.
> **Open** Year-round. Check in: call for time. Check out: call for time.
> **Getting there** Notting Hill Gate, Ladbroke Grove and Holland Park tube stations are all less than a 10min walk away.

The shabby brio is carried through into the rooms upstairs; they're a tad worn, and most of them are very small, but they're clean, with en-suite showers and storage space, and certainly a brilliant deal for anyone who's here to soak up the nightlife and the location and not spend too much time in their lodgings. Rooms at the back are far quieter. The so-called "bridal suite", with its four-poster bed, gives you the most space, while the cosy maisonette apartment (not as fancy as it sounds) has French windows from the master bedroom out onto a roof terrace.

The New Inn

This may not be the smartest corner of St John's Wood, but it's quiet and perfectly safe, and just minutes away from the huge green swathe of Regent's Park. Hotel guests have their own entrance, so needn't walk through the bar to get in and out – but the pub itself, an unreconstructed, unpretentious Greene King boozer, is friendly enough that it will feel like your own local after a night or two.

You'll be given a warm welcome by landlady Jan or one of her staff, and led through narrow corridors to your lodging. Don't come looking for fussy flourishes

> **The New Inn, 2 Allitsen Rd, London, NW8 6LA** ☎020 7722 0726, Ⓦ newinnlondon.co.uk.
> **Price** 3 en-suite doubles, 2 en-suite twins, all £85.
> **Facilities** Internet. Breakfast, lunch and dinner available. Bar. Café. TVs in rooms.
> **Open** Year-round. Check in: 2pm. Check out: 11am.
> **Getting there** St John's Wood tube station (Jubilee line) is a 10min walk away.

or boutique styling: everything here is kept basic, clean and simple. Beds are very comfortable, and rooms – especially Room 2 and Room 3 – far larger than you would normally expect in this price range. More remarkably still, the en-suite bathrooms are huge. Breakfast (continental £6; full English £9) is served in the pub, where you can also get inexpensive Thai food, and the cafés, shops and patisseries of St John's Wood High Street are just five minutes' walk away. A well-kept secret and a wonderful bargain.

EAST ANGLIA

With its huge skies and flat, empty landscapes, East Anglia can feel a world apart. The M11 from London to Cambridge is the sole motorway in this easternmost corner of England; driving, you'll spend most of your time on winding lanes that take you on long, lovely routes through open countryside, or on coastal roads cut off from the sea by a swathe of salt marshes, woodlands and dunes. Train connections, on the other hand, are surprisingly good – particularly from London, with fast services to Ely, Cambridge, Norwich and King's Lynn – and the very useful Coasthopper bus service along the North Norfolk coast connects with the train.

Inland Suffolk, or "Constable country", boasts quintessentially English scenery, its picture-postcard old villages lined with half-timbered medieval and Tudor buildings painted the distinctive "Suffolk pink". Beautifully preserved Lavenham, with its renowned restaurants and gastropubs, is perhaps the most famous of the county's old wool towns, and while it has gone steadily upmarket – as has much of the Suffolk coast, studded with well-heeled towns like Southwold and Aldeburgh – there are places to stay nearby where you can relish the charm without suffering the astronomical prices.

Norfolk, known above all for being pancake-flat, is another fine holiday destination, whether you want to rent a barge on the Broads, take a city break in historic Norwich, or explore the footpaths and nature reserves of the otherworldly coast. For the most part, this shoreline has yet to scale the gentrified heights of Suffolk's coast, and it has a number of very good-value budget accommodation options – a couple of superb hostels, and some very inexpensive B&Bs – minutes from the sea and a few hours from London.

The other two counties in this chapter may not pack such a punch, but should not be overlooked. Cambridgeshire, of course, is dominated by its university town, but accommodation here is pricey. Head instead to the small villages a short drive away, which offer rural peace and affordable luxury. Or focus instead on historic Ely, a laidback little city with a glorious Norman cathedral, which is less expensive than Cambridge, and richly deserves a stay in its own right. Much-maligned Essex, meanwhile, can claim its own share of pretty hamlets – which tend to be far less expensive than those in the counties west of the capital, and are equipped with some great inns and B&Bs – and, in handsome Colchester, boasts the oldest town in England.

EAST ANGLIA

NAME	LOCATION	PAGE	REAL BARGAIN	TREAT YOURSELF	FAMILY-FRIENDLY	GREAT RURAL LOCATION	OUTDOOR ACTIVITIES	GREAT FOOD AND DRINK	DORMS	PUBLIC TRANSPORT
29 Waterside	Ely	31	④							✓
Bell Inn and Hill House	Horndon-on-the-Hill	33	⑪	✓	✓				✓	
Charlie Brown's	Colchester	30	⑩					✓		✓
Deepdale Backpackers Hostel	Burnham Deepdale	27	①	✓		✓	✓	✓		✓	✓
Manor Barn and Farmhouse	Happisburgh	32	②	✓			✓	✓		
Milden Hall	Milden	35	⑧			✓	✓	✓	✓	
Oak House	Gislingham	32	⑤			✓	✓	✓		
The Old Chapel	Horseheath	34	⑦		✓		✓			
Old Red Lion	Castle Acre	28	③	✓		✓	✓	✓	✓	✓
Poplar Farm	Sproughton	35	⑨				✓			
YHA Blaxhall	Blaxhall	26	⑥			✓	✓	✓		✓	

From top left *Bell Inn and Hill House* (see p.33); *Charlie Brown's* (see p.30); *Oak House* (see p.32); *Deepdale Backpackers Hostel* (see p.27) **Previous page** The Great Ouse, looking towards Wiggenhall St Peter

The watery terrain of RSPB Minsmere, one of two great birdwatching spots near *YHA Blaxhall*

YHA Blaxhall

YHA Blaxhall enjoys the best of both worlds. Tucked just behind the Suffolk Coast, it's in a wonderful area for cycling and hiking, with great birdwatching at the RSPB reserve of Minsmere, a watery terrain of reedbeds, scrub and dunes, and Orfordness National Nature Reserve, a shingle spit rich in sea lavender. It's a splendid spot for culture hounds too – the sense of solitude is palpable, but it's just down the road from Snape Maltings, which hosts the Aldeburgh music festival in June and a calendar of musical events year-round.

Occupying a former school, the YHA has high ceilings that give a welcome sense of space. Most of the spick-and-span dorms share bathrooms – the sole en suite, with six beds, is often used by families. An overflow dorm in the garden has bunk space for eight – it's big, and private, but a bit of a trek to the bathrooms. The star of the show is the double/triple room, which has cheery yellow walls, bright prints and garden views, and makes a lovely little hideaway. You can self cater in the well-equipped kitchen, while the airy dining room offers wine, beer and inexpensive, crowd-pleasing breakfasts and suppers. The lounge, with French doors onto the small garden, is comfy, if a tad dated – and it's roomy enough that you can sit and read if you prefer not to socialize.

YHA Blaxhall, Heath Walk, Blaxhall, Woodbridge, Suffolk, IP12 2EA ☎0845 371 9305, Ⓦyha.org.uk.
Price 1 double/triple with shared (disabled access) bathroom £31–41. Dorms: 2x4, 5x6 (1 of which is en suite), 1x8. Dorm beds £19.40–23.40, except in the eight-bed dorm, which is £10 per person.
Facilities Dinner available. Kitchen facilities. On-site parking. Breakfast available. Bar. Games/common room. Garden. Lockers.
Restrictions Good disabled access.
Open Year-round. Check in: 5pm. Check out: 10am.
Getting there *YHA Blaxhall* is around 3 miles west of the A12 on the B1078.

Deepdale Backpackers Hostel

BURNHAM DEEPDALE

Everything about this bright, friendly place is just right. Perfectly sited for the birdwatching, bracing beach walks and the fresh shellfish feasts found along the marshy north Norfolk coast, it's just strides from the coastal path and an easy hop from vast Holkham Bay and the lovely seaside village of Blakeney, with its seal-spotting trips. Surprisingly, too, for this remote patch of the country, transport connections are exemplary (the Coasthopper bus stops outside). There's a petrol station and handful of shops next door – including a small supermarket, and a caff for when you don't feel like cooking – with the excellent *White Horse* seafood restaurant in nearby Brancaster Staithe.

Spread across a couple of converted stables, the accommodation is spotless, cheery and stylish, painted in bold colours, with polished wooden floors and high beamed ceilings. Private rooms offer astonishing value, from secluded attic nooks to a light, dog-friendly double/triple with its own little patio, while the roomy dorms couldn't be more comfy. You're asked to be quiet after 10pm – a characteristically thoughtful touch. There's a sunny patio with barbecues and picnic benches, a huge kitchen, and a sunken living room whose local art, wood-burning stove and oversized lampshades give it real charm. All this, plus impeccable eco-credentials and an idyllic campsite offering tipis and yurts: budget accommodation doesn't get much better.

Deepdale Farm, Burnham Deepdale, Norfolk, PE31 8DD ☎01485 210256, ⓦdeepdalebackpackers.co.uk.
Price 1 double £30–60, 1 twin £30–60, 3 triples £45–80, 2 quads £50–90. Dorms: 2x6, 1x8 £10.50–15. Six-bed dorms cost £60–90 as a family room. Prices are at the highest at Xmas and in high summer. All rooms are en suite.
Facilities Internet. Kitchen facilities. On-site parking. Cafe. Shop. Games/common room. Garden. Lockers.
Restrictions Dogs allowed. Good disabled access.
Open May close for a short period in mid-winter. 2-night minimum at weekends for rooms; no minimum stay for dorms. Check in: 2pm. Check out: 10am.
Getting there Burnham Deepdale is about 25 miles northeast of Kings Lynn on the A149; a useful Coasthopper bus service runs regularly between Hunstanton and Cromer – and often from King's Lynn train station, too – stopping at the hostel as it heads along the north Norfolk coast.

From left Bold colours at *Deepdale Backpackers Hostel*; the grand sweep of Holkham Bay

Old Red Lion

CASTLE ACRE

There's something magical about this simple, welcoming spot. Painted deep red and covered in Virginia creeper, the *Old Red Lion* sits just outside a gatehouse in the medieval walled village of Castle Acre in northwest Norfolk. Set around a little green, with teashops, pubs and a couple of shops, this pretty place is a few strides from the long-distance Peddars Way footpath – an ancient route from Suffolk to the north Norfolk coast – and a perfect stop-off for walkers and cyclists. A splendid twelfth-century castle, featuring some of the best village earthworks in the country, is practically on your doorstep, and there is an impressive eleventh-century priory just around the corner. Mostly, though, the magic comes simply from staying here – not quite a hostel, not quite a B&B, but with the best of both worlds and more besides.

The *Old Red Lion* was once a pub, but you'd never know it. Owner Alison Loughlin has lived here (in a separate area) for nearly forty years, teaching yoga and welcoming travellers from around the world, and her warmhearted, alternative style infuses the whole place. You enter through a suntrap courtyard, paved with pebble mosaics, to the main building, where a warren of rooms, from twins to a ten-bed dorm, offer simple, cosy lodgings – all pine furnishings and floorboards, colourful duvets and kilim rugs. Photos and framed prints – from Bertrand Russell via Shakespeare to Gustav Klimt – line the walls, and there's a stove-warmed snug filled with books.

> Old Red Lion, Bailey Street, Castle Acre, Norfolk, PE32 2AG ☎01760 755557, ⓦoldredlion.org.uk.
> **Price** 2 twins with shared bathroom £50, 2 doubles with shared bathroom £60, 1 en-suite double £70. Breakfast included. Dorms: 1x10, 1x6, both with shared bathroom, £22.50 (£21 for more than one night). Dogs are welcome for £5 extra.
> **Facilities** Kitchen facilities. On-site parking. Breakfast available. Games/common room. Garden.
> **Restrictions** Dogs allowed.
> **Open** Year-round. Check in: flexible. Check out: flexible.
> **Getting there** Castle Acre is 4 miles north of Swaffham on the A1065. The hostel is 75 yards downhill from the Bailey Gate in the village centre. The nearest train stations are King's Lynn and Downham Market, both around 15 miles away.

The largest dorm offers eight cheerily curtained-off wooden bunks and two single beds. The smaller dorm, with three bunks, is simpler, with large wooden drawers for storage. There's also a sky-blue double and two smaller twins in rosy pink and sunny yellow. The bathroom and a couple of shower rooms are shared; they're nothing fancy, but all are clean, bright and well equipped. For a little more privacy, consider the two doubles in the annexe: downstairs, a charming room with accessible toilet; upstairs a light-flooded hideaway with a Mediterranean feel and a lovely en-suite shower.

The wholefood breakfast – muesli, fruit, bread, spreads and yoghurt – is a self-service affair, and there's a small kitchen for guests' use. Eat in the courtyard, or the large, airy Garden Room – this often gets hired by groups, so later on in the day you may find yourself rubbing shoulders with artists or massage practitioners. Evenings are best spent in the village, relaxing in the *George and Dragon* with a local ale and good locally sourced food. Back at your lodgings, sit out in the courtyard and stare at the stars, or curl up in the snug with a book. You may have the place to yourself, or you may find yourself chatting to walkers, cyclists and alternative therapists. The *Old Red Lion* follows its own rules, full of charm and character: surrender to its quirks to discover something utterly unique.

Clockwise from top left The *Old Red Lion*'s stove-warmed, comfortable snug; its red-painted exterior; the suntrap courtyard; Castle Acre's eleventh-century priory; what it says on the tin

Charlie Brown's offers sophisticated rooms in a medieval house

Charlie Brown's

COLCHESTER

Occupying a medieval building in the oldest town in England, *Charlie Brown's* has wisely resisted the urge to go chintzy. Instead, it's filled with vintage pieces, from antique blanket boxes to an Art Deco iron bed, with abstract art on the walls, contemporary bathrooms and jewel-coloured throws and cushions providing gorgeous flashes of colour. It has a warm, organic feel too, respectful of the building's great age, with rough-hewn wooden beams, softly plastered walls, seagrass flooring and thriving green plants.

Each room feels different. The four-poster room is bold and strong, the unfussy lines of the bed echoing the beams and the quirky slope of the floor. There's an airier, more contemporary feel to the mulberry room, but this looks directly onto the road, so can be noisier. The green room is smaller, but has two spectacular beds, and its private bathroom is larger and a little fancier than the en suites in the other two. You can spend a happy few hours learning about the town's Roman past in Colchester Castle Museum, and there are lots of good restaurants: just down the road from *Charlie Brown's*, the Tudor pub *Rose and Crown* and the brasserie *Old Siege House* are both recommended.

Charlie Brown's, 60 East Street, Colchester, Essex, CO1 2TS ☎01206 517541, ⓦcharliebrownsbedand breakfast.co.uk.
Price 2 en-suite doubles £60 and £65 (can be used as family rooms, £80 for 2 adults and 2 children). 1 double/twin/triple with private bathroom £50/£60/£70. Breakfast included.
Facilities Internet. On-site parking. Garden. TVs in rooms.
Restrictions Dogs allowed.
Open Closed Christmas and New Year. Check in: flexible. Check out: 10am.
Getting there *Charlie Brown's* is about 30min walk from Colchester train station; taxis and buses (#2, #62 or #78) are plentiful. It's slightly nearer Colchester Town station (15min walk, no taxis), which is on a branch line. There are parking spaces for up to 3 cars; mention when booking.

29 Waterside

29 Waterside boasts one of the most desirable locations in Ely, the pint-sized cathedral city that gazes over the Cambridgeshire fens. On an attractive old street just ten minutes' walk from the magnificent Norman cathedral and – as the name suggests – seconds away from the Great Ouse, it's a splendid base for exploring the city: the river is delightful here, with a winding footpath, friendly geese and ducks parading around a little green, good waterside teashops, pubs and restaurants, and a splendid arts centre and cinema, the Maltings, just around the corner.

> 29 Waterside, Ely, Cambridgeshire, CB7 4AU ☎01353 614329, ⓦhomepages .nildram.co.uk/~dtooth.
> **Price** 1 en-suite double £75.
> **Facilities** On-site parking. Garden.
> **Open** Closed 31 Jan. Check in: flexible. Check out: flexible.
> **Getting there** Ely is 14 miles northeast of Cambridge on the A10. *29 Waterside* is a 10min walk from Ely train station, which has connections to Cambridge and London King's Cross.

The house, converted from two eighteenth-century cottages, is cosy and cute, with lots of original details, and the one guest room, with an attractive Victorian-style en-suite shower, offers all the comforts you might need. Above all, though, it's the easy charm of the owners that really appeals. Charlie and Jude Chaldcraft are the most natural of hosts, and will endeavour to make your stay as comfortable as you could possibly wish. Breakfast is a relaxed, flexible affair – you'll be served whatever you fancy (within reason), and can eat either in the old beamed dining room or, in warmer weather, in the dinky walled garden, which is also the domain of the friendly resident rabbit.

Ely's magnificent cathedral is a few minutes' walk from cosy, cute *29 Waterside*

Oak House

Entering this fifteenth-century farmhouse in deepest Suffolk is like entering a fairy tale. But don't come expecting country-cottage twee. Owners Kathy and Tom Brooke are still in the process of a painstaking restoration, respecting the timeworn, wonky beauty of the building while enlivening it with their own magpie aesthetic. Jaunty 50s lampshades, candles in teacups, Indonesian masks, a vintage accordion – that offbeat style may look effortless, but everything is placed with wit and love. Only one room, the largest, has an en suite – a burlesque boudoir extravaganza with a claw-foot tub. Climbing a crazily narrow staircase brings you to a couple of snug doubles under the eaves – the floors slope even more dramatically here than elsewhere, and in one corner the door and the medieval beams have been painted shocking pink. Breakfast is taken in the brick-floored kitchen; you can also dine here, with the

Oak House, Mill St, Gislingham, Suffolk, IP23 8JT ☎ **01379 788959,** ⓦ**oakhousesuffolk.co.uk.**
Price 2 doubles with shared bath £55, 1 double with private bathroom £70, 1 en-suite double £110. Breakfast included.
Facilities Internet. Lunch and dinner available. On-site parking. Games/common room. Garden. TVs in rooms. Bike hire.
Restrictions Dogs allowed.
Open Year-round. Check in: flexible. Check out: noon.
Getting there Gislingham is around 18 miles northeast of Bury St Edmunds and is accessible from the A14 and A12. The nearest train stations are Diss and Stowmarket (both about 9 miles away), from where there are buses.

family or privately. The home-cooked food, served in a typically idiosyncratic and cheery dining room, is simple and delicious. If you can drag yourself away, head out to explore the quaint village of Gislingham and a variety of lovely rural walks and cycle rides; Tom, a keen wild swimmer, can direct you to some splendid swimming spots nearby.

Manor Barn and Farmhouse

There's an edge-of-the-earth feel to this remote stretch of Norfolk. It's a superb area for cycling, and its unspoiled beaches – including Horsey, with its resident seals – rarely get crowded. Happisburgh itself, literally falling into the sea, is a dramatic spot, its roaring waves slowly eating into the village's shored-up cliffs – and recent archeological finds here have provided the earliest evidence of human habitation in Britain.

This lovely B&B makes a perfect base. In the main house – a handsome part-Tudor, part-Georgian family home – choose between a grand en-suite double/ twin or a charming double, bathed in light, its beautiful bathroom boasting a roll-top bath and shower. The thatched sixteenth-century barn is a delightful bolt hole, with its own guest lounge and three simple, comfortable en-suite bedrooms. One has a four poster, while the two on the upper floor, with high vaulted ceilings, feel private and serene. Big breakfasts are

Manor Farmhouse, Happisburgh, Norfolk, NR12 0SA ☎ **01692 651262,** ⓦ**manorbarnnorfolk.co.uk.**
Price Barn: 3 en-suite doubles £55. Farmhouse: 1 en-suite double £70. 1 double with private bathroom £55. Breakfast included. Discounts for longer stays.
Facilities Internet. Dinner available. On-site parking. Games/common room. Garden. TVs in rooms.
Restrictions No children under 7.
Open Farmhouse open mainly in summer. Barn open all year, but self-catering only at Xmas and New Year. Check in: call for time. Check out: flexible.
Getting there Happisburgh is 17 miles from Norwich and 9 miles northeast of Wroxham off the A149. The B&B lies a mile inland on the Stalham side of Happisburgh.

served in the main house, around a communal table in the wood-panelled dining room. Hostess Rosie Eldridge couldn't be nicer, going out of her way to give guests as relaxed a stay as possible.

Clockwise from top left *Oak House*'s en-suite double and exterior; the bar at *Bell Inn*; ivy-covered *Hill House*

Bell Inn and Hill House

HORNDON-ON-THE-HILL

This fifteenth-century hilltop tavern was once on the main route between London and Colchester, and still has the warmth of a wayfarer's inn. Owned by the same family for 75 years, it's now a superb, friendly gastropub, with a warren of rooms in the ancient building and eleven more in the Georgian *Hill House* next door. You get real luxury for your money here, and at less than an hour's drive from London, it makes a great getaway for capital dwellers. There are pretty walking trails nearby, and you're just a hop away from Henry VIII's Tilbury Fort on the Thames Estuary.

Above the pub, five opulent suites are dedicated to formidable women from Lady Hamilton to Josephine; all are huge, and might feature a sleigh bed, a four-poster or a clawfoot tub. Tilting walls, gnarled beams and thick plaster walls attest to the building's age, while widescreen TVs, comfy sofas and luxurious bathrooms provide modern comforts. In *Hill House*, you're spoilt for choice: three upmarket motel-type rooms with modern wetrooms; an amazing two-level suite with a spiral staircase and a stunning bathroom; a light, modern, Far-Eastern-themed option; or the funky little Captain's Cabin, with a mezzanine bed. Room 6 has a medieval vibe and an office annexe; Room 5, tucked away in the attic, is rustic and charming.

The Bell Inn, High Road, Horndon-on-the-Hill, Essex, SS17 8LD ☎01375 642463, ⓦbell-inn.co.uk.
Price 3 en-suite doubles £50. 7 en-suite doubles £60. 6 larger suites £75 during the week, £85 at the weekend. Breakfast £5–10.
Facilities Internet. Dinner available. On-site parking. Lunch available. Breakfast available. Bar. Café. Garden. TVs in rooms.
Restrictions Dogs allowed. Good disabled access.
Open Closed Christmas Day and Boxing Day. Check in: 2pm. Check out: 11am.
Getting there Horndon-on-the-Hill is an hour's drive from London, just off the A13, about 5 miles from the M25 and 5 miles southwest of Basildon.

The Old Chapel

Tucked behind an unassuming facade on an unassuming lane in a quiet Cambridgeshire village, the Old Chapel combines all the comforts of a luxury hotel with the warmth of a friendly B&B. You're just 12 miles from Cambridge here, and it makes a superb base.

Hosts Ian and Alex Rose are "people" people and their elegant home, while impeccable, reflects their delightful lack of pretension. The cosy lounge, book-stuffed library and leafy conservatory just beg to be curled up in, and easy country walks head off from the end of the back garden. Bedrooms – also filled with books – are fabulous, with super-comfortable beds, fresh-as-can-be linens, pretty throws, fat cushions, fresh flowers and luxuriant carpets. No detail has been missed. Even the tea- and coffee-making facilities include a cafetiere and fresh coffee, tins of biscuits and big bowls of fruit. Robes are provided, along with a raft of unexpected extras – the bathrooms brim with fancy toiletries, hairspray, deodorant and toothbrush rechargers. Oh, and did we mention the sauna? Breakfast is eaten in the heart of the house, the huge kitchen – the actual Old Chapel – which centres on a convivial communal table and is warmed by a wood-burning stove. You'll leave feeling nourished, revived and relaxed.

The Old Chapel, West Wickham Rd, Horseheath, Cambridgeshire, CB21 4QA
☎01223 894027, ⓦtheoldchapelbandb.co.uk.
Price 1 double with private bathroom £75, 1 en-suite double £80, 1 single with private bathroom £55. Breakfast included.
Facilities Internet. On-site parking. Garden. TVs in rooms.
Open Year-round. Check in: flexible. Check out: flexible.
Getting there Horseheath is around 12 miles southeast of Cambridge, off the A11; there's a bus (13/13A) from Cambridge.

The Old Chapel's book-stuffed library and fabulous bedrooms

Milden Hall

This charming part of Suffolk, at the heart of East Anglia's medieval cloth trade, is famed for its historic and unfeasibly picturesque half-timbered villages. Tucked down a quiet lane 3 miles or so from Lavenham – one of the prettiest villages of all, with its splendid old pubs and restaurants – *Milden Hall* offers an idyllic base. Prepare yourself, as you sweep up the long driveway, for something special: this sixteenth-century hall farmhouse, given an elegant Georgian makeover, makes a stunning first impression. Yet, crammed with old books and magazines, historical prints and paintings, comfy period furniture and offbeat personal heirlooms, this is above all a family home, humming with life. The smallest guest room, a twin, is quite large enough, but the other two are enormous. The star is the Adams Room, with its fine Georgian woodwork, lofty ceilings and vast windows overlooking ancient meadows. While the bathroom's not luxurious, everything is comfortable, and the locally sourced, organic breakfasts are delicious. The grounds stretch for 500 acres, with farmland, woods and nature trails to explore. The family, conservationists and ecologists, can lend you bikes and arm you with a map – their love for the place is infectious.

Milden Hall, Milden, near Lavenham, Suffolk, CO10 9NY ☎ 01787 247235, ⓦ thehall-milden.co.uk.
Price Adams and Gallery doubles £70–90. Becker twin £65–80. Lower rates are for 2-night and midweek stays. 1 bathroom/toilet and 1 additional toilet shared between the three rooms. Breakfast included.
Facilities Internet. On-site parking. Games/common room. Garden. TVs in rooms. Bike hire available.
Open Occasionally closed during the owners' holidays. Check in: 4pm. Check out: 10am.
Getting there *Milden Hall* is 3.5 miles southeast of Lavenham. The front drive is on a sharp bend on the B1115 between Milden crossroads and Little Waldingfield. Sudbury, 15min away by taxi, is the nearest station.

Poplar Farm

Poplar Farm is one of that fine British breed: a sprawling, cosy traditional farmhouse. There are lots of arty touches, fresh flowers in all the rooms, a pair of very friendly dogs and books everywhere you look. It's worn in places, as the best-loved homes are, and hostess Sally Sparrow will welcome you like a friend. Though surrounded by countryside, you're just ten minutes' drive from Ipswich, and well placed for the Stour Valley's half-timbered villages and Constable connections. All three guest rooms in the main house – a twin with beamed walls, a light room large enough for a family and a smaller, quieter double – have super-soft cotton quilts and cheery rugs. An annexe in the courtyard holds another, more modern room: your own private hideaway, with, get this, your own private sauna. Make sure to spend time pottering about the five acres of grounds – the rambling wooded gardens reveal lovely hidden corners (and a secluded yurt), with fruit, veg and flower patches, and rescue hens pecking at the soil. If you're feeling sporty, you can use the tennis courts or take a dip in the pool – luxuries that are just the icing on the cake at this splendid little spot.

Poplar Farm, Poplar Lane, Sproughton, near Ipswich, Suffolk, IP8 3HL ☎ 01473 601211, ⓦ poplarfarmhousesuffolkbb.eu.
Price 3 doubles with private bathrooms £65, 1 courtyard en-suite double £65. Breakfast included.
Facilities Internet. On-site parking. Games/common room. Garden. TVs in rooms.
Restrictions Dogs allowed.
Open Year-round. Check in: call for time. Check out: 11am.
Getting there *Poplar Farm* is just off the A12, around 10min drive west of Ipswich, the nearest train station, with connections to London Liverpool Street and Norwich.

SOUTHEAST ENGLAND

Curling itself around London in a broad sweep, the Southeast takes in a varied range of destinations, from the cheap-and-cheerful resorts of the Kent coast to the refined villages of Oxfordshire. Kent, Sussex and Hampshire are the most obvious holiday spots; here you'll find the ancient cathedral town of Canterbury, the foodie area (it's gastropub heaven) around the arty little seaside town of Whitstable, and Brighton, which lords it over the otherwise quiet Sussex coast with its cosmopolitan restaurants, funky shops and lively nightlife.

There are pockets of blissful peace and quiet in the southeast, too: the South Downs National Park – Britain's newest, which stretches from Hampshire to East Sussex – offers fine walking on the South Downs Way, while the New Forest, where wild ponies roam free and dappled paths head off from village greens into the woods, can feel like a world apart. On the southern edge of the forest, the remote stretch of coast between the Isle of Wight and Bournemouth has its own breezy charms, fringed with shingle beaches and tidal marshes. Even the commuter belt counties of Surrey and Buckinghamshire, commonly dismissed as little more than well-heeled suburbs of London, offer sweet pockets of rural charm perfect for pretty

country walks – and some quirky old hostels to use as a base.

In Oxfordshire, most visitors are heading for the county town, with its dreaming spires, but plenty of picturesque villages nearby offer good-value, less crowded alternatives. The Isle of Wight, meanwhile, a quick hop from the mainland, has done a lot in recent years to shake off its fogeyish reputation and serves its increasingly youthful visitors – here for the festivals, the beaches and the nightlife – rather well.

You can pay a lot in this region, much of which is covered by the home counties, where prices – for anything – aren't low, and rooms less than £90 rare. But we've dug out some real gems here, offering fantastic value. The fact that most are within a couple of hours of London – making them particularly appealing as weekend destinations for capital-dwellers – makes it worth considering visiting mid-week, when everything is quieter and many places drop their prices as a matter of course. Road connections with London are good, with the main roads sprawling out from the M25, but it'll take longer than you might expect to drive east to west – from Canterbury to the New Forest for example. The railway fills in the gaps, and in many cases – notably on the route from London to the Sussex coast – hopping on a train will be far faster than driving.

SOUTHEAST ENGLAND

NAME	LOCATION	PAGE		REAL BARGAIN	TREAT YOURSELF	FAMILY-FRIENDLY	GREAT RURAL LOCATION	OUTDOOR ACTIVITIES	GREAT FOOD AND DRINK	DORMS	PUBLIC TRANSPORT
arthouse b&b	Canterbury	44	15						✓		✓
The Big Sleep	Eastbourne	46	13			✓					✓
The Cherry Tree	Kingston Blount	49	8				✓				
Court Hill Centre	Wantage	51	3				✓	✓		✓	
The Falkland Arms	Great Tew	47	4				✓		✓		
Kasbah	Isle of Wight	48	6						✓		✓
Kipps	Brighton	43	12	✓					✓	✓	✓
The Linen Shed	Boughton under Blean	40	14		✓	✓			✓		
One Broad Street	Brighton	43	11			✓			✓		✓
Vinegar Hill Pottery and B&B	Milford on Sea	50	2		✓	✓	✓				
Wetherdown Lodge	Petersfield	51	7				✓	✓	✓	✓	
Wych Green Cottage	Bramshaw	41	1		✓	✓	✓	✓	✓		
YHA Jordans	Jordans	49	9				✓	✓	✓	✓	
YHA Oxford	Oxford	50	5			✓			✓	✓	✓
YHA Tanners Hatch	Dorking	46	10				✓	✓	✓	✓	

Clockwise from top left *Vinegar Hill Pottery and B&B* (see p.50); The Needles, Isle of Wight; *Wych Green Cottage* (see p.41); fish and chips in Brighton **Previous page** The South Downs near Pulborough, West Sussex

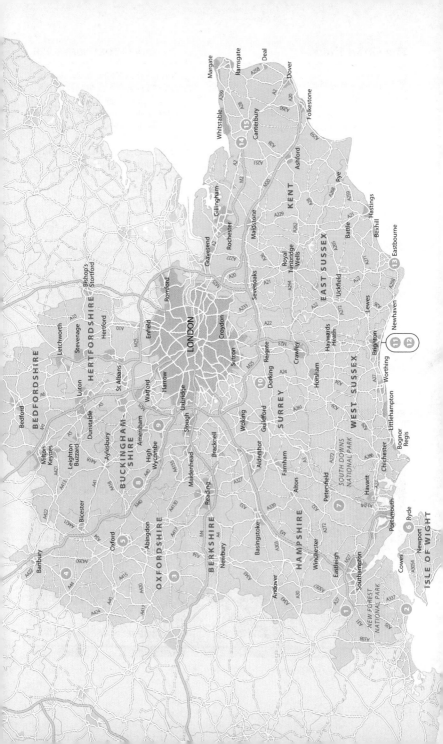

The Linen Shed

This dove-grey clapboard house, raised above the street behind a lush front garden, is not your standard B&B. The house itself, fashioned from a couple of vintage Nissen huts, has been imaginatively restored – light floods in through skylights and French windows, while bare floorboards, weathered wood, muted eau-de-nil and chalky hues create a soft, welcoming feel. As for the decor – everything has a story, from the old velvet sofas to the sewing-machine factory chairs in the kitchen. Warmly welcomed by Vickie and Graham Miles, and perhaps their two tabby cats, you'll instantly feel at home – make a cuppa, pop a bottle in the fridge, and linger awhile on the back veranda. Staying in one room – dazzling in powder grey and white, with Deco-style glass cabinets and a wall of retro mirrors – you'll share the bathroom with your hosts. The other two, larger rooms have a French provincial feel and their own beautiful antique bathrooms nearby. For dinner, head a few miles to the coast and dine on oysters at Whitstable, or splash out at the *Sportsman* gastropub in Seasalter. This corner of Kent is foodie heaven – even the local pub is a cut above, serving good real ales and tasty meals. Save room for Vickie's gourmet breakfasts, though; and prepare yourself for a wrench when it's time to leave.

> **The Linen Shed, 104 The Street, Boughton under Blean, Kent, ME13 9AP** ☎01227 752271, Ⓦthelinenshed.com.
> **Price** 1 double with shared bathroom £80. 2 doubles with private bathroom £85/£90. Breakfast included.
> **Facilities** Internet. On-site parking. Garden.
> **Restrictions** Dogs allowed.
> **Open** Open year-round. Check in: flexible. Check out: 11am.
> **Getting there** Boughton lies 3 miles east of Faversham and 7 miles southwest of Whitstable, less than a mile from Junction 7 of the M2. There are hourly trains from London Victoria to Selling train station, 10min drive away.

You'll feel right at home in Kent's imaginatively restored *Linen Shed*

Wych Green Cottage offers bucolic charm and great breakfasts in the heart of the New Forest

Wych Green Cottage

BRAMSHAW

Watch out for the piglets! And the ponies. And the sheep. Oh, and the peacock. You'll weave your way through a host of nonchalant animals to get to *Wych Green Cottage*, which lies in a glorious spot in the heart of the New Forest. Local horses and pigs wander freely down dappled lanes and across village greens; you may even come across a group of them settled contentedly in the middle of the road. It couldn't be more idyllic – you'd never guess that the M27 is minutes away – and the house itself is delightfully traditional with beams and leaded windows.

Rooms here are small, comfy and quiet, decorated country-cottage style with modern touches. Two self-contained units in the flower-filled back garden offer more space, and privacy, with little outdoor seating areas. Thoughtful details abound throughout, with mini-fridges, fresh milk, CD players (with CDs), sewing kits, ironing boards and decks of cards. The *Green Dragon*, a couple of miles away, serves delicious home-cooking and real ales, while in the morning a *Wych Green* breakfast – big bowls of fresh berries with yoghurt, a full English with eggs from their own chickens, and mountains of toast with home-made jams – will set you up for a day's walking or cycling in the forest.

Wych Green Cottage, Bramshaw, Hampshire, SO43 7JF ☎023 8081 2561, Ⓦwychgreencottage.co.uk.
Price 1 en-suite double in the main house £75 (£70 per night for more than 1 night). 1 en-suite single in the main house £45. 2 en-suite doubles in the back garden £75. Breakfast included. A three-bedroom detached cottage, sleeping 5, can be booked as B&B (prices on application).
Facilities Internet. On-site parking. Garden. TVs in rooms.
Open Year-round. Check in: 4pm. Check out: 10am.
Getting there Wych Green is in the north of the New Forest on the B3079, near the village of Bramshaw; junction 1 of the M27 is just 10 miles away.

Clockwise from top Sun and shingle on Brighton Beach; supercool comfort at *One Broad Street*; the Royal Pavillion; outside *One Broad Street*

Kipps

There are some party hostels in Brighton, the bohemian queen bee of the staid Sussex coast, but this delightful place isn't one of them. Homely and exceptionally friendly, *Kipps* has more of the feel of a small European hotel than an institutional hostel or a grungy-but-cool backpackers. They have socials here, for sure – but they're based around cake and movies rather than karaoke and bikini nights. A lot of effort has gone into making *Kipps* welcoming even to people who don't usually stay in hostels: communal spaces are neat and clean, with dashes of style – a Banksy theme on one floor, nautical memorabilia on another – and the rooms, though slightly worn in places, are cheerily decorated. Many are en suite, while others have shower cubicles and basins. The location is splendid, very near the sea and just minutes away from the bars, shops and restaurants of the Lanes. It's also an appealing place to hang out – you can gaze upon Brighton Pavilion from the lounge (which has a computer, Wii and DVDs) or chat to fellow guests in the bar and tiny roof terrace.

Kipps, 76 Grand Parade, Brighton, East Sussex, BN2 9JA ☎01273 604182, Ⓦkipps-brighton.com.
Price 6 doubles/twins with shared toilet but shower and basin in room from £62. 1 en-suite double from £66. 1 single with shared toilet from £32. Dorms: 2x10 en suite from £19.50. Rates 25–30% lower Oct–March. Breakfast included for rooms, £1–2 for dorms.
Facilities TVs in rooms. Kitchen. Bar. Games/common room. Lockers. Internet.
Open Year-round. 2-night minimum stay at the weekend. Check in: 2pm. Check out: 11am.
Getting there *Kipps* is opposite the Royal Pavilion, 12min walk from the train station and 5min from the bus station. You can reserve a parking permit in advance (£6/24hr), or there are meters behind the hostel on William St (free 6pm–9am and Sun). More free parking is about 10 minutes' walk away.

One Broad Street

Brighton's B&Bs are some of the most expensive in the country, and the quality can be poor. There's no need to throw your money away, though: *One Broad Street*, a supercool and very comfy bolthole a seashell's throw from the beach, offers excellent value. The airy rooms use dazzling whites and splashy bright colours to create a sunny modern ambience, with funky touches like chocolate bars, cheery crockery and swanky White Company toiletries in the (small) bathrooms. If you're not bothered about a sea view, ask about the upstairs suite, which gives you lots of space and, with its attic windows, a view of the stars. Being so central, on the edge of Kemp Town, *One Broad Street* can get noise from the street

One Broad Street, 1 Broad St, Brighton, East Sussex, BN2 1TJ ☎01273 699227, Ⓦonebroadstreet.com.
Price 7 en-suite doubles £80–89 depending on season. Breakfast included.
Facilities Internet. TVs in rooms.
Restrictions No children under 16.
Open Closed Dec & Jan. 2-night minimum stay at the weekend, 3-night minimum on bank holidays. Check in: call for time. Check out: 10am.
Getting there The B&B is a 15min walk from the train station, less from the bus station. If driving, ask about a residents' permit (£6 per day).

at weekends – but, with a characteristically thoughtful touch, earplugs are supplied in the room, and most guests don't find it a problem. The breakfasts, which include home-made granola and a good range of locally sourced produce, are hearty and healthy – a delicious way to kick-start a full-on day of seaside fun.

arthouse b&b

CANTERBURY

The *arthouse*, occupying an old red-brick fire station built around a lofty arched courtyard, has a superb location – it's on Canterbury's B&B avenue, London Road, a hop away from the ancient town centre – but very little in common with its chintzy neighbours. The name says it all – owned by artists and designers Anna and John Taylor, the house bears more resemblance to a funky gallery or a retro magazine shoot than a guesthouse. Their quirky work fills the space with personality and style: from the moment you step into the hallway, adorned with witty paintings, a trio of women's coats hung as art and jelly-bean-bright modern chandeliers, you know you're in for a cool and intriguing experience. The set up is unusual, too. Anna and John live in their own modern home and studio at the end of the garden. Guests, therefore, have the run of the light-filled *arthouse*, which has two large double rooms – each with private shower rooms – a communal lounge, an open-plan dining area and a small kitchen where you can prepare hot drinks and snacks. One bedroom, airy and feminine with a funked-up vintage feel, faces the back courtyard and has a rather luxurious shower room right next door. The second, lined with John's wordplay artpieces, is cheaper but larger, the pay-off being that it faces onto the road and that its simple private bathroom is down two flights of stairs. Plush, colourful robes are provided to take off the edge.

In the homely living room, where Elvis shares space with contemporary paintings and quirky ceramics, you can settle in front of the TV, flick through a fine selection of magazines and books, or simply gaze around you at the wonderful decor. There's a modern walled courtyard out back for when the weather's nice.

The walk into Canterbury centre takes just a few minutes, leading you through the medieval walls into the pedestrianized core. The main draw is the magnificent Norman cathedral, but there are plenty of museums and historic sights, too, and wandering the narrow streets, lined with perilously tilting half-timbered houses, is a pleasure in itself. The presence of the university

keeps things lively at night, whether you're after funky veggie restaurants, cool café-bars or ancient inns with real ales and log fires.

In the morning, Anna will lay out an organic continental breakfast for you in the dining room which you can eat as and when (and where) you wish. If you're feeling sociable you might chat to your fellow guests, but there's plenty of space if you prefer solitude. Relaxation is key at the *arthouse*: over and above all the amazing surroundings, it's the profound sense of feeling at home that defines this magical spot.

> **arthouse b&b, 24 London Road, Canterbury, Kent CT2 8LN** ☎01227 453032, Ⓦarthousebandb.com.
> **Price** 2 doubles with private bathrooms £60 and £65, breakfast included.
> **Facilities** Internet. Kitchen. On-site parking. Games/common room. Garden.
> **Open** The B&B may close when the owners take their holidays. Check in: flexible. Check out: flexible.
> **Getting there** *arthouse b&b* is a 10min walk from Canterbury West train station, with hourly fast trains to London St Pancras.

A design for living at Canterbury's intriguing *arthouse*

YHA Tanners Hatch

Your first glimpse of *Tanners Hatch*, a lovely seventeenth-century cottage conversion surrounded by rambling roses and mature trees, is a moment of pure delight – this must be one of the prettiest YHAs in the country. Just a couple miles from the old town of Dorking, the hostel is on National Trust property in the Surrey countryside, and the wooded grounds offer bucolic views across the rolling fields. Paths lead to the Edwardian estate of Polesden Lacey, and the RHS Wisley Garden is nearby. Inside, it's the very definition of cosy – it can be a squeeze at peak times, but the friendly, all-muck-in-together atmosphere is part of the appeal and the low beamed ceilings and creaky narrow stairs attest to the building's age. There's a little kitchen (it's self-catering only) and a snug living room, and you're welcome to make campfires and stoke up barbecues in the woods. The three dorms, tucked under the eaves, are small, and the toilet/shower block is outside. There's no TV or internet, and mobile reception is patchy. Pure, peaceful bliss.

YHA Tanners Hatch, off Ranmore Road, Dorking, Surrey, RH5 6BE ☎0845 371 9542, ⓦyha.org.uk.
Price Dorms: 1x7, 2x9. £16.40–24.40. Camping £5.50–9.50 per person.
Facilities Kitchen. Shop. Games/common room. Garden.
Open Year-round. Check in: 5pm. Check out: 10am.
Getting there Tanners Hatch is 3.5 miles northwest of Dorking, half a mile along a woodland track from the nearest road. Coming by car, park at the Denbies Hillside National Trust car park on Ranmore Road and walk through the woods for 15min. You can also walk the 2 miles from Box Hill and Westhumble train station, which has regular services to London Victoria.

The Big Sleep

A Hollywood-backed designer budget hotel occupying an old Trusthouse Forte on the Eastbourne seafront? This shouldn't work. But it does, if you can embrace the eccentricities. Unsung Eastbourne, best known for its retirement homes, is sleepy but charming with a long, wide shingle beach. Just strides away from Beachy Head, it's a splendid spot for anyone looking for peace and quiet on the Sussex coast – and it even has an airy modern art gallery, the Towner, for rainy days. Wend your way through the *Big Sleep*'s unpromising institutional corridors to surprisingly funky rooms, each one different in size and layout, but most decorated on the same lines: clean white with blocks of pastel blue or pink. The faux-fur curtains and photos of John Malkovich (he's one of the backers) might raise an eyebrow, but the spotless bathrooms, comfortable beds and big windows more than compensate. Go for a suite if you can; all of these have sea views, some have retro leatherette rocking-chairs, one has a standalone claw-foot tub, and a few themed options, with gorgeous statement wallpaper, stray from the minimal design concept.

The Big Sleep, King Edwards Parade, Eastbourne, East Sussex, BN21 4EB ☎01323 722676, ⓦthebigsleephotel.com.
Price Standard rooms: 27 doubles/twins (1 disabled) from £55, 2 triples £79–99, 10 singles £40–55. Sea-view suites: 4 doubles, 2 triples, 4 family rooms from £99. All en suite. Breakfast included.
Facilities Internet. Bar. Games/common room. TVs in rooms.
Open Year-round. Check in: 3pm. Check out: 10am.
Getting there The Big Sleep is a 10min walk from Eastbourne train station, with services to London Victoria and Brighton. There is on-street parking nearby; drivers can buy residents' parking permits from the hotel for £1 per day.

The Falkland Arms

GREAT TEW

You couldn't find a prettier English village than Great Tew, its thatched cottages, meandering lanes and flower-filled gardens tucked away in peaceful countryside near Chipping Norton and just 20 miles from Oxford. And you'd be hard pushed to find a prettier English pub than the *Falkland Arms*, the sixteenth-century inn that lies at its heart. While it has charm in spades – flagstone floors, settle benches, log fires, vintage tankards dangling from gnarled timber beams – this warm, sociable place has avoided the tweeification that smothers so much of the Cotswolds. Young families, American tourists, Oxford students and the CAMRA crew gather around rough-hewn tables to

The Falkland Arms, The Green, Great Tew, Oxfordshire, OX7 4DB ☎01608 683653, ⓦfalklandarms.co.uk.
Price 5 en-suite doubles £60–90. Breakfast included.
Facilities Internet. On-site parking. Bar. Garden. TVs in rooms. Lunch and dinner available.
Open Year-round. Check in: 1pm. Check out: 11am.
Getting there From Chipping Norton take the A44 and the A361, then turn right onto the B4022 for Great Tew. *The Falkland Arms* is on the village green.

enjoy Wadworth beers and herby fruit wines, honest pub grub (from chunky pork pies to creamy risottos) and even old-fashioned snuff, which is sold behind the bar. The bedrooms are rustic, a little time-worn, and certainly not slick, but each has its charm and the fanciest have four-posters. The attic, reached by a creaky winding staircase, is the largest, and the quietest, while those directly above the bar are best for anyone who is here more to while away a long, happy evening in one of the country's finest pubs than to get a quiet night's sleep. Things can get pretty loud, especially on Sundays, when there's live folk music.

Clockwise from top left Quirky idiosyncrasy at *The Big Sleep*; a country idyll at *YHA Tanners Hatch*; inside and outside the charming *Falkland Arms*

Kasbah

With its music festivals and cool campsites, the Isle of Wight has shaken off its fusty image in recent years; *Kasbah*, at the end of Ryde's lively Union Street, makes a hip little base. It's handy, too: across the road from the hovercraft and catamaran terminals, and with good transport connections to the rest of the island. The name evokes Morocco – and tin lanterns, North African plates, and mosaic-tiled tables make a healthy show – but there's also a more general chill-out feel to this comfy, youthful bar/restaurant. It's popular, and unless you take one of the pricier attic rooms you'll probably hear the downstairs revelry until the wee hours. But for anyone who wants to hang out, listen to acoustic bands at the weekend, and sip cocktails on the tiny back terrace with its tinkling fountain, it's a friendly option. The rooms are a good size and look great, with exotic flourishes – opulent scatter cushions, mosaic sinks, jazzy floral wallpaper – that allow you to forgive the tired-looking carpets. Those on the top floor are quietest, and have sea views. Incidentally, the wood-and-brick exterior, which looks rather medieval, in fact dates from 1900, when it was built as a blacksmiths' shop. Just another little quirk in the fabric of this idiosyncratic little spot.

Kasbah, 76 Union St, Ryde, Isle of Wight, Hampshire, PO33 2LN ☎**01983 810088,** 🌐**kasbahryde.com.**

Price 5 en-suite doubles £75, 1 en-suite twin £75, 2 en-suite doubles with sea view £80, 1 en-suite family room (sleeps five) £109. Breakfast included.

Facilities Internet. Bar. Café. Garden. TVs in rooms. Lunch and dinner available.

Open Year-round. Check in: 2pm. Check out: noon.

Getting there The *Kasbah* is at the end of Union Street near the pier, a few min walk from the hovercraft and ferry terminals (with services to Portsmouth and Southsea), Ryde train station and bus stops.

Clockwise from top left The jazzy design in the bedrooms of the *Kasbah* is matched in the pub downstairs; this hip little spot is well situated for you to enjoy both town and country

YHA Jordans

A cute little Chilterns lodging hidden in the woods near a quiet Quaker village, this hostel, in operation since 1933, offers good old-fashioned YHA charm. Sipping coffee on the flowery deck in the morning, serenaded by birdsong and the wind in the trees, it's hard to believe you're just 5 miles from a tube station. Many guests drive to Amersham and take the underground to London; after a long day's sightseeing, it's a delight to return to this country retreat. You could happily pass a day or two here: there's good walking nearby, through the Chiltern hills, the village has a couple of historic Quaker sights and Seer Green, just a mile away, has a gastropub, the *Jolly Cricketers*. The four small dorms are fresh, clean and light and there's a compact, well-stocked kitchen and a cosy dining area. It's self-catering, with a sociable buzz guaranteed over supper. Outside, you can chill out on a sofa on the deck, chat at the bench tables or, best of all, warm your hands around the crackling campfire.

YHA Jordans, Welders Lane, Jordans, Beaconsfield, Buckinghamshire, HP9 2SN ☎0845 371 9523, ⊛yha.org.uk.
Price Dorms: 2x5, 2x6 £22.40 (£51–59 for exclusive use by family or group). Limited camping space in summer.
Facilities Internet. Kitchen. On-site parking. Shop. Games/common room. Garden. Breakfast available
Restrictions No children under 3. Curfew 11pm.
Open Year-round. Check in: 5pm. Check out: 10am.
Getting there Buses stop at Chalfont St Peter, just over a mile away, and trains at Seer Green, a mile away. Driving, leave the M40 at Junction 2, taking the A355 exit to Beaconsfield. The hostel is around 2.5 miles from the exit.

The Cherry Tree

The Buckinghamshire/Oxfordshire borders, dotted with well-heeled villages and within striking distance of both Oxford and London, are notoriously pricey, which makes these rooms, in a barn conversion behind a village pub just 2 miles from the M40, something of a find. The barn, footsteps from the pub itself is very private. Rooms are small, but have everything you need – en-suite shower/bath, tea-making facilities, TV – and those on the top floor have floor-to-ceiling windows. Effort has gone into making each look stylish and attractive, with luxurious coverlets and large modern paintings contrasting with rustic wooden beams and warmly painted walls. There are glitches

The Cherry Tree, High Street, Kingston Blount, Oxfordshire, OX39 4SJ ☎01844 352273, ⊛cherrytreepub.net.
Price 2 en-suite doubles, 2 en-suite twins, £50. Breakfast included.
Facilities Internet. On-site parking. Bar. TVs in rooms. Lunch and dinner available.
Open Closed 2 weeks a year when the proprietors take a holiday – see website. Check in: call for time. Check out: 10am.
Getting there Kingston Blount is on the B409 a couple of miles north of the M40 near Thame and can be reached from Junctions 5 or 6.

– the shower may lose pressure, and you may have to squeeze around the bed to get to the bathroom – but at these prices you're getting a good deal. The pub itself is handsome, traditional on the outside, but minimal and airy within, with abstract art on the walls and stripped wooden floors. It's cosiest in the winter, when a real fire warms the place up and there are games to play by the fireside. Beers include Brakspear, the local ale, and their homely pub grub – fish and chips, sausage and mash – is good value.

Vinegar Hill Pottery and B&B

There's an end-of-the-road feel to Milford on Sea, an unassuming village on a shingly stretch of beach at the edge of the New Forest. Here, tucked down a leafy lane, you'll find *Vinegar Hill*, a B&B and pottery attached to the home of David and Lucy Rogers and their young children. David's vivid blue pottery and gorgeous handmade sinks adorn every room, and artistic flourishes abound. The Garden Room is a bargain, with a double bed (two singles can be added), a lounge with TV/DVD-player, a gorgeous Mexican-tiled bathroom and a little patio with an irresistible gypsy caravan. The Hayloft, meanwhile, reached by a (steep) spiral staircase, is a romantic eyrie. All fresh white bedlinen and light wood, this soothing room has no TV – nothing, in fact, to distract from the peace and quiet. *Vinegar Hill* is just ten minutes' walk from the village centre and its handful of good restaurants, and, via a riverside footpath through the woods, the same distance to the sea. Keyhaven, to the east, offers a nature sanctuary, tidal marshes and bracing seaside walks.

Vinegar Hill Pottery and B&B, Vinegar Hill, Milford on Sea, Hampshire, SO41 0RZ ☎01590 642979, ⊛davidrogerspottery .co.uk.

Price Garden room sleeps 2–6: en-suite double £85, plus £15 per person for 1–2 extra single beds, plus gypsy caravan £60. Hayloft: en-suite double £75. Breakfast included.

Facilities Internet. On-site parking. Garden. TVs in rooms. Bike hire.

Open Year-round. Check in: 4pm. Check out: 10am.

Getting there Vinegar Hill lies southwest of Lymington about 12 miles south of Lyndhurst, and is accessible via the A337 and B3058.

YHA Oxford

Right next to the train station, and an easy walk from Oxford's colleges and museums, this huge purpose-built YHA provides a very decent base for exploring the town. It's less of a party hostel than the other independent hostels in Oxford – both of which are nearby – and far larger, offering comfortable rooms, a TV lounge and a quieter library/work area. Most accommodation is in six-bed dorms, which are gratifyingly roomy and all en suite; the decor is no-fuss, with plain pine bunks, each with a light, plus storage and hanging space, lockers and large windows. The smaller rooms, which range from one single to a number of four-beds, have TVs. A couple of the doubles have outside balconies, and there are a few cheaper options that share bathrooms. The restaurant and 24hr café, though they wouldn't win any style awards, serve solid food at reasonable prices, and you can use the cosy, sociable self-catering kitchen if you prefer to rustle up something yourself. The little garden at the back is a nice place to take your food or a bottle of beer from the bar; a relaxing spot to take time out from sightseeing.

YHA Oxford, 2a Botley Road, Oxford, Oxfordshire, OX2 0AB ☎0845 371 9131, ⊛yha.org.uk.

Price Dorms: 21x6 £18–25.65, all en suite. Rooms: 1 single with shared bathroom £28–31, 4 twins with shared bathroom £53–59, 8 en-suite twins £53–61, 1 en-suite triple £48–73, 12 en-suite four-bed rooms £53–81.

Facilities Internet. Kitchen facilities. Bar. Café. Shop. Games/common room. Garden. TVs in rooms. Lockers. Breakfast, lunch and dinner available.

Open Year-round. Check in: 3pm. Check out: 10am.

Getting there The hostel is behind Oxford train station, a 5min walk from Oxford University. The nearest free parking is 10min walk away.

Wetherdown Lodge

It's no surprise, perhaps, that the Sustainability Centre, owned by the Earthworks Trust charity and dedicated to low-impact living, should be in this lovely spot, surrounded by 55 acres of woodland, wildflowers and chalk grassland at the edge of the South Downs. The fact that it's housed in the old HMS *Mercury* naval base, a complex of ugly buildings decommissioned in the 1990s, might feel more incongruous, but sits perfectly with their sustainable agenda. Hostel-style accommodation is provided by *Wetherdown Lodge*, once the barracks for Navy trainees. It's utilitarian but comfortable, with simple rooms heated by a biomass boiler fired with woodchip fuel. Floors are covered with natural marmoleum (made from jute, chalk and linseed oil) and triple-glazing keeps things snug. Many guests are attending courses at the centre – and there are lots of good events for kids – but anyone is welcome, and the communal lounge is a sociable spot. They have camping facilities, too, including tipis and yurts. The lodge has a small kitchen, while the on-site *Beech Café* serves home-made cakes and veggie lunches.

Wetherdown Lodge, Droxford Rd, East Meon, Petersfield, Hampshire, GU32 1HR ☎01730 823549, ⓦsustainability -centre.org.
Price 3 rooms sleep 2, 11 rooms sleep 3. Possible to convert some into a family room. All cost £23 per adult sharing, £26 single, and £13 per child aged 5–13. All have shared bathrooms. Breakfast included.
Facilities Internet. Kitchen. On-site parking. Café. Games/common room. Garden. Bike hire. Lunch available.
Open Year-round. Check in: call for time. Check out: call for time.
Getting there The centre is 7 miles southwest of Petersfield, accessible from the A3 (Clanfield exit). The nearest train station is Petersfield, from where you can catch buses to Clanfield (#37) or East Meon (#52 or #67), both of which are 2 miles away. There are also buses from Portsmouth (#41/X41) to Clanfield.

Court Hill Centre

Just a few strides from the long-distance Ridgeway National Trail, near Wantage in Oxfordshire, this friendly hostel provides a restful haven at the end of a bracing day's walking or cycling. Housed in a group of restored timber barns, it sits on one of the best stretches of the trail, a 7-mile walk from the ancient site of White Horse Hill. Rooms in the bunkhouse are plain, clean and comfortable, and some have wonderful, sweeping views of the Berkshire Downs; there's a drying room, laundry and cycle shed for guests' use. The communal kitchen is small but has the essentials – you may prefer to fill up on the hearty meals on offer in the dining room. There's also a tea-room, its walls lined with local information, offering scones, ice cream and home-made cakes, as well as a

Court Hill Centre, Letchombe Regis, Oxfordshire, OX12 9NE ☎01235 760253, ⓦcourthill.org.uk.
Price Dorms: 1x2, 6x4, 1x5, 1x13, 1x15, £17.50. Breakfast £5.50, dinner £8.50.
Facilities Kitchen. On-site parking available. Café. Garden. Lunch available.
Open Year-round. Check in: 5pm. Check out: 10am.
Getting there The hostel is accessible by foot from the National Ridgeway Trail. The nearest train station is Didcot Parkway, 10 miles away; buses run from the station to Wantage, which is 2 miles from the centre. If driving, follow the signs to Wantage from Junction 14 of the M4.

pretty courtyard garden surrounded by the hostel's barn buildings. It's all rather relaxed – there's even a sunken chill-out area next to the restaurant, with a log fire – and deliciously quiet if you happen not to coincide with a school group.

SOUTHWEST ENGLAND

Devon, Cornwall, Dorset, Somerset and Wiltshire form one of the most alluring regions in the country, with pristine stretches of coast, soaring cathedrals, mysterious prehistoric sites, lush countryside and idyllic villages. Their obvious appeal means demand for accommodation is high, particularly in the summer-holiday paradise of Devon and Cornwall, and prices are correspondingly on the steep side. But don't stay away: there are plenty of good hostels and some stunning and affordable B&Bs here, in buildings that range from a restored fisherman's cottage to a cliffside listening station and an eighteenth-century chapel.

Indeed, Devon and Cornwall are popular for a host of very good reasons. You can taste the surf in brash Newquay, stare out at the sea-lashed Lizard Peninsula from a remote hostel, check out the local seafood from a bargain B&B in Padstow and stay above a funky café in Dartmouth or in a former pilchard press in St Ives. It's surprisingly easy to find an end-of-the world feel in this idiosyncratic and beautiful part of the world, whether you're chasing King Arthur legends on the North Cornish coast or catching a ferry to the Isles of Scilly.

Dorset and Wiltshire may be lower key, but welcoming B&Bs let you explore quintessentially English villages, coastal resorts and chalk escarpments, while the cathedral and medieval streetscape of Salisbury shouldn't be missed. Wells in Somerset has an equally magnificent cathedral, and Glastonbury comes replete with Biblical tales and fine old buildings. In the cities, check out Bristol's art, restaurants and pubs from a hip grainhouse-conversion hostel, or base yourself in a honey-coloured Georgian terrace in handsome Bath, home to a huge medieval abbey and the compelling remains of a Roman bathhouse and temple.

There are some excellent hostels across the Southwest for those on tighter budgets, often in grand, remote converted structures, and most offering family rooms and cooking facilities. The region's B&Bs, meanwhile, can be first rate, whether they're in beach towns or rustic locations. Throughout the region – and especially as you go further west – it pays to book in advance. School holiday periods are of course especially popular and most places will hike their prices up. But an out-of-season visit can be a real pleasure in this temperate region, particularly for surfers and those keen to check out the lively towns and cities.

SOUTHWEST ENGLAND

NAME	LOCATION	PAGE		REAL BARGAIN	TREAT YOURSELF	FAMILY-FRIENDLY	GREAT RURAL LOCATION	OUTDOOR ACTIVITIES	GREAT FOOD AND DRINK	DORMS	PUBLIC TRANSPORT
Belmont B&B	Bath	56	26						✓		✓
Café Alf Resco	Dartmouth	61	21	✓	✓	✓					
Canon Grange	Wells	73	24			✓					✓
The Cobbles	St Ives	71	5		✓			✓	✓		✓
Coombe House	Lyme Regis	65	22						✓		✓
Donkey Shoe Cottage	Clovelly	60	17			✓					
Evergreen	Isles of Scilly	64	1								✓
Falmouth Backpackers	Falmouth	62	9						✓	✓	✓
Glastonbury Backpackers	Glastonbury	63	23							✓	
Myrtle Cottage	Porlock	70	20		✓		✓				
NorthShore	Bude	59	15				✓	✓	✓	✓	
Ocean Backpackers	Ilfracombe	64	18	✓				✓		✓	✓
Old Chapel Backpackers	Zennor	74	2			✓	✓	✓	✓	✓	
The Old Forge	Compton Abbas	60	28		✓	✓	✓				
Original Backpackers	Newquay	67	8					✓		✓	✓
South Quay	Padstow	67	11						✓		✓
St Ives Backpackers	St Ives	71	4	✓					✓	✓	✓
Truro Lodge	Truro	73	10	✓		✓				✓	✓
Turret Hotel	Lynton	66	19			✓					✓
White Hart	Bath	56	27	✓					✓	✓	✓
Wyndham Park Lodge	Salisbury	70	29			✓					✓
YHA Boscastle	Boscastle	57	14					✓		✓	
YHA Boswinger	Boswinger	58	12				✓	✓		✓	
YHA Castle Horneck	Penzance	68	3							✓	✓
YHA Elmscott	Hartland	63	16				✓	✓		✓	
YHA Lizard Point	The Lizard	65	6				✓	✓		✓	
YHA Narrow Quay	Bristol	59	25						✓	✓	✓
YHA Perranporth	Perranporth	69	7					✓		✓	
YHA Tintagel	Tintagel	72	13				✓	✓		✓	

Previous page Logan Rock, Porthcurno

Belmont B&B

It may not have quite as much character as the *White Hart* (see below), but if you're looking for a classic B&B with cooked breakfasts and some great views, the *Belmont* is a fine alternative. It's set on a long terrace of honey-coloured Georgian houses a short walk north of the city centre, and is efficiently run by a couple who have been here for over thirty years. Decor is traditional, with striped wallpaper and carpets, and the original fireplaces have been retained. Front rooms are double-glazed to ensure quiet, and back rooms have a wonderful steep view over lines of tall terraces and the green hills beyond the city. There's a bright breakfast room downstairs where a full English or continental breakfast is made to order, and a large upstairs lounge with TV. Stroll down Lansdown Road to peruse the excellent Topping & Company bookshop and then continue straight ahead for the sights: the fifteenth-century abbey, the restored Roman baths and the Georgian Pump Room.

Belmont B&B, 7 Belmont, Lansdown Road, Bath, Somerset, BA1 5DZ ☎01225 423082, Ⓦbelmontbath.co.uk.
Price 2 doubles with shared bathroom £50, 4 en-suite doubles £70, 1 en-suite triple £85. Breakfast included.
Facilities Internet. TVs in rooms.
Open Year-round. Check in: flexible. Check out: 10am.
Getting there Lansdown Road is immediately north of the city centre, a 20min walk from the adjacent train and bus stations. The owners can advise on the best parking nearby.

White Hart

The budget rooms at the *White Hart* are a hidden gem. Just out of Bath city centre, a short walk from the train station, the pub sits on an attractive street of cafés and small shops, a sculpted white hart above its door. The pub food is excellent and the place has been sympathetically modernized, with sturdy pine tables, bright vases of flowers, a gleaming wooden bar and art on the walls. Out back there's an abundant terrace garden, tumbling with roses and geraniums in summer – it's a lovely spot for a long, relaxed Sunday lunch. From here you access the hostel – dorms plus private rooms – which are plain but clean and comfortable, with a basic breakfast of toast and cereal served in the pleasant communal kitchen. Guests have a key to the garden door, meaning they are free to come and go outside pub hours. Despite the pub setting the atmosphere is restful and welcoming – the *White Hart* is more gastropub than rowdy boozer. And its residential location means you're free of the city crowds, though close to the sights and the most graceful and elegant Georgian architecture in the country.

White Hart, Widcombe Hill, Bath, Somerset, BA2 6AA ☎01225 313985, Ⓦwhitehartbath.co.uk.
Price 1 single £25, 1 twin £40, both with separate bathrooms. 1 en-suite double £50, 1 large en-suite double £70 (£80 if used as a triple). 24 beds in 5 dorms, £15. Breakfast included.
Facilities Internet. Kitchen. Bar. Garden. TVs in rooms. Lunch and dinner available.
Open Open year-round. Check in: flexible. Check out: 11am.
Getting there Arriving by rail, go to the rear of Bath Spa, through the taxi tunnel, and cross the river via the footbridge. Over the pedestrian crossing, turn left onto Claverton St (Widcombe Parade). Walk past the shops and you'll see the *White Hart*.

YHA Boscastle

The tiny Cornish settlement of Boscastle has always been shaped by water. It was once a very active fishing village, and its rugged stone harbour, hemmed in by steep hills, remains undeniably picturesque. The place achieved unwanted fame in 2004, when the river flooded – a video in the visitor centre shows the scale of the disaster, but miraculously nobody was killed. Since then this touristy little place, much of it owned by the National Trust, has rebuilt and regained its status as a delightful stop for a harbourside stroll and a local ice cream, and the sturdy stone youth hostel, right in the heart of things, is lapped by gentler tides. Dorms (including three- and four-bed options, which are good for families) are in the eaves, with beams overhead and single wooden beds as well as bunks. There's a cosy lounge, good self-catering facilities and nearby pubs to linger in once the day-trippers have departed the

YHA Boscastle, Palace Stables, Boscastle, Cornwall, PL35 0HD ☎0845 371 9006, ⓦyha.org.uk.
Price Dorms: 1x3, 1x4, 1x5, 2x6. £23.40 per person.
Facilities Internet. Kitchen. Games/common room.
Open Dec–March only available for exclusive hire. Check in: 10am. Check out: 5pm.
Getting there The B3263 Tintagel to Bude road passes close by – the hostel is the last building on the right-hand side at the top of the slipway. Parking is in the public car park (250m from the hostel). Coming by public transport, take the #595 bus from Bude to Boscastle or the #594 from Wadebridge to Boscastle.

village – the volume of the crowds can make this feel rather like a show village by day. The South West Coastal Path, which stretches around the coast from Somerset to Dorset, is easily accessible, and the hostel will give you contacts for the wealth of outdoor activities nearby, from sailing and surf schools to kayaking and fishing.

YHA Boscastle sits at the heart of the pretty but resilient village of the same name

YHA Boswinger

Located in an isolated and rugged corner of Cornwall near St Austell, crisscrossed by narrow country lanes, this is a great get-away-from-it option for families. The spacious hostel is set in a former farmhouse just a ten-minute walk from the gorgeous sandy expanse of Hemmick beach. The dorms are bright and clean, with sturdy wooden bunks and wardrobes, and the dinner menu offers fish'n'chips and a long list of other hearty staples made using Cornish produce. There's a small dining room, a spacious lounge and games room with long wooden tables, and plenty of outside space for eating and playing ball games. Boswinger itself is tiny, but the restored nineteenth-century Lost Gardens of Heligan are just down the road, and this is a great base for cycling and rambles. The hostel provides lots of information on both, including cycle routes to the Eden Project (you get £3 off the entry fee if you don't arrive by car). Pentewan Cycle Hire (Ⓦpentewanvalleycyclehire .co.uk) will deliver bikes to the hostel for you, and the hostel also has details on nearby snorkel safaris. West of Boswinger is the surfers' beach of Porthluney Cove, backed by Caerhays Castle, a location for the BBC's 1979 take on *Rebecca*.

YHA Boswinger, Boswinger, Cornwall, PL26 6LL Ⓣ0845 371 9107, Ⓦyha.org.uk.
Price Dorms: 3x2, 4x4, 3x6, £21.40.
Facilities Internet. Kitchen. On-site parking. Games/common room. Garden. Bike hire. Breakfast, lunch and dinner available.
Open Nov–March only available for exclusive hire. Check in: 5pm. Check out: 10am.
Getting there From the A390 (St Austell) take the B3273 towards Mevagissey. After 5 miles turn right at the top of the hill and follow signs for Gorran. After 4 miles fork right to Boswinger (follow brown tourist signs). The hostel is situated in Boswinger hamlet, just below *Seaview International* campsite. It's an easy 20min walk from the nearest bus stop at Gorran Churchtown, where the bus from St Austell drops off.

Clockwise from top left Bright and breezy *YHA Boswinger*; *NorthShore*'s exterior; Bude's Summerleaze beach

YHA Narrow Quay

The occasionally frumpy spirit of the YHA is nowhere to be seen in this cool grainhouse conversion on the quay in Bristol, right at the social heart of this dynamic city. The building's airy interior is sliced through by two mezzanine floors, one housing a lounge with sofas, well-stocked bookshops and a flatscreen TV, and one with a canteen-style restaurant. From here you look down to the lively café-bar on the ground floor, which attracts ordinary punters as well as YHAers. Throughout, the whitewashed brick walls, rubber floors and artful graffiti give an appropriately hip city-centre feel. On the top floor rooms house 134 people, in a combination of singles, twins, family rooms and dorms. There's a comfy lounge at the back of the building, a games room with pool table and telly, a self-catering kitchen and handy facilities like a cycle lockup. Turn left out of the building and in a few steps you're at the acclaimed Arnolfini Gallery, which showcases contemporary British and international art.

YHA Narrow Quay, 14 Narrow Quay, Bristol, BS1 4QA ☎0845 371 9726, ⓦyha.org.uk.
Price Dorms: 26x4, 2x5, 4x3, from £21.40. 2 twins from £42, 3 triples from £56.
Facilities Internet. Kitchen. Bar. Café. Games or common room. Breakfast, lunch and dinner available.
Open Year-round. Check in: flexible. Check out: 10am.
Getting there By bus, alight at Malborough Street Coach Station, follow directions for the harbour and pick up finger post signs to the hostel (15–20 min walk). From Bristol Temple Meads train station, walk towards the city centre and follow finger post signs to hostel (10-15min walk). Drivers should leave the M4 and take the M32 to Bristol. There's parking on Prince Street, the road behind Narrow Quay.

NorthShore

Bude may feel a liitle more ordinary and suburban than the likes of St Ives, but the crashing breaks of nearby beaches of Crackington Haven, Crooklets and Duckpool are much loved by surfers, who will find a friendly welcome at the laidback NorthShore backpackers'. The red brick house itself, on a residential street a few blocks back from the beach, is pretty grand, featuring parquet floors, stained glass and a wooden staircase. The couple who run the hostel live here too, giving it a family feel – you're encouraged to help keep the large kitchen clean and tidy, but otherwise are free to do what you want. There's a spacious and comfortable lounge, a big dining room, a large well-equipped kitchen, a pool table and two computer terminals. It's an old building, and the slamming of the wooden doors upstairs can be a pain, but the rooms are characterful and cosy. Foodies should book ahead for an excellent dinner at the Life's a Beach café or the restaurant on Summerleaze Beach (☎01288 355222), a stroll away from the hostel. Would-be surfers can ask at the tourist office for details of lessons and equipment hire.

NorthShore, 57 Killerton Road, Bude, Cornwall, EX23 8EW ☎01288 354256, ⓦnorthshorebude.com.
Price 3 doubles with separate bathrooms from £38, 1 en-suite twin from £38, 1 triple with separate bathroom from £50. Dorms: 4x2, 2x6, from £14.
Facilities Internet. Kitchen. On-site parking. Games/common room. Garden.
Open Year-round. Check in: flexible. Check out: 10am.
Getting there Fairly regular buses run the 40 miles to the nearest major train station, Exeter St David's. Drivers can access the town via the A39, which hugs the north Cornwall coast. The hostel is on Killerton Road, just south of the golf course in the centre of Bude.

Donkey Shoe Cottage

The vertiginous Devon fishing village of Clovelly is so popular that visitors have to park at its entrance and pay an entry fee to take the long steep walk down to the appealing harbour. If you book ahead to stay at *Donkey Shoe Cottage*, you can park and access the village for free – and sample the charms of its cobbled streets once the crowds of visitors have left. The town is delightfully car-free and carefully preserved – the main mode of transport is still the donkeys whose footwear has given the cottage its

> **Donkey Shoe Cottage, 21 High Street, Clovelly, Devon, EX39 5TB** ☎01237 431601, Ⓦdonkeyshoecottage.co.uk.
> **Price** 1 double room, 1 twin room, 1 triple. £30 per person per night. Breakfast included.
> **Open** Year-round. Check in: 1pm. Check out: 10am.
> **Getting there** The nearest station is Barnstable, from where there are buses for Clovelly. The village is signposted off the A39.

name. The B&B is in a pretty, whitewashed old house on the main street, with gable attic windows and tubs of bright flowers outside. Inside, the decor is on the old-fashioned side – this is not a luxury option – but the rates are reasonable and the welcome friendly, and the double room at the top of the house has sea views. You can eat at one of the two hotels – the *New Inn* or the *Red Lion* – on the quay, and there are several chintzy tearooms in the village. If you take to the coastal path, the beach at Mouth Mill to the west of Clovelly, with its rock archways, is a good destination for a swim.

The Old Forge

The *Old Forge* combines the genteel delights of the English B&B – afternoon tea, huge breakfasts and open fires – with the pleasures of farmyard life. When we visited there was a litter of tumbling labradoodle puppies as well as a new foal. Tim and Lucy Kerridge run the place with great care and attention to detail, and their conversion of the early eighteenth-century farmhouse buildings is both sympathetic and stylish. Inside the main body of the house there's a cosy sitting room for guests, with comfy sofas, games and local maps. The bedrooms are colourful but elegant, with oak beams, wrought-iron beds, patchwork quilts, radios and tea-making facilities, while the self-contained apartment in the old Smithy, complete with blacksmith's tools and artefacts, has a galleried

> **The Old Forge, Chapel Hill, Compton Abbas, Dorset, SP7 0NQ** ☎01747 811881, Ⓦtheoldforgedorset.co.uk.
> **Price** 1 family room (with single and double bed) £80, 1 double £75, 1 single £40 – breakfast included. 2 self-catering apartments, both doubles, £175–350 for a 3-day break, depending on the season.
> **Facilities** Games/common room.
> **Open** Year-round. Minimun stay 3 days in the apartments. Check in: flexible. Check out: flexible.
> **Getting there** From Shaftesbury, take the A350 south to reach Compton Abbas. *The Old Forge* is at the entrance to the village, on the left-hand side.

bedroom, a sitting room with wood-burning stove and a kitchen and bathroom, as well as a pergola wreathed with honeysuckle and a grape vine. The picture-book village of Compton Abbas is preserved by the National Trust in memory of Thomas Hardy, who immortalized the area's lush chalk downland and ancient settlements as the fictional kingdom of Wessex. Near Compton Abbas is one of Britain's best known chalk figures, the naked Cerne Abbas giant, who has been making heads turn for centuries.

Clockwise from top left Bohemian comfort and delicious breakfasts at *Café Alf Resco*; all the pleasures of the country at *The Old Forge*; simple charm under the eaves at *Donkey Shoe Cottage*

Café Alf Resco

This great little café, B&B and apartment in beautiful Dartmouth is a real bargain. Downstairs, the buzzy café itself (open 7am–2pm) looks like it should be on the Left Bank; it serves Devon yoghurt, home-made granola, local sausages and excellent coffee from a Gaggia machine, as well as hosting the odd jazz night. The guest rooms are accessed from the other side of the tall Victorian house – avoid the place if stairs are not your thing. There's an elegant double with an LCD TV, and next door is a bunk room for two, often used to sleep kids while their parents enjoy the luxury of the double room. But the star of the show is upstairs, a beautiful self-catering apartment with wooden walls and ceiling, a neat galley kitchen, a miniature balcony with views of the River Dart and a ship's cabin bathroom. With its cushions, wood-burning stove and attractive antique furniture, the style is uncontrived bohemian chic.

Café Alf Resco, Lower Street, Dartmouth, Devon, TQ6 9AN ☎01803 835880, Ⓦcafealfresco.co.uk.
Price Apartment for 2 £65 (£85 with breakfast). 1 twin bunk room £55, 1 double £75, breakfast included. No credit cards. All rooms are en suite.
Facilities Internet. Kitchen. On-site parking. Café. TVs in rooms.
Open Year-round. Check in: flexible. Check out: flexible.
Getting there The most scenic way to get to Dartmouth is to go by train to Paignton, and then take the steam train. There are regular buses from Torbay, Totnes and Plymouth. The A380 and A3022 connect Dartmouth with Exmouth and the M5. The café is on Lower Street, just back from the river.

Owners Peter and Kate Ryder will find babysitters and can advise on boat trips and outings in the area. Dartmouth itself is a prosperous town with a deep harbour and some remarkable buildings, including the seventeenth-century timber-framed Butterwalk. Refreshingly low on tourism, it still thrives on fishing and freight, plus the presence of the Royal Naval College.

Clockwise from top left *YHA Elmscott* is walking distance from the rugged North Devon coast; the *YHA's* neat, appealing garden; sociable *Falmouth Backpackers* boasts a charming central location

Falmouth Backpackers

With a quiet location on a Falmouth back street, this is a hostel with a home-from-home feel – the owner lives in the tall terraced house herself and keeps a friendly eye on the place. Downstairs there's a spacious lounge and a kitchen with an Aga, making it a good spot for self-caterers, though a simple complimentary breakfast is provided. The communal space makes this a sociable hostel, which welcomes all sorts of travellers, though many are here for kayaking and other watersports. Upstairs, the rooms have pictures, lamps and patterned duvets; the owner has plans to convert an attractive upstairs bedroom into a budget double. From the hostel you can walk to the wide sandy town beach in a couple of minutes – its grandeur comes as a surprise given the urban setting – and the lively cafés, pubs and shops of the town centre are also a short walk away. Falmouth gets mobbed with visitors in summer, but it's still an active cargo port and has a likeably lived-in feel. Aside from beaches, watersports and a burgeoning arts scene, the main attraction is the Maritime Museum, which showcases an impressive display of craft, suspended in mid-air.

Falmouth Backpackers, 9 Gyllynvase Terrace, Falmouth, Cornwall, TR11 4DL ☎01326 319996, ✆falmouth backpackers.co.uk.
Price 4 dorms, each housing 4–6, £19 per person. 1 en-suite double £50. 1 twin/triple £21 per person.
Facilities Kitchen. On-site parking. Games/common room. Garden.
Open Year-round. Check in: flexible. Check out: 10am.
Getting there From the A30 take the A39 via Truro to Falmouth. Stay on the A39, heading towards the castle, and turn right into Gyllyngvase Road and then left into Gyllyngvase Terrace. The train station, with regular connections to Plymouth and Exeter, is 200m away.

Glastonbury Backpackers

You enter this well-located backpackers up a spiral staircase from the *Crown Inn*, an old coaching inn right in the heart of Glastonbury that has late-night openings and big screens for sports. The hostel has no curfew, and the vibe is more suited to young travellers than families: the proximity of the pub means the basic dorms can be noisy, so come for the party or prepared with earplugs. Glastonbury is now synonymous with the music festival, but there are plenty of other things to explore. Just a few steps from the hostel are the ruins of the abbey, which dates back to the seventh century and houses what is said to be the tomb of Arthur and Guinevere – something taken by local mystics (of which there are many) as evidence to identify Glastonbury as Avalon. Dominating the town is the Tor, a distinctive conical hill a mile or so from the centre, which was once a pilgrimage destination and still offers great views that on a clear day stretch to the Welsh mountains. This all ensures that a counter-cultural, New Age vibe is very much in evidence: shops are packed with healing crystals, and organic and veggie food fills the menu of many local restaurants and cafés.

Glastonbury Backpackers, 4 Market Place, Glastonbury, Somerset, BA6 9HD ☎01458 833353, ⓦglastonburybackpackers.com.
Price 26 dorm beds, £16.50. 6 twins and doubles, some en suite, £55–60.
Facilities Internet. Kitchen. Bar. Games/common room.
Open Open year round. Check in: 2pm. Check out: 10am.
Getting there The easiest way to arrive by public transport is to take the train to Castle Cary, from where you can take a bus or taxi to Glastonbury. Drivers should leave the M5 at Bridgewater on the A39.

YHA Elmscott

This former school house a short walk from the wild north Devon coast was once owned by the YHA, but was taken over by local farmers who run it with the help of YHA-trained volunteers. It's an enticing spot – a flagstoned building, built in the 1870s, with an attractive walled garden. Inside, it's plain but comfortably furnished, with a pleasant communal dining room with TV and a lounge where you can play board games. The simple dorms are upstairs and there's one twin room; a neighbouring annexe offers a basic self-catering kitchen. A tiny shop sells tinned foods, but note that there's no breakfast provided and this is a pretty isolated spot – the nearest village is Hartland, around three miles away, which has pubs and a café. To the west, atmospheric Hartland Quay is backed by slate cliffs, and was a major port until it was smashed by storms in 1887 – you can have a pint at the *Wrecker's Retreat Bar*, and look across to Lundy Island, while a mile to the south there's surfing at Speke's Mill Mouth. Many visitors, though, aren't tempted from the hostel itself – the well-tended garden, with its benches and flowerbeds, is a lovely spot on a summer evening.

YHA Elmscott, Hartland, Devon, EX39 6ES ☎0845 371 9736, ⓦelmscott.org.uk/youth-hostel.asp.
Price Dorms: 3x4, 3x6. 1 twin room. £18–23 per person, depending on the season.
Facilities Kitchen. Shop. Games/common room. Garden.
Restrictions Curfew 10.30pm.
Open Year-round. Check in: 5pm. Check out: 10am.
Getting there Turn off the A39 just north of *West Country Inn* and follow signs along the lanes. If you're walking from Hartland, continue to the west end of Fore Street and pick up the footpath to Elmscott (3.5 miles) through The Vale.

Ocean Backpackers

Iflracombe isn't the coolest seaside destination in Devon, having retained the quaint but bustling feel of an Edwardian resort, but its blue-painted backpackers, built by a master boatman in 1860 and located in the well-preserved centre near the bus station and harbour, gives it a dash of style for budget travellers. The cave-like whitewashed sitting room has huge sofas, a TV, computers and games, there are six solar-heated showers and a kitchen and dining area with long communal wooden tables. Upstairs, there are dorms and two private rooms : a family room for four and a spacious four-poster double with sea views that's a true bargain. The atmosphere is welcoming, relaxed and curfew-free, and while no breakfast is served, they do provide free tea and coffee and you'll find plenty of cafés nearby. Aside from strolling around town, watching boats nip in and out of the harbour and enjoying some fishing and swimming, visitors can take the coastal path east to explore a series of attractive coves and inlets; there's surfing at Woolacombe, Croyde, Saunton and Putsborough. Further afield, you can take a cruise from Ilfracombe to tiny, car-free Lundy Island, great for bird- and seal-spotting.

Ocean Backpackers, 29 St James Place, Ilfracombe, Devon, EX34 9BJ ☎01271 867835, ⓦoceanbackpackers.co.uk.
Price The 38 dorm beds start at £12 in winter, rising to £15 on summer weekends. The en-suite double is £38, and the en-suite family room starts at £50.
Facilities Internet. Kitchen. On-site parking. Games/common room.
Open Open year-round. Check in: flexible. Check out: 10am.
Getting there From the M5, drivers should take the A361 signposted Barnstaple, then follow signs to Ilfracombe. Barnstable is the nearest train station: from here there are regular buses to Ilfracombe.

Evergreen

The scattered Isles of Scilly boast Neolithic remains, seals, dolphins, puffin and tales of shipwrecks and piracy; exotic gardens flourish in their temperate climate. The slow and relaxed pace makes these remote islands feel a world apart, something enhanced if you take the long ferry journey. The archipelago's biggest settlement, tiny Hugh Town, is home to *Evergreen*, a compact, pretty building, one of a row of colourwashed fisherman's cottages over 300 years old, boasting an abundant front garden with bench seating. On the ground floor is a dining room and a lounge for guests, with a TV and lots of local books and leaflets; the five plainly furnished, clean and comfortable rooms sit above. The town is dotted with pubs and cafés and is a walker's paradise, with trails heading off in all directions. A boatman calls in to the cottage at breakfast to tell guests about "off-island" trips, taking in Tresco, with its famous Abbey Gardens, or St Martins, ringed by white powder beaches.

Evergreen, The Parade, Hugh Town, Isles of Scilly, TR21 0LP ☎01729 422711, ⓔevergreen.scilly@btinternet.com.
Price 2 doubles, 2 twins, 1 single, all £40 per person April–Oct, £32 per person Nov–March. All rooms are en suite. Breakfast included.
Facilities Internet. Games/common room. Garden. TVs in rooms.
Open Year-round. Check in: flexible. Check out: 10am.
Getting there The Isles of Scilly can be accessed on the Scillonian ferry from Penzance, which runs to Hugh Town (it takes around 15min to walk from the ferry terminal to the heart of town, where the B&B is located). More expensive Skybus flights connect Land's End, Newquay, Exeter, Bristol and Southampton with St Mary's, where they are met by buses heading to Hugh Town. See ⓦislesofscilly-travel.co.uk.

YHA Lizard Point

The Lizard, the southernmost village in England, sits at the farthest point of the Lizard Peninsula, an exposed, treeless and wave-lashed stretch of coast, its tip guarded by an eighteenth-century lighthouse. The YHA – once a Victorian hotel – sits just east of the lighthouse, and offers spectacular views over tumultous Lizard Point. The remoteness, combined with the grandeur of the whitewashed buildings, can make you feel you're in your own private mansion if you hire the place out of season. The rambling complex has dorms and family rooms, as well as a common room, kitchen, dining room, laundry and BBQ area. You can take a tour of the lighthouse itself, or follow the coast path northwest from here to reach dramatic Kynance Cove with its sheer cliffs and stacks. Strong currents mean the cove is not recommended for swimming, but there are diving schools nearby. Windsurfing, scuba diving and dolphin spotting are all possible to the east in the village of Coverack. The Lizard itself is not the most characterful of villages, but you can get pub meals at *Top House* pub or self-cater at the hostel (bring supplies), and enjoy the romance of being at one of the most far-flung points of the British Isles.

YHA Lizard Point, Lizard Point, Cornwall, TR12 7NT ☎0845 371 9550, ⓦyha.org.uk.
Price Dorms: 2x4, 2x5, 1x6. 2 triples with shared bathroom. £21.40 per person per night.
Facilities Internet. Kitchen. On-site parking. Shop. Games/common room. Garden.
Open Only available for exclusive hire Nov–March. Check in: 5pm. Check out: 10am.
Getting there Head past Truro to Helston, and take the A3083 signposted to Lizard. Once at Lizard Point, follow the signs for the National Trust car park. The youth hostel is next to the lighthouse. Buses run between The Lizard and Helston, which has connections to Truro and Falmouth.

Coombe House

This friendly B&B is located in an imposing Blue Lias stone house just back from the sea in Lyme Regis. Just two rooms overlook its walled courtyard, both simply and elegantly furnished with white walls and bedspreads, while, in a nicely indulgent touch, the breakfast of fruit, cereal and home-made bread and jam is brought to your room on a trolley. Despite being a popular stop on the tourist trail, the town is a unique and lovely place to hole up. Waves crash onto the pebble beach, colourful Victorian and Regency villas stretch decorously along the seafront and ammonites stud The Cobb, the harbour wall immortalized in *The French Lieutenant's Woman* by John Fowles and Jane Austen's *Persuasion*. The cliffs near town were the site of the discovery, in 1811, of the 30ft dinosaur skeleton that now looms large in the National History Museum in London.

Coombe House, 41 Coombe Street, Lyme Regis, Dorset, DT7 3PY ☎01297 443849, ⓦcoombe-house.co.uk.
Price 1 en-suite double, £33 per person. 1 en-suite twin, £29 per person. Breakfast included.
Facilities Garden.
Open Open year-round. Check in: flexible. Check out: 10am.
Getting there The nearest station is 5 miles away in Axminster, from where there are hourly buses to Lyme Regis. Drivers should leave the M5 at Taunton or Wellington. Head down the main street (Broad Street) and turn into Combe Street at the traffic lights – the only set in Lyme. *Coombe House* is about 70 yards along on the right.

Turret Hotel

The *Turret Hotel*, a grand red-stone Victorian villa topped by a Gothic pointed turret, is historic as well as beautiful: it was built in 1890 by the designer of Lynton's famous cliff railway, which links the village with the harbour, 600ft below. The spick and span B&B is run with warmth and efficiency by Scottish owner Nancy Wayman, who is justly proud of the high-ceilinged en-suite rooms, decorated in a formal, traditional style – floral curtains and patterned wallpaper and bedlinen – that's broadly in keeping with the age of the house. Downstairs is a spruce dining room, where full English and full veg breakfasts are served, along with home-made marmalade, porridge and kippers. Altogether, it's a reassuringly old-fashioned and cosy B&B. The little North Devon town itself is a sedate and charming resort; with its steep surrounding hills it was likened to Switzerland by nineteenth-century visitors, and a dash of romance was added when it featured in R.D. Blackmore's *Lorna Doone*. Distinguished by its grandiose Victorian architecture, independent shops and galleries, it's also a great base for rambles on Exmoor and visits to nearby surfing beaches.

Turret Hotel, 33 Lee Road, Lynton, Devon, EX35 6BS ☏01598 753 284, ⊕turret hotel.co.uk.
Price 4 en-suite doubles £60–70 (depending on room size), 1 en-suite twin £64. Breakfast included. Discounts for long stays.
Facilities Internet. On-site parking. TVs in rooms.
Open Year-round. Check in: flexible. Check out: 10am.
Getting there From Barnstaple, accessible by train from Exeter, take bus #309 or #310 to Lynton. The town is on the A30, which hugs the North Devon coast.

Clockwise from left The exterior of the *Turret Hotel*; the hotel offers beautiful views of the coast; inside, the attractive rooms feature floral curtains and smart wallpaper

Original Backpackers

Brash, sprawling Newquay isn't one of Cornwall's sedate seaside towns: indeed, it revels in its resort status. But this is Britain's surf capital, and relaxed *Original Backpackers* does a great job of making its wave-obsessed clientele feel at home. It's a bed-only dorm, with no breakfast or cooking facilities (each dorm has a kettle so you can make a cuppa), but the excellent central location ensures you're just a short walk from umpteen cafés, pubs and shops. The hostel overlooks Towan Beach, the most central of the town's 7 miles of sand, meaning you can get up and out with your board within minutes. Outlets throughout the town rent and sell surfing gear, and you can get lessons at 🌐britsurf.co.uk – if you want to escape the crowds, try going south to the dunes of Crantock Beach, or the caves and rock arches at Perran Beach. Walkers can make use of the South West Coastal Path,

> Original Backpackers, 16 Beachfield Avenue, Newquay, Cornwall, TR7 1DR
> ☎01637 874668, 🌐originalbackpackers.co.uk.
> **Price** Dorms: 1x3, 1x4, 3x6; 2 twin rooms with shared bathrooms. May & Sept £20 per person; June–Aug £25 per person; Oct–April £15 per person.
> **Open** Year round. 2 nights minimum stay on bank holidays. Check in: flexible. Check out: 10am.
> **Getting there** The hostel is located in the centre of Newquay. Buses head to St Austell and beyond, and Newquay station has trains to Par, which connect with services to Plymouth and London Paddington. Drivers should leave the A39 at St Columb Major, taking the A3059 to Newquay.

heading south to Holywell Bay to see its rocky headland's tidal estuary and mudflats or north to Padstow and the dramatic cliffs and stacks of Tolcarne, Lusty Glaze and Watergate Bay.

South Quay

PADSTOW

Enclosed by the Camel estuary, its harbour bobbing with fishing boats, Padstow is one of Cornwall's prettiest coastal villages. The crowds are consequently on the high side, but the centre is refreshingly low on cars and the summer promenade round the harbour, especially as the sun goes down, is buzzy and enjoyable. *South Quay* B&B is a bargain given its location, right by the water; you're likely to be greeted by Fitz, a tenacious Jack Russell, at the front door of the tall, Victorian house. The back double bedroom is a good bet if you're on a budget – it's prettily decorated in pink and white with a stencilled grape vine and shares a spacious bathroom with the brisk owners. The gem here, though, is the en-suite top bedroom, which has a tiny terrace under the gable of the house where you can sit and survey the lively goings-on of the

> South Quay, Padstow, Cornwall, PL28 8BY
> ☎01841 532383, 🌐southquaybedandbreakfastpadstow.co.uk.
> **Price** Rear double with shared bathroom £60 (single occupancy £45). Top bedroom £74, with discounts for longer or midweek stays. Breakfast included.
> **Facilities** Internet. Garden. TVs in rooms.
> **Open** Year-round. Check in: flexible. Check out: flexible.
> **Getting there** The nearest rail station is at Bodmin Parkway, with services to Exeter and London Paddington. There is a bus service from here to Padstow, timed to meet train arrivals. By car, leave the A39 just west of Wadebridge and take the A389 north to Padstow.

harbour. You'll find the famous Rick Stein restaurant and café nearby; some think that the village has become too much of a fiefdom, but the houses, pubs and cafés, hung with flower baskets in summer, still exercise a great deal of charm.

YHA Castle Horneck

Set in woodland around 25 minutes' walk from town, the YHA is Penzance's best budget option and buzzes with families, hikers and surfers in high season. It's in a recently restored Georgian manor, and offers rather swisher accommodation than many YHAs. Some of the grand original features, such as ornate fireplaces, have been retained, but it's also thoroughly modern, with a stylish restaurant and bar, a well-furnished lounge, table football and an excellent self-catering kitchen. There are doubles, twins and family rooms as well as dorms, and all rooms are simply furnished and spotlessly clean. Penzance lacks the charm of St Ives on the north coast, but it's an active working port, and a terrific base for boat trips along the coast and out to the Isles of Scilly. You're well positioned to visit the dramatic rock-cut Minack Theatre as well as stunning St Michael's Mount, or just to spot seals, dolphins and even sharks in the nearby waters. There are sand beaches nearby, as well as the clifftop coast path – a

great way of exploring the area. And in West Penwith – the furthest extreme of the Cornish coast – you can visit a superb array of Neolithic remains: barrows, quoits and stone circles.

YHA Castle Horneck, Alverton, Penzance, Cornwall, TR20 8TF ☎0845 371 9653, ⓦyha.org.uk.
Price Dorms: 6x2, 1x3, 1x4, 2x5, 11x6, 1x8, from £23.40.
Facilities Internet. Kitchen. Café. Games/common room. Garden. Breakfast, lunch and dinner available.
Open Year-round. Check in: 10am. Check out: 5pm.
Getting there Penzance is served by regular trains from London and the rest of the region. Walkers and cyclists should go through town centre and past the YMCA, turn right along Castle Horneck Road and cross the bypass, then take the driveway on the left. Penzance is just off the A30 – drivers should follow the bypass and turn at the *YHA Castle Horneck* sign. Do not go through the town centre.

Georgian *YHA Castle Horneck* has a well-furnished lounge and grand original features

Views don't come much better than those at *YHA Perranporth*, a former listening station in Cornwall

YHA Perranporth

The plain low hostel building may not be a thing of great beauty from the outside, but this former listening station on an attractive stretch of Cornwall's north coast has a clifftop location and sweeping sea views which would make a boutique hotel turn green with envy. Throughout, everything is neat and appropriately shipshape, and the large picture windows make the best of the dizzying vista down to wide and sandy St Agnes beach, protected by life guards. There's an attractive wood-ceilinged lounge hung with bright flags, and the wooden bunks in the compact dorms are sturdy and comfortable. A small kitchen provides all you need for self-catering; Perranporth and the adjoining lively, sprawling village of St Agnes feature grocers, butchers and greengrocers. And the hostel has plenty of information about local activities: walking the coastal path, surfing, coasteering, kite sports, kayaking, climbing and abseiling. Many will be happy to just soak in the Atlantic surf views, gazing over 3 miles of sandy strands and looking out for seals and dolphins – this is one hostel where you should definitely bring some binoculars.

Perranporth YHA, Droskyn Point, Perranporth, Cornwall, 0845 371 9755
☎0845 371 9755, ⓦyha.org.uk.
Price Dorms: 2x4, 2x8, £23.40 per person.
Facilities Kitchen. Games/common room. Garden.
Open Nov–March open for exclusive hire only. Check in: 5pm. Check out: 10am.
Getting there The A3075 connects Perranporth and Newquay. From Perranporth, take the B3285 southwest, and turn right into Tywarnhale Road, then left at the sign. You can also take local bus services between Newquay and Perranporth. The hostel is beyond a locked gate and small parking area on the coastal footpath. No vehicle access, except for loading and unloading.

Myrtle Cottage

Sporting a long thatched roof, rugged whitewashed walls and tall central chimney, sixteenth-century *Myrtle Cottage* feels like it's sprung straight from the pages of a storybook. Inside, the four rooms have pretty traditional furniture, wonky wooden beams and floral fabrics. An excellent full English breakfast is served by the friendly owners, including eggs and bacon from local farms, or you can opt for kippers. The B&B sits on the high street of the charming North Devon village of Porlock, alongside rows of other thatch-and-cob cottages. Located in a dip surrounded by the steep and dramatic Exmoor hills, this picturesque place featured in the romantic novel *Lorna Doone*. Its other literary association is less fortunate: the opium-induced inspiration in which Coleridge wrote "Kubla Khan" was interrupted by a plodding person from Porlock. There are few formal sights in the village, but it's a lovely place for a potter, and the surrounding hills are great for lengthy hikes.

Myrtle Cottage, High Street, Porlock, Devon, TA24 8PU ☎01643 862978, Ⓦmyrtleporlock.co.uk.
Price 1 double, 1 twin (both £27.50 per person, £30 single occupancy), 1 family room with 1 double and 1 single bed (from £60), 1 family room with 1 single, 1 double, plus 2 fold-out settees (£20 per person). All rooms are en suite; breakfast included.
Facilities On-site parking. Garden. TVs in rooms.
Open Year-round. Check in: flexible. Check out: 10am.
Getting there Porlock is west of Minehead on the A39. Drop down the hill into the village, and head down High Street, passing the church on the left. You'll see the post office on the left – the B&B is opposite. Buses run from Minehead.

Wyndham Park Lodge

With its ancient street plan, jigsaw of medieval, Georgian and Victorian houses and soaring thirteenth-century cathedral, prosperous Salisbury is full of interest, as well as being a great base for some prehistoric sights. Tucked away on a pretty residential back street, red-brick *Wyndham Park Lodge* is a warm and welcoming B&B where the owners have retained the Victorian sash windows, fireplaces and fittings, and decorated the rooms with antique furniture. There are three double rooms, two upstairs and one at the back of the house, which has its own entrance and private patio; this is decorated in soft primrose, pink and pistachio hues. Breakfast is full English or veggie, plus there's home-made marmalade, yoghurt, fresh fruit, kippers and pancakes. You're under ten minutes' walk from the town here – the spire of the cathedral, the tallest in England, its prominent landmark. It's a 2-mile walk from the town to hillside Old Sarum, a dramatic Iron Age fort, and – equipped with an OS map – you can make the hike to Stonehenge; approaching across the fields rather than by road is an unforgettable experience.

Wyndham Park Lodge, 51 Wyndham Road, Salisbury, Wiltshire, SP1 3AB ☎01722 416517, Ⓦwyndhamparklodge.co.uk.
Price 2 en-suite doubles £65–75, 1 en-suite triple £70–85 depending on the season. Breakfast included.
Facilities Internet. On-site parking. Garden.
Open Year-round. Check in: flexible. Check out: 10am.
Getting there Salisbury's train station, with decent connections to London, Exeter, Cardiff and Bristol, is half a mile west of the town centre on South Western Road; the bus station is close to the market square in the centre on Endless Street. The city is between the M3 to the north, the M4 to the south.

The Cobbles

This sparkling former fisherman's cottage and pilchard press enjoys a superb setting in the Downalong area of St Ives, backing onto wide, surfy Porthmeor Beach. The whitewashed B&B boasts neat sash windows and derives its name from the cobbled pavement outside, which is decorated with tubs of succulent plants. Inside, everything is compact and shipshape: there's a small neat dining room, and two doubles, a twin and a single, stylishly but simply decorated in pale colours. Breakfast consists of a full English with local sausages, alongside fresh fruit salad, juices and cereals or porridge. You're perfectly placed to explore the art heritage of St Ives, once the home of artists such as Ben Nicholson and Barbara Hepworth. A short stroll away is the town's Painting School (Ⓦstivesartschool .co.uk), recently reopened after a state of the art renovation and with imaginative short painting and drawing courses, and the Art Deco grandeur of the Tate. You can rent wet suits and boards on Porthmeor Beach, whose wide extent also makes it great for running and games.

The Cobbles, 33 Back Road West, St Ives, Cornwall, TR26 1NL Ⓣ01736 798206, Ⓦthecobbles.co.uk.
Price 2 doubles, 1 twin, 1 single, all en suite, £40–50 per person. Breakfast included. Book well in advance.
Facilities Internet. On-site parking. TVs in rooms.
Open Open year-round. Minimum stay 2 nights in summer. Check in: flexible. Check out: 10am.
Getting there St Ives can be reached by train via the scenic branch line from St Erth; the journey takes around 6hr from London. To reach it by car, take the A30 to St Erth, and then the A3074. Driving on the narrow streets is no fun, so use the long-stay car park above the town. Following signs for Tate St Ives will bring you you close to the B&B.

St Ives Backpackers

Located in a grand former Wesleyan school, *St Ives Backpackers* is slap-bang in the middle of the vibrant little beach town. It's in the process of a much-needed revamp which should captialize on the high ceilings and fine proportions of the building. You ring the buzzer to gain access to the lofty communal area, accessed via a flight of stairs, which has DVDs, a tuck shop, a pool table and sofas as well as the hostel reception. There are double and twin rooms as well as dorms, with the accent firmly on a young surf-orientated crowd. Downstairs are the shower rooms, a communal kitchen with a big wooden table, and a courtyard garden that's used for BBQs in summer. Ask the owner about the hostel's discount card, which will give you good deals on eating, drinking and surfboard, wetsuit and boat hire. The hostel is pretty much in the heart of St Ives, within easy walking distance of the beaches, the Tate, Hepworth's studio and the coastal path.

St Ives Backpackers, Street-an-Garrow, St Ives, Cornwall, TR26 1SG Ⓣ01736 799 444, Ⓦwww.backpackers.co.uk/st-ives/.
Price 11 dorm rooms, £11.95–17.95, depending on the season. 2 doubles and 2 twins with shared bathrooms, £13.95–19.95 per person.
Facilities Internet. Kitchen. Shop. Games/common room. Garden.
Open Open year-round. Check in: 5pm. Check out: flexible.
Getting there St Ives can be reached by train via the scenic branch line from St Erth; the journey takes around 6hr from London. To reach St Ives by car, take the A30 to St Erth, and then the A3074. Driving on the narrow central streets is no fun, so use the long-stay car park above the town. The hostel is in the centre of town, near the public library.

Experience that end-of-the-world feeling at *YHA Tintagel*

YHA Tintagel

If you want to really get away from it all, this cliff-top hostel could be the spot. It's accessed via a series of increasingly narrow and bumpy minor roads that lead towards the north Cornish coast, and located on Glebe Cliff, just west of Tintagel Castle. The fortress is said to be the place of King Arthur's conception but, although an air of mystery clings to the rugged ruins, the thirteenth-century castle is too recent to have a plausible claim. The low white buildings of the hostel were once the local quarry manager's cottage, and have been simply and sympathetically renovated. There's a common room and a kitchen; you can buy a few supplies here, but it's best to stock up before you come – the village of Tintagel is a somewhat desultory place, with just gift shops and a handful of cafés. The hostel enjoys spectacular coastal views over Dunderhole Point, and is ideal for outdoor types, being right on the South West Coast Path route; you can also cycle the North Cornwall Trail or pedal around the lanes and heathland of Bodmin Moor. The wild coastline is great for watersports: there's a surf school at Polzeath, plus sea- and wreck-fishing and kayaking opportunities. At the end of the day, you can relax at the hostel and take in the stunning sea views.

YHA Tintagel, Dunderhole Point, Tintagel, Cornwall, PL34 0DW ☎0845 371 9145, ⊕yha.org.uk.
Price 1 twin room. Dorms: 2x4, 2x6. Beds £21.40.
Facilities Kitchen. On-site parking. Games/common room. Garden.
Open Year-round. Check in: 5pm. Check out: 10am.
Getting there To reach Tintagel village, leave the A39 and take the B3314 and then the B3263. From Tintagel continue on the B3263 to Tregatta. Turn right along the narrow lane, then take the very rough, unlit track to hostel. On foot, follow the road to Tintagel church, then take the path to the hostel.

Truro Lodge

The owner of this relaxed Truro hostel – the town's mayor – hasn't quite got round to putting up a sign, though he's been welcoming guests for several years. That's characteristic of this distinctly uncommercial operation, down a quiet street just outside the town centre, which feels much more like a family home than a conventional hostel. The Grade II listed villa itself dates back to 1840 and has a long, tangled front garden, a pretty terrace and a spacious sitting room. Guests are welcome to use the handsome, old-fashioned kitchen, which has a pulley to dry clothes and an Aga, while upstairs there's a huge bathroom with a fine clawfoot bath, marbled fireplace and wooden floors, adding to the sense of slightly faded grandeur throughout. There are no TVs in the rooms, and none are en suite, so if you're fond of lots of creature comforts it's not for you. But Truro Lodge is full of architectural character and domestic charm, a million miles from a bland hotel chain.

Truro Lodge, 10 The Parade, Truro, Cornwall, TR1 1QE ☎01872 260857, Ⓦtrurobackpackers.co.uk.
Price 1 single £25, 2 doubles £38, 1 four-bed family room £65, 1 four-bed dorm £18.
Facilities Internet. Kitchen. Games/common room. Garden.
Open Open year-round. Check in: flexible. Check out: flexible.
Getting there Truro is at the junction of the A39 and the A390, and is well connected to the rest of Cornwall by bus and train: it's on the line between Exeter and Falmouth which runs parallel to the south coast. The hostel is just east of the town centre and fronts onto Malpas Road – your best access is from there.

Canon Grange

Canon Grange has an idyllic location in the heart of the beautiful town of Wells: the B&B backs on to the cathedral green, so there's nothing between you and the magnificent wide facade of the cathedral – one of the high points of English Gothic – but a swathe of neatly clipped grass and some strolling visitors. The tall, sixteenth-century B&B's front faces a quiet city street that leads down to a square where a market is held every Wednesday and Saturday. Inside, things are almost as impressive – *Canon Grange* is grandly decorated with antiques, bedspreads and exposed medieval beams, and the most upmarket room, the "Walnut Suite", has gleaming wooden beds and exposed black beams. The other four options are spacious and attractive, and the prices are good value given the location and plush decor. The ground-floor breakfast room is done out in traditional style with lace tablecloths and china, and mornings bring fresh fruits salads, fresh orange juice and cooked English and veggie breakfasts. The result is a great central base from which to explore this sedate, historic town in the shadow of the Mendip Hills.

Canon Grange, Cathedral Green, Wells, Somerset, BA5 2UB ☎01749 671800, Ⓦcanongrange.co.uk.
Price 4 en-suite doubles, 1 double with shared bathroom, £60–70, 1 family room sleeping up to 3, £70–85. Breakfast included.
Facilities Internet. Garden.
Open Year-round. Check in: flexible. Check out: 10am.
Getting there Wells is on the A39, about 20 miles south of Bristol; there are buses from Bristol and Bath, but no train station. The B&B is in the heart of Wells, directly opposite the cathedral.

Old Chapel Backpackers

ZENNOR

The *Old Chapel Backpackers*, a likeable base in the Cornish village of Zennor – home to great walks, rumours of mermaids and a superb pub – gets a thumbs up on all fronts. The hostel is housed in a handsome stone chapel, and run with vigour and enthusiasm by a friendly young team. The downstairs café is a destination in its own right for walkers and tourists, with large slabs of home-made cake, colourful art on the walls and a zingy bistro feel; eat here or at the trestle tables outside, surrounded by tubs of flowers. Upstairs, bedrooms still have their original round-arched windows and shutters. The wooden bunks in the dorms are sturdy and handsome, and there's an excellent family room/ double with a double bed and two bunks. The place is impeccably clean and all in all offers the perfect pitstop for a coastal walk – be sure to book in advance as it's justly popular.

> **Old Chapel Backpackers, Zennor, Cornwall, TR26 3BY** ☎ **01736 798307,** Ⓦ **backpackers.co.uk/zennor/page2.htm.**
>
> **Price** 30 dorm beds £18 . 1 family room (with 1 double and 2 bunk beds) £70, £50 if occupied by a couple.
>
> **Facilities** Internet. On-site parking. Café. Games/common room. Garden. Breakfast and lunch available.
>
> **Open** Year-round. Check in: 5pm. Check out: 10am.
>
> **Getting there** Zennor sits just short of the coast, 4 miles west of Penzance; take the B3306. The village is on the bus route between St Ives and Penzance.

There are no facilities for self-catering, though the café serves breakfast and provides packed lunches as well as dishing up filling curries, lasagne and quiches, plus soups, salad and even cream teas. The bright yellow café lounge has a TV and a collection of DVDs, should you need them.

Zennor itself, a rugged hamlet 4 miles west of St Ives, is a compelling place; one-time resident D.H. Lawrence compared the sea surrounding the "tiny granite village nestling under high shaggy moor-hills" favourably to the Med. He lived here with his German wife Frieda, though unhappily they were hounded out under suspicion of being enemy spies. Be sure to have a peek inside the ancient church of St Senara (from whom the village derives its name), which features a 500-year-old wooden chair carved with a mermaid. The unusual and very unsecular object is said to have been inspired by the legend of a local chorister, lured into the sea by a mermaid who loved his singing.

Next door to the hostel is an excellent thirteenth-century pub, the *Tinner's Arms*, which offers regular folk evenings and serves local ales and upmarket pub food. Intriguing walks lead off in all directions – you'll soon notice ancient stone cattle grids embedded in the fields, and the area is dotted with hugely impressive Neolithic stone tombs. The imposing Zennor quoit, just east of the village, is the largest Neolithic dolmen (chamber tomb) in Britain. All in all, the village and nearby sea cliffs have an appealing end of the world feel, but with the big added bonus of promixity to the galleries, restaurants and shops of St Ives.

One option to reach the enticing golden beaches, galleries, restaurants and shops of St Ives from Zennor is to walk along a particularly dramatic, demanding and rocky stretch of the coastal path. Give yourself a break and take the bus back to the village for the return trip, perhaps nursing a restorative pint of real ale at the *Tinner's Arms* before turning in for a peaceful night's sleep at this most attractive of hostels.

Clockwise from top left The *Tinner's Arms* is a great spot for a local ale; traditional exterior and lively interior at the *Old Chapel Backpackers*; the hostel is located near golden beaches and cliff-top walks

THE MIDLANDS

For many, the Midlands is synonymous with the large industrial centres of Birmingham, Leicester and Coventry. But this wide swathe of the country, from the Welsh border to the Lincolnshire Fens, also takes in some of England's most rural and picturesque counties in Derbyshire, Staffordshire, Shropshire, Herefordshire and Warwickshire, and includes the wild and open Peak District as well as the lush landscapes and impossibly pretty villages of the Cotswolds. The counties to the east are less enticing, but we've included options that allow you to explore the handsome hilltown of Lincoln, as well as the fens and Sherwood Forest. And while Birmingham might not feature on a conventional tourist itinerary, it's an energetic and culturally vibrant city with a lot to offer.

There are some superb hostels and B&Bs in the region, many located in lush countryside or attractive towns and villages. Across the board, we've tried to identify intriguing buildings for you to hole up in: an Elizabethan half-timbered house in lovely Bishop's Castle, a farmhouse near Matlock with a fifteenth-century kitchen, a YHA in a Victorian Gothic pile overlooking the Wye and a stylish Japanese-style capsule hotel in Birmingham. The region's B&Bs are high on home

comforts: most use local produce to concoct an excellent filling breakfast to set you up for the day. Many hostels, meanwhile, sit in historic properties that belie their bargain rates – you can pay as little as £10 to stay at a surprisingly swish Peak District country house in Hartingdon.

Indeed, with most of the Midlands a little off the tourist trail, you'll find prices reasonable and visitor numbers not overwhelming. One exception is the Cotswolds, whose venerable villages, built in honey-coloured stone, are irresistible, as crowds of visitors testify. And the gritstone ridges and limestone crags of the Peak District draw plenty of walkers, who are well served by village B&Bs and fine hostels.

On the border of Wales, Herefordshire and Shropshire, with their chalk ridges, dense hedgerows, meandering rivers and flower-filled meadows, are almost as appealing. In sharp contrast, Birmingham is notorious for its ringroads and 1960s architectural monstrosities, but it's a cultural magnet and also has a core of fine Georgian and Victorian buildings, great galleries and good shopping.

THE MIDLANDS

NAME	LOCATION	PAGE		REAL BARGAIN	TREAT YOURSELF	FAMILY-FRIENDLY	GREAT RURAL LOCATION	OUTDOOR ACTIVITIES	GREAT FOOD AND DRINK	DORMS	PUBLIC TRANSPORT
Birmingham Central Backpackers	Birmingham	81	10						✓	✓	✓
Bloc	Birmingham	81	9						✓		✓
Bunns Croft	Moreton Eye	90	3				✓				
Fern Cottage	Pucklechurch	93	7			✓					
Machado Gallery	Barford	80	16			✓					
Manor Farm	Dethick	85	17			✓	✓	✓			
The Porch House	Bishop's Castle	82	2						✓	✓	
St Anne's	Painswick	92	8			✓	✓		✓		
St Clement's Lodge	Lincoln	88	20						✓		✓
Stoop House Farm	Butterton	84	11			✓	✓	✓			
The Wheatsheaf Inn	Ludlow	89	4						✓		✓
White House	Folkingham	87	21			✓					
Willoughby House	Norwell	91	19			✓					
YHA Clun Mill	Clun	84	1				✓	✓		✓	
YHA Hartington Hall	Hartington	87	12	✓			✓	✓	✓	✓	✓
YHA Ravenstor	Millers Dale	90	13			✓	✓	✓		✓	✓
YHA Sherwood Forest	Edwinstowe	86	18				✓	✓		✓	
YHA Stow-on-the-Wold	Stow-on-the-Wold	95	14			✓			✓	✓	
YHA Stratford-upon-Avon	Alveston	80	15				✓		✓	✓	✓
YHA Welsh Bicknor	Ross-on-Wye	94	6				✓	✓	✓	✓	
YHA Wilderhope Manor	Longville in the Dale	89	5	✓			✓	✓		✓	
YHA Woody's Top	Ruckland	94	22							✓	

From left *St. Clement's Lodge* (see p.88); *YHA Stow-on-the-Wold* (see p.95) **Previous page** Lincoln

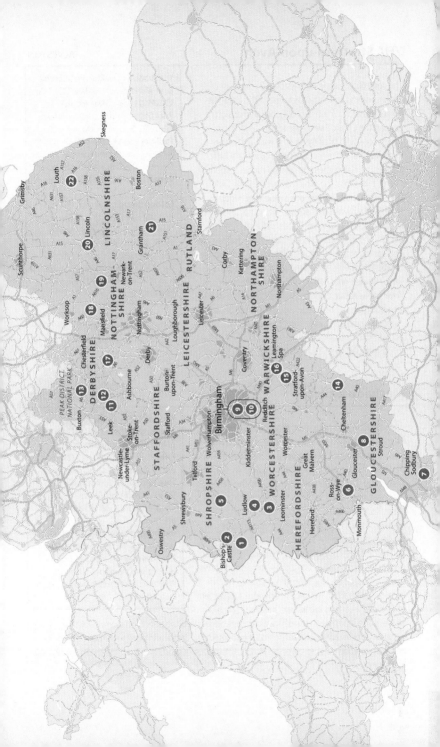

YHA Stratford-upon-Avon

The commuter village of Alveston – 2 miles east of Shakespeare's birthplace – is home to this attractive hostel, located in a substantial Georgian mansion. Beyond the Classical white facade, the YHA has a cheery look with brightly painted walls and plenty of communal space and sweeping grounds which are ideal for ball games and general running around. There's bike rental too, which is handy for the fairly flat ride into Stratford (otherwise there are regular buses). The town's Shakespeare connection means that it's jam-packed year-round, and you'll find plenty of sights – the Birthplace Museum and Anne Hathaway's Cottage are the classic stops, while Hall's Croft explores Elizabethan medicine and thirteenth-century Holy Trinity Church houses the Bard's grave. Of course, the Royal Shakespeare Company is based here too, and its repertory nature means you can see a range of plays – not all by the great man – over the course of a few days. Another attraction is the eating scene: aside from umpteen pubs and restaurants, beamed and ancient *Lambs* on Sheep Street is highly recommended for its hearty meat dishes and English puds.

YHA Stratford-upon-Avon, Wellesbourne Road, Alveston, Warwickshire, CV37 7RG ☎0845 371 9661, Ⓦyha.org.uk.
Price Dorms: 10 twin rooms, 2x3, 7x4, 7x6, 2x8, 1x10 £15.40 per person.
Facilities Internet. Kitchen. On-site parking. Bar. Café. Games/common room. Garden. Bike rental. Breakfast and dinner available.
Open Year-round. Check in: flexible. Check out: 10am.
Getting there From Junction 15 of the M40, take the A429 south and follow signs to Charlecote Park, then turn right onto the B4086; the hostel is less than 2 miles from here on the right. Stratford-upon-Avon station, with services to London Marylebone, is 2.5 miles away – buses #15, #18 and #18A head to the hostel.

Machado Gallery

Barford's long, low brick-built *Machado Gallery* is an elegantly furnished treasure-trove of art and antiques. The sculptor owner sees herself as continuing a craft tradition that started in the artisan joiner's workshop here in the mid-eighteenth century, and the gallery itself features changing exhibitions of paintings, prints, ceramics and textiles. The two large B&B rooms are decked out with Turkish carpets, simple antiques and quality linen, while the studio room, with its skylights and arched French windows, is particularly light-filled and attractive. Breakfast comprises home-made bread and marmalade and locally sourced produce for the continental buffet or full English (there's a supplement of £6.50 for a cooked breakfast). Outside, you can sit by the pond in the walled and moated garden and soak in the tranquil village vibe. Barford is a good base for Warwick, with its splendid early medieval castle, and don't miss the wonderfully eccentric tearoom in Lord Leycester Hospital. You're also a short drive from the theatres, pubs and restaurants of Stratford-upon-Avon.

Machado Gallery, 9 Wellesbourne Road, Barford, Warwickshire, CV35 8EL ☎01926 624061, Ⓦmachadogallery.co.uk.
Price Studio room £95, Room 1 £89, Room 2 £79. Continental breakfast included.
Facilities Internet. Breakfast available. Games/common room. Garden.
Open Year-round. Check in: flexible. Check out: 10am.
Getting there From Junction 15 on the M40 take the A429 towards Wellesbourne. Take the first left turn to Barford, cross the old bridge and the mini roundabout into Wellesbourne Road and *Machado* is 55yds on the left-hand side.

Birmingham Central Backpackers

If it's budget backpacker Birmingham you're after, then this is the spot for you. This hostel in a former pub is located on a wide and rather desolate street of warehouses near the coach station, but don't be put off: the family-owned place is a warm and welcoming traveller's hub. It's very much geared to the youth market, its brick interior heaped with spinning globes, piles of DVDs, games and knickknacks, a large-screen telly and a dizzying paint job. There's a small kitchen for self-catering – no meals are available in the hostel. Despite the somewhat grungy vibe, it's impeccably clean, and one nice touch is the little courtyard garden with a ping pong table and tubs of flowers, with huge brick railway arches looming impressively overhead. Sleeping options comprise private rooms, mixed and female dorms and an eight-bed "pod dorm" with individual reading lights, lockers and comfy mattresses. Sinuous Selfridges, with its futuristic metallic cladding, is just up the road, and you're within walking distance of Chinatown, plus galleries, excellent clubs, live-music venues and restaurants.

> **Birmingham Central Backpackers, 58 Coventry Street, Birmingham, B5 5NH** ☎0121 643 0033, ⓦbirmingham centralbackpackers.com.
> **Price** Dorms £12.50–30, depending on dorm size. 1x4, 6x6, 1x8, 1x12 (all mixed); 2x6 (female); 1x8 (pod dorm). 2 singles £30, 2 twins £44, 1 triples £66, 1 quad £88. Light breakfast included.
> **Facilities** Internet. Kitchen. On-site parking. Bar. Games/common room. Garden. TVs in rooms. Lockers.
> **Open** Year-round. Check in: flexible. Check out: flexible.
> **Getting there** The hostel is located on the corner of Oxford and Coventry streets, a 5min walk from Birmingham Central coach station and a 15min walk from Birmingham New Street station.

Bloc

With more than a dash of visual style and wit, *Bloc* brings the Japanese capsule-hotel concept to Birmingham's lively, swish Jewellery Quarter. True to its name, the building is a block, but not a featureless one – one whole side is occupied by a glassed-in reception and sitting area, with cool graphics, cube-shaped light fittings and bright furniture. The style throughout is economy chic, and they've cleverly made savings on space but not on the quality of the furnishings and fittings, meaning this is a million miles from threadbare budget accommodation. The rooms are undeniably small – some have windows while others have blinds which just conceal a wall – but comfortable enough for a good night's sleep. Each room incorporates a flat-screen TV and a ship-cabin-style wetroom with an impressive power shower, plus there's an eco-friendly a/c system and neat under-bed storage. The only communal space is the reception and an ironing room, but for under £10 the hotel will order a cute breakfast in a box for you from a nearby café. And the historic Jewellery Quarter, otherwise out of the reach of budget travellers, makes a great weekend base.

> **Bloc, Caroline Street, Birmingham, B3 1UG** ☎0121 212 1223, ⓦblochotels.com.
> **Price** 73 en-suite doubles £50–65.
> **Facilities** Internet. TVs in rooms. Breakfast available.
> **Open** Year-round. Check in: flexible. Check out: 10am.
> **Getting there** The hotel is located at the northeastern side of the city centre, just north of the grassy square surrounding St Paul's Church; it's a 20min walk from Birmingham New Street station. *Bloc* has a discount deal with the nearby NCP car park.

The Porch House

BISHOP'S CASTLE

The Porch House, unmissably grand on the sloping main street of the Shropshire town of Bishop's Castle, is a stunning example of Elizabethan domestic architecture: a stay here is a treat for history lovers or anyone with a penchant for old buildings. The huge, half-timbered house was built in 1564 – the year of Shakespeare's birth – and the basic structure of wattle and daub and huge oak beams survives, along with a more sober eighteenth-century extension at the back. By the late 1970s the building was in a poor state, thanks to damp and death-watch beetles, and English Heritage sponsored a restoration – look out for the modern sculptures of children on the façade. In 2002 the house was bought by Gill and John Lucas, who run the place as a relaxed and welcoming B&B.

The Porch House, 33–35 High Street, Bishop's Castle, Shropshire, SY9 5BE ☎01588 638854, Ⓦtheporchhouse.com.
Price 2 en-suite doubles £70–80, breakfast included. 2 self-catering apartments £230–240 (weekend), £270–280 (week) in high season.
Facilities Internet. On-site parking. Games/common room. Garden. TVs in rooms.
Open Year-round. Sat night only bookings not normally available. Check in: flexible. Check out: 11am.
Getting there Bishop's Castle is just off the A468 south of Shrewsbury. The nearest railway station is 12 miles away at Craven Arms.

The eponymous porch itself is very imposing; beyond this, the area that was the courtyard has been glassed to create a light-filled hallway. Otherwise, amazing old features remain intact: wonky, gleaming oak floorboards, time-worn timber framing and stone floors filched around 1700 from the castle up the hill. There's even a cabinet with medallions featuring Napoleon, left by a prisoner of the Napoleonic Wars who was billeted here. Upstairs, the en-suite rooms are spacious, prettily furnished and full of character and interest; there's a large dining room for guests and a garden, and the owners also rent out two self-contained apartments in the house. For breakfast there's cereal and porridge, plus the local butcher's

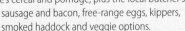

sausage and bacon, free-range eggs, kippers, smoked haddock and veggie options.

The little town itself is a total gem – it was a planned town in 1087, and the original layout of long plots divided by lanes and facing onto a main street is still discernible. At the top of the street are the remnants of the castle itself; further down you'll find a hotpotch of historic houses, excellent pubs and independent shops. It's a lively place – the pubs often host good folk and jazz nights, and there's a general market every Friday, a farmer's market every third Saturday of the month and flea and collectors' markets on the first Saturday of the month. The nearby walking on the chalk ridges of the Shropshire Hills is superb, and you're surrounded by magnificent stately homes such as Powis Castle and fairytale Stokesay.

Clockwise from top left *The Porch House*'s prettily furnished bedrooms; the sunroofed stairwell, once the home's courtyard; the half-timbered exterior stands out even in Bishop's Castle's pretty streets

Stoop House Farm

Butterton is a fine Peak District village, with its ancient stone houses, precipitous streets, rocket-like church spire and traditional pub. And comfortable *Stoop House Farm*, at its heart, is the perfect place from which to explore the village, as well as Staffordshire's moorlands and Derbyshire's peaks. The owners of this eighteenth-century working farm offer B&B in the house and self-catering in the converted stable in the grounds. The B&B room enjoys its own private entrance, and features a fine eighteenth-century bed carved with Welsh dragons. There's a swish modern bathroom, while the guest sitting room features oak beams, deep armchairs scattered with cushions, a tall stone fireplace and sweeping views from the breakfast table, where you'll be served with bacon and sausages from the local butcher. Outside, guests enjoy their own patch of the garden with outdoor seating. The equally stylish converted stables have flagstone floors, a modern timber roof and staircase, chunky wooden furniture and a well-equipped kitchen. If you can tear yourself away, you'll find trails in all directions taking you into superb walking country, as well as Butterton's *Black Lion* pub with its open fires, pool table and walkers' bar.

Stoop House Farm, Butterton, Staffordshire, ST13 7SY ☎ 01538 304486, W stoophousefarm.co.uk.
Price 1 en-suite double £70. Stables (sleep 4) £400–600 per week. Breakfast included.
Facilities Internet. On-site parking. Games/common room. Garden.
Open Year-round. Check in: flexible. Check out: flexible.
Getting there The A53 runs from Stoke and the M1 to Leek. From here, take the A523 then the B5053. Pass Onecote and take the second turning on your right to Butterton. Once in the village, head past the village shop; after 100yd take the right fork.

YHA Clun Mill

Set in the prime walking country of the south Shropshire hills, this little hostel occupies a unique property: a restored seventeenth-century watermill in the unspoilt village of Clun. You can still see the old mill machinery, and the building enjoys a pretty location in its own grounds on the edge of town. Inside, lots of old features have been retained: there's a rugged flagstone floor, dark timbers in the ceilings and exposed stonework in the small dorms, which have sturdy bunks and wooden floors: the lounge/dining room has a woodburning stove for cooler days. Otherwise it's an austere option, which suits the outdoorsy clientele. The hostel is a terrific base for walking and cycling, within striking distance of Offa's Dyke, a trail leading along the King of Mercia's ancient boundary wall, the looping 140-mile Shropshire Way, and the Devil's Chair rock formation on the Stiperstones ridge. Clun is surrounded by high chalk ridges and features a ruined Norman castle and a traditional pub, the *White Horse*, while further forays can be made to fantastical Stokesay Castle, the ancient town of Ludlow (see p.89), and historic hippie haven Bishop's Castle (see p.82)

YHA Clun Mill, The Mill, Clun, Craven Arms, Shropshire, SY7 8NY ☎ 0845 371 9112, W yha.org.uk.
Price Dorms: 2x4, 1x7, 1x8 £19.40.
Facilities Kitchen. On-site parking. Games/common room. Garden.
Restrictions Curfew 10pm.
Open Year-round. Check in: 5pm. Check out: 10am.
Getting there Clun is on the A488, southwest of Shrewsbury. From Clun High Street (B4368) go to the end of Ford Street, turn right and then left. The hostel is 220yd on the right, past Memorial Hall. The nearest train station is 8 miles away at Craven Arms.

Manor Farm

The phrase "steeped in history" is overused, but it fits the bill for *Manor Farm*, an enticing B&B in the quiet Derbyshire countryside. Originally built in 1403 and still a working sheep farm, it was once the home of Sir Anthony Babington, source of the infamous Babington Plot against Elizabeth I, which led to the death of Mary Queen of Scots and his own grisly execution, aged 25. The house was rebuilt in 1670, the original building providing enough stone to construct the next-door church, an icehouse and the outbuildings, which now comprise the hamlet of Dethick. In more recent times, the house was home to Alison Uttley, who wrote the engaging *Traveller in Time* (1939) based on the Babington Plot. The ancient open kitchen has dark beams and huge fireplaces, and the guest rooms are the result of an impeccably eco-friendly makeover, soothingly decorated with pale linen, antique furniture and super-comfortable beds. Breakfasts here use local produce and the B&B's own veg and fruit. The lively, thoughtful owner will advise on the wealth of hiking and cycling in the Dales and the Peak District and on stately homes nearby, and in the evening you can cross the fields for a meal and a pint at the pub *Jugg and Glass*.

Manor Farm, Dethick, nr Matlock, Derbyshire, DE4 5GG ☎01629 534302, Ⓦwww.manorfarmdethick.co.uk.
Price 5 en-suite twins and doubles £80–85. 1 twin/double with separate bathroom which can be booked with one of the en-suite rooms for a total of £120–145. Breakfast included.
Facilities Internet. On-site parking. Garden.
Open Year-round. Check in: 4pm. Check out: 10am.
Getting there Dethick is a 15min drive west of the M1. Take Junction 28 and take the A615, turning at Tansley Crossroads for Dethick Lane. The owner will collect guests from the train station at Matlock, which has services to Derby and Nottingham.

Clockwise from top left *Manor Farm*; Babington remembered; outdoor seating; indoor dining

Clockwise from top left YHA Sherwood Forest's dining room; its chunky exterior; seventeenth-century White House has an elegant interior; White House, seen from the village green

YHA Sherwood Forest

EDWINSTOWE

Kids will love getting this close to Robin Hood's woodland realm – this purpose-built hostel is set by Edwinstowe village cricket pitch, right on the edge of Sherwood Forest. Both the visitor centre and the vast Major Oak – 16m high, at least 800 years old and described in legends as sheltering Robin and the Merry Men – are just a few minutes' walk away.

The hostel itself is a substantial barn-like building, housing eleven small dorms and two two-bed rooms plus an airy dining room and a decent kitchen for self-caterers. It's a great place for families with small kids to entertain, with a garden for running around, a TV room with board games and a Wii. There's a bike store too – you'll probably want to bring or hire bikes as this is ideal cycling territory. The visitor centre has details on cycling, hiking and spotting some of the forest's trees, although it's worth bearing in mind that, for all its legends, Sherwood Forest itself has been much reduced – a larger stretch of the same ancient woodland is accessible at Clumber Park, 6 miles to the north. Back at the hostel, the village of Edwinstowe provides a Co-op, pubs and cafés, and a swimming pool, a handy option for rainy days.

YHA Sherwood Forest, Forest Corner, Edwinstowe, Nottinghamshire, NG21 9RN ☎0845 371 9139, ⓦyha.org.uk.
Price 2 twin rooms, 11x4 dorm beds, £22.40 per bed.
Facilities Kitchen On-site parking. Games/common room. Garden. Bike rental. Breakfast and dinner available.
Restrictions Curfew 11pm.
Open Year-round. Check in: 3pm. Check out: 10am.
Getting there From Junction 28 on the M1, take the A38, turning on to the A6075 for Edwinstowe just before Mansfield. Follow signs in the village centre for the hostel. The nearest train station is 8 miles away at Mansfield, while bus #33 runs from Nottingham to Edwinstowe.

White House

Many B&Bs make the claim of being a home from home, but seventeenth-century *White House*, genuinely has that feel – in a home that's grander than most people can aspire to. The rooms are painted in sympathetic colours and furnished with Georgian antiques, paintings and prints, but the feel is lived-in rather than precious. A breakfast including local eggs and bacon is served in the front dining room with its stone fireplace, rush mat floor and high windows, while at the back of the house there's a delightfully snug sitting room for guests with a parquet floor and a wood-burning stove; in summer you can sit out in

White House, 25 Market Place, Folkingham, Lincolnshire, NG34 0SE ☎01529 497298, ✆bedandbreakfast folkinghamlincolnshire.co.uk.
Price 1 en-suite double and 1 en-suite double/twin £70. Adjoining single £30–50.
Facilities Internet. On-site parking. Games/common room. Garden. TVs in rooms.
Open Year-round. Check in: flexible. Check out: flexible.
Getting there Folkingham is halfway between Lincoln and Peterborough on the A15.

the lush garden with swifts flying overhead. The bedrooms are comfortable and stylish – the downstairs double has a four-poster, the adjoining single can accommodate a child or extra adult and the prettily decorated upstairs room can be used as a double or a twin. Folkingham itself is quiet, but makes a good centre for trips to an array of nearby historic homes, including Belton House, Belvoir Castle, Burghley House, Grimsthorpe Castle and Doddington Hall.

YHA Hartington Hall

A drive across the bare, windswept and often misty expanses of the Derbyshire dales can leave you feeling very far from civilization. All the more surprising, then, to arrive at the attractive limestone and gritstone village of Hartington, set on a gentle hillside, and find elegant seventeenth-century *Hartington Hall*. This is a flagship property for the YHA, having been upgraded to something approaching a country-house hotel. Downstairs there's a bar, a lively restaurant and a comfortable lounge. Upstairs are the dorms and rooms, all cosily fitted out with en-suite shower rooms and individual reading lights. This is an old building, but the restoration has left many architectural features intact, including a sloping wooden door leading to a double room where Bonnie Prince Charlie is reputed to have slept. Most visitors here are bent on exploring the outdoors, as you're right in the heart of the Peak District National Park. At the end of the day, a hearty hostel

Hartington Hall, Hall Bank, Hartington, Derbyshire, SK17 0AT ☎0845 371 9740, ✆yha.org.uk.
Price 5 singles, 5 twins, 3 doubles, 4 triples. Dorms: 10x4, 3x5, 2x6 beds, 1x7, 3x8. £22.40 per person, with substantial discounts for walk-ins.
Facilities Internet. Kitchen. On-site parking. Bar. Games/common room. Garden. Breakfast, lunch and dinner available.
Open Year-round. Check in: flexible. Check out: 10am.
Getting there Hartington is off the A515 between Ashbourne and Buxton on the B5054; Hall Bank is the first road on the left as you enter the village. The Bowers bus #442 runs between Ashbourne and Buxton (accessed by hourly trains from Manchester Piccadilly), passing through Hartington.

meal and a pint at the bar are the perfect pick-me-up, and the village is lovely for an evening wander, with its duckpond, Georgian houses, rustic cottages and thirteenth-century church.

St Clement's Lodge

Get past its bland lower district, and Lincoln has the magic of an Italian hill town. You ascend aptly named Steep Hill, past a jigsaw of medieval houses and shops, to the mighty twelfth-century cathedral with its high façade of sculpted panels and – just five minutes' walk beyond – cosy *St Clement's Lodge*. The foursquare villa was built in 1989, and its wisteria-clad exterior has Victorian-style good looks, while the rooms inside are spacious and modern. The owners are friendly and capable, happy to chat or to leave you to enjoy some peace, and rooms are simply but attractively decorated and feature king-size beds. Breakfast, served in the downstairs dining room, is a big event – as well as the usual options you can enjoy poached haddock, smoked salmon, kippers, kidneys or liver. The owners have plenty of recommendations for what to see and do: as

St Clement's Lodge, 21 Langworthgate, Lincoln, Lincolnshire, LN2 4AD ☎01522 521532, 🌐stclementslodge.co.uk.
Price 2 en-suite doubles, 1 twin with separate bathroom £70. Breakfast included.
Facilities Internet. On-site parking. Games/common room. Garden. TVs in rooms.
Open Year-round. Check in: flexible. Check out: flexible.
Getting there From the A1 take the A15 to Lincoln. Turn left at the traffic lights by the cathedral. Trains run to York, Leeds and London King's Cross – from the station, take Steep Hill past the cathedral, then follow Eastgate and take a left fork onto Langworthgate.

well as the star attractions of the cathedral and the castle with its ancient walls, there's the twelfth-century Jew's House – the medieval town had a flourishing Jewish population – and plenty of traces of Roman Lincoln to discover. It's a thriving, upmarket place, with excellent boutique shopping and independently owned cafés, pubs and restaurants: try *Café Zoot* for lunchtime salads and hearty supper dishes, *Gino's* for pizza and pasta in lively surroundings.

Clockwise from left Lincoln Cathedral; the wisteria-clad front of *St. Clement's*; the lodge's downstairs dining room

YHA Wilderhope Manor

From the darting swallows nesting in the porch to the creaking sixteenth-century floorboards, *Wilderhope*, located on the wooded escarpment of Wenlock Edge, is one of the YHA's most historic and atmospheric properties. It's undeniably spartan – although a planned redevelopment may smarten things up – but offers a unique opportunity for a budget stay in an ancient property. Built in 1586 as a manor house, *Wilderhope* remained in the same family until 1742, but its condition deteriorated until a 1930s restoration by the Cadbury family that made it a National Trust property but guaranteed it would also operate as a hostel. Inside, the original plasterwork and panelling remains remarkably intact, and there's a magnificent flagstoned dining room (where full meals are served) with a huge fireplace, a rugged basement bar and a couple of ancient spiral staircases. The dorms feature gleaming, wonky wooden floors and lattice windows with tinted views of Wenlock Edge, whose beauty inspired A.E. Housman and Vaughan Williams. You're likely to encounter lots of walkers and cyclists here – it's a staging post on the route from Land's End to John O'Groats. On a summer evening, the stone terrace outside is a perfect spot to relax.

YHA Wilderhope Manor, Longville in the Dale, Shropshire, TF13 6EG ☎0845 371 9149, ⓦyha.org.uk.
Price Dorms: 1x3, 1x4, 2x5, 1x6, 2x10, 2x12 £13.
Facilities Internet. Kitchen. Bar. Café. Shop. Games/common room. Garden. Breakfast and dinner available.
Open Year-round, but Feb–Oct open weekends only. Check in: 3pm. Check out: 10am.
Getting there From Shrewsbury, take the A458 southeast. Just before Much Wenlock, turn right onto the B4371 towards Church Stretton. Continue for 6 miles to Longville in the Dale, take the first left and continue up the lane. As you approach the brow of the hill, the hostel drive is on your left.

The Wheatsheaf Inn

The half-timbered, weathered-stone houses of Ludlow gather round a rambling ruined castle that sits above the Teme and Corve rivers. If you want to soak up the atmosphere, *The Wheatsheaf* is hard to beat: located at the foot of Broad Street in the shadow of Ludlow's only remaining medieval gate, the pub has been serving pints for nearly 300 years. The interior retains some of the old features: timbered ceilings, rough stone walls and an open fire. Upstairs are five snug en-suite rooms, brightly decorated and comfortable. A full English and buffet breakfast is available in the morning, served in the restaurant by the bar. You're well placed here for a visit to the impressive, ruined castle which still rises high above the town. The town's other attractions include the Church of St Laurence, with its fifteenth-century stained glass, and the Jacobean hotel *Feather*, featuring a fantastical carved wooden facade. The town is a bit of a foodie hotspot: try acclaimed *Mr Underhills*, by the castle ramparts, if you're feeling flush, or head to *The Olive Branch* on the Bull Ring for light daytime meals.

The Wheatsheaf Inn, Lower Broad Street, Ludlow, Shropshire, SY8 1PQ ☎01584 872 980, ⓦthe-wheatsheaf-inn.co.uk.
Price 4 en-suite doubles, 1 en-suite twin £70. If used as family room: 2 adults & 1 child £85, 3 adults £100. Breakfast included.
Facilities Bar. TVs in rooms. Dinner available.
Open Year-round. Check in: flexible. Check out: 10am.
Getting there Ludlow is on the A49 south of Shrewsbury, and is on the train line between Hereford and Shrewsbury. The inn is a 10min walk from the station.

YHA Ravenstor

With its Potterish name, country-house facade, great views and sweeping 70-acre grounds, *YHA Ravenstor* is one of the grandest hostels in the Peak District. The building itself, ringed by mature trees, is owned by the National Trust but has been given a bright makeover, featuring a lounge with log fire, cheerful dorms and a good self-catering kitchen. This is a terrific base for walkers, with hikes and cycle rides from the front door: it's located on White Peak Way, which cuts through Dovedale, the 200-mile Pennine Bridleway and the Monsal cycling trail. The grounds lead into Tideswell Dale nature reserve, where you can see wild flowers such as orchids and cowslips. And the village of Tideswell itself, a few minutes' walk away, has a lofty church known as the Cathedral of the Peak, built in the fourteenth century and featuring the altar tomb of an Agincourt knight. Other nearby highlights include Chatsworth with its sweeping fountain-filled gardens, and – at the other end of the scale – the heart-

YHA Ravenstor, Millers Dale, Buxton, Derbyshire, SK17 8SS ☎0845 371965, Ⓦyha.org.uk.
Price 3 twins from £35. Dorms: 1x3, 4x4, 1x5, 3x6, 1x7, 2x8 from £17.40.
Facilities Internet. On-site parking. Shop. Games/common room. Garden. Breakfast and dinner available.
Open Year-round. Check in: 5pm. Check out: 10am.
Getting there The nearest train station (with regular services to Manchester) is 8 miles away in Buxton; buses #65 and #66 run from here to Tideswell. By car, from the M1 take Junction 29 towards Chesterfield and follow the brown signs to Chatsworth House. Join the A623 at Baslow and turn left to Tideswell after 8 miles. Go through Tideswell, and the hostel is on the left after 1.5 miles.

stopping rollercoasters of Alton Towers. The food at the YHA is pretty good; otherwise head to the *Red Lion* in nearby Litton for real ale and generous portions of traditional pub food.

Bunns Croft

Bunns Croft is as picturesque an English country cottage as you could imagine. The fifteenth-century building is cruck-framed, its huge oak timbers arcing inwards to support the roof, and the weathered wood and ochre exterior is encircled by herbaceous borders, an abundant herb garden and rambling roses. Inside, there are stone floors, cast-iron beds in cosy rooms and rich colours on the walls. The gentle hills of the surrounding area are crisscrossed by country lanes and walking trails: after an award-winning, locally sourced organic breakfast at the B&B, you might want to explore the Mortimer Trail, which runs from Ludlow to Kington. Moreton Eye is just north of the market town of Leominster, whose wide main street is lined with ancient houses and shops. There's also a "black and white villages" trail, named for the county's

Bunns Croft, Moreton Eye, Herefordshire, HR6 0DP ☎01568 615836, Ⓦbedandbreakfastnationwide.com /leominster-bunns-croft-2359.html.
Price 1 en-suite twin, 1 double with private bathroom, both £70–80. 2 singles with private bathrooms from £35. Breakfast included.
Facilities Internet. Garden. Dinner available.
Open Year-round. Check in: flexible. Check out: 10am.
Getting there From Leominster take the A49 towards Ludlow for 4 miles. In the village of Ashton, turn left towards Luston. *Bunns Croft* is a mile from the main road on the right-hand side.

timber-framed buildings, and you're in a good spot to visit the local medieval churches as well as stately homes such as eighteenth-century Berrington Court. Back at the B&B, the owner will provide an excellent three-course dinner for around £25.

Willoughby House's rooms and suites are soothingly decorated and well equipped

Willoughby House

NORWELL

The village of Norwell sits between Nottingham and Lincoln, a few miles east of Sherwood Forest. It's a drowsy place, but the medieval church of St Lawrence and the *Plough Inn* add some interest and this large, confident three-storey B&B, set just off the A1, is an attractive stop-off. The brick farmhouse was built in 1780, and its interior is made welcoming with a bold and beautiful Georgian colour scheme: in the dining room the open fire, gleaming wooden furniture and chandelier are set off with poppy-red walls, while the bedrooms are done out in more soothing shades. There are antique paintings, china and carpets throughout, but vibrant colours and an eclectic mix of traditional and contemporary pieces give the place a chic feel. There's a spacious double with extra-long bath; a twin with a large leather sofa and granite fireplace; and a suite with two rooms in the raftered loft, which share a bathroom. The annexe, in a restored granary in the grounds, has a master bedroom with its own wood-burning stove, roll-top bath, beamed ceiling and sofa (dogs are allowed in the annex). The English, veggie and Continental breakfasts, made with fresh local produce, are a big draw. Nearby Southwell has an twelfth-century minster with rocket-like spires and an intriguing, poignant sight: a substantial nineteenth-century workhouse owned by the National Trust.

Willoughby House, Main Street, Norwell, Nottinghamshire, NG23 6JN ☎01636 636266, Ⓦwilloughbyhousebandb .co.uk.

Price 1 double with private bathroom, 1 en-suite double/twin, 1 en-suite annexe room £80–85. 1 suite with double and twin rooms and bathroom, from £140 if booked together, £80 if booked individually. £10 weekend supplement may apply. Breakfast included.

Facilities Internet. On-site parking. Garden. TVs in rooms.

Open Year-round. Check in: flexible. Check out: flexible.

Getting there Leave the A1 two exits north of Newark, following signs to Norwell. In the village, pass the church, and the next turn on the left is School Lane. Stay on Main Street, and you'll see the B&B on your left.

St Anne's

This eighteenth-century wool merchant's house offers charming B&B in the heart of Painswick, which grew rich on the trade. It's decked out with antiques, and the ground-floor twin room and two doubles – one with a four-poster – combine traditional decor with home comforts; guests can relax on the sofa in the dining room where there's an open fire. The organic, locally sourced breakfasts include home-made jam and bread – indeed, their whole smallholding is organic, just part of a well-thought-out green policy that also sees them use renewable energy for their electricity. The owners welcome walkers and cyclists in particular, providing picnic lunches, and will help with lifts if you don't have you own transport. The ancient grey limestone buildings of Painswick make it one of the prettiest villages in the Cotswolds – which is saying a lot. There's an excellent old pub in the form of the CAMRA-acclaimed *Royal Oak*, a good village deli, a timber-framed post office, a Norman church with tabletop tombs and 99 yew trees and the oldest bowling green in England. Perhaps the biggest draw though is the village's flamboyant early eighteenth-century Rococo garden, dotted with statues and follies and housing a magnificent symmetrical kitchen garden.

St Anne's, Gloucester Street, Painswick, Gloucestershire, GL6 6QN ☎01452 812879, ✆st-annes-painswick.co.uk.
Price 2 en-suite doubles, 1 en-suite twin £70. Breakfast included.
Facilities Internet. Games/common room.
Open Year-round. Check in: 5pm. Check out: 10am.
Getting there The village is easily accessed from the M5: leave the motorway at Gloucester, and take the B4073 for Painswick.

Clockwise from top left Like many local buildings, *St Anne's* is made from local limestone; ready for breakfast; the charming bedrooms combine traditional decor with home comforts

Fern Cottage offers home-grown breakfasts and a warm welcome in Gloucestershire

Fern Cottage

PUCKLECHURCH

Fern Cottage has to be one of the friendliest B&Bs in Britain, with a genuinely caring attitude to guests that extends to helping with lifts and advice about sights and restaurants. The owners ask that you phone to make a booking, so they can ascertain what you want from your visit. This little smallholding – a farm with converted stables where the guestrooms are located – sits close to Bristol, near the pleasant walking and cycle route that links the city with Bath's Roman remains and Georgian cityscape. The surrounding countryside isn't dramatic, but the garden has fruit trees, secluded seating and views of nearby Siston Court, a Tudor stately home. Here you'll also find a chalet-like building with a hot tub, a nicely eccentric and luxurious touch. The award-winning B&B's generous breakfasts are decidedly home grown: eggs come from their chickens, they serve their own jams, and sausages and bacon come from a farm across the fields. Two of the four en-suite doubles have small sitting rooms, and the dining room in the main house is always open to guests. Throughout, the decor is impeccable and comfortable, and there are binoculars in each room so you can spot birds and visiting deer.

Fern Cottage, 188 Shortwood Hill, Pucklechurch, Gloucestershire, BS16 9PG
☎0117 937 4966,
🌐ferncottagebedandbreakfast.co.uk.
Price 4 en-suite doubles £78–83.
Facilities Internet. Garden. TVs in rooms. Breakfast available.
Open Year-round. Check in: 4pm. Check out: 10am.
Getting there Leave the M32 at Junction 1 and follow signs towards Kingswood. At Emersons Green carry on until you come to the Dramway roundabout. Take the slip road on the left for Pucklechurch. Carry on for a mile to the top of the hill until you see on the left a sign showing Pucklechurch straight on. The signposted driveway is on the right-hand side immediately opposite.

YHA Welsh Bicknor

Don't be fooled by the name – you're still just in England at this romantic Herefordshire property, though Monmouth and the Welsh border are just a couple of miles to the east. The approach to the hostel, on foot, by car or even by canoe, is unforgettable. It's in the heart of the extensive private estate, and the tall Victorian Gothic building is reached by a plunging narrow driveway which zigzags through the trees – the spire peeking through belongs to the abandoned estate church – to bring you to river level. Beyond the house itself, a former rectory, is a small riverside campsite, the gently flowing Wye and – at night – the twinkling lights of nearby pubs which you can access in around 20 minutes' walk. Inside, the hostel is old-fashioned but congenial and attractive.

YHA Welsh Bicknor, Welsh Bicknor, nr Goodrich, Ross-on-Wye, Herefordshire, HR9 6JJ ☎01594 860300, ⓦyha.org.uk.
Price Dorms: 2 twins, 6x4, 4x6, 2x8, 1x10 £17.40–23.40.
Facilities Kitchen. On-site parking. Bar. Games or common room. Garden. Breakfast available.
Restrictions Curfew 11pm.
Open Year-round. Check in: 5pm. Check out: 10am.
Getting there From the A40 between Ross on Wye and Monmouth, turn left to signposted Goodrich. In Goodrich, turn left opposite *Jolly's*. Follow the road for 1.5 miles and when it splits, take the right-hand track.

There are a couple of lounges with river views, rooms are named for types of tree, and there's a good self-catering kitchen set by a courtyard garden. A big breakfast is served in the dining room downstairs, an excellent way of preparing yourself for a day hiking the Wye Valley Walk, or for some paddling on the river itself: ask at the hostel about canoe and kayak hire nearby.

YHA Woody's Top

YHA Woody's Top is well off the beaten track in the Wolds, in a quiet northeastern corner of Lincolnshire, 25 miles from Lincoln. The quirky name comes from Mr Wood's Top Barn, which is what it was when the YHA took on the extremely basic property in 1948. One of the organization's more modest acquisitions, it's a plain little brick building, set in a corn field, with simple dorms, a spartan sitting room and a well-equipped kitchen. Mainly comprising four-bed dorms, tranquil *Woody's* is a good choice for families on a budget, and the open valleys and rolling chalk hills round about make for excellent cycling: the landscape is undramatic but absorbing, and dotted with ancient

YHA Woody's Top, Ruckland, Louth, Lincolnshire, LN11 8RQ ☎0845 371 9546, ⓦyha.org.uk.
Price Dorms: 3x4, 1x6 £20. 1 twin £54, exclusive use of four-bed dorm £92.
Facilities Kitchen. Shop. Games/common room. Garden.
Open Only open for private hire Sept–May. Check in: 10am. Check out: 5pm.
Getting there The hostel is just off the A16 between Boston and Louth. Leave the A16 at Burwell, turn left at the crossroads and the hostel is 330yd on the right, at the top of Ruckland Hill.

villages. Nearby Ruckland features the tiny Victorian church of Saint Olave, while immediately north is the market town of Louth, a handy spot for picking up supplies – the hostel is self-catering only. This was the location of the short-lived Lincolnshire Rising against Henry VIII, which resulted in the local vicar being hung, drawn and quartered, a grisly event marked by a plaque in the surprisingly grand late medieval church. The church café is great for home-made cakes, there are several pubs, and the *Priory* serves good Modern British food.

Seventeenth-century *YHA Stow-on-the-Wold* is a handsome hostel in the Cotswolds

YHA Stow-on-the-Wold

This stylish hostel is the only YHA hostel in the Cotswolds, an area better known for country-house hotels and chintzy B&Bs. Appropriately enough, it's pretty posh as hostels go, located in a beautiful seventeenth-century Grade II-listed house right in the centre of Stow-on-the-Wold. The little market town is one of the area's tourist honeypots and gets swamped with coach tours, but even this can't erode the charm of its grand old buildings, spruce tearooms, antique shops and narrow lanes – the latter designed for corralling sheep into the main square. The hostel itself is on the square, with a smart café/dining room looking out onto the action. There's a lounge with toys, games, books and TV, and a garden at the back

YHA Stow-on-the-Wold, The Square, Sheep Street, Stow-on-the-Wold, Gloucestershire, GL54 1AT ☎0845 371 9540, ⊛yha.org.uk.

Price 1 single room and dorms: 2x4, 4x6, 1x7, 1x8 £21.40.

Facilities Internet. Kitchen facilities. On-site parking. Bar. Café. Games/common room. Garden. Lunch and dinner available.

Open Year-round. Check in: 5pm. Check out: 10am.

Getting there From the M4, take the A419 past Swindon before turning onto the A429; the YHA is signposted from the main road.

featuring a kids' play area. The dorms and rooms are spotless, with chunky wooden bunks and beds, you can self-cater in the well-equipped kitchen and there's also a laundry. If you don't fancy cooking, the best place for cakes and a cuppa is the *Cotswold Garden Tearoom*, while the *Eagle and Child* is good for classy bar food.

SOUTH WALES

South Wales has long felt overlooked and undertouristed compared with similarly spectacular regions of wild coast and countryside such as the West Country. In fact, it wasn't so long ago that your budget accommodation options could be summed up as either chintz and doilies or boots and bunkrooms. No longer. Today anyone on a budget can opt for modest boutique style in historic coaching inns or smart stays in traditional seaside resorts. Visitors can escape to cottagey farmhouses, quirky B&Bs behind the beach and hostels that appeal for their style as much as location.

So what's behind this transformation in Welsh hospitality? You could say it's a consequence of parliamentary devolution, which has reinvigorated South Wales since 1997 – nowhere more so than in Cardiff. Europe's youngest capital is enjoying its boisterous teenage years, full of energy and optimism, and has acquired a number of city-centre hostels to house weekend visitors. You could equally argue that the upping of budget-stay standards is a trickle-through consequence of gentrification as more and more downshifters have come west in search of the good life. Whatever the cause, whether town or country, budget accommodation in South Wales now matches anything across the border – except perhaps in the prices.

If this smartening up is new, the essence of a stay in South Wales remains unchanged. There are the same pristine white beaches and ragged coastlines in Pembrokeshire and on the Gower peninsula, from St David's Head and Barafundle Bay to Rhossili's epic, cliff-bookended sweep of sand. And the walking hills of the Brecon Beacons National Park have lost none of their allure, from exhilarating peaks like Pen-y-Fan, the highest mountain in southern Britain, to pretty valleys like the Usk around Crickhowell. There are even still some overlooked regions such as Carmarthenshire, pillowed in gorgeous countryside that is tailormade for simply dropping off the radar.

Nor has the influx of goose-down duvets and wi-fi hubs had a detrimental effect on that most traditional of Welsh virtues, a warm welcome. Charming hosts with time to chat are as much a part of the South Wales experience as home-made cake on arrival or breakfasts of locally sourced produce. The best budget stays in the region are highly personal affairs, where you are treated less as a client in a hotel chain than a welcome guest in someone's home. Indeed, the budget hotel chains haven't really cottoned on to the region yet. Being overlooked isn't always a bad thing.

NAME	LOCATION	PAGE		REAL BARGAIN	TREAT YOURSELF	FAMILY-FRIENDLY	GREAT RURAL LOCATION	OUTDOOR ACTIVITIES	GREAT FOOD AND DRINK	DORMS	PUBLIC TRANSPORT
Aberporth Express	Rhydlewis	112	⑧			✓		✓			
Bay House	Tenby	115	⑦		✓				✓		✓
Beacons Backpackers	Bwlch	101	㉓					✓		✓	✓
Beili Neuadd	Rhayader	111	⑲	✓	✓		✓	✓		✓	
Bridge Café	Brecon	100	⑳	✓					✓		✓
The Cawdor	Llandeilo	104	⑮		✓				✓		✓
The Coach House	St David's	114	③					✓	✓	✓	✓
The Crescent	Swansea	115	⑯				✓		✓		✓
Dolgoch Hostel	Dolgoch	102	⑱				✓	✓		✓	
Ffynnon Fendigaid	Rhydlewis	113	⑩		✓		✓				
Hay Stables	Hay-on-Wye	103	㉕	✓					✓		✓
Llanthony Priory	Llanthony	108	㉗				✓	✓			
Mandinam	Llangadog	106	⑰		✓		✓	✓			✓
The Old School Hostel	Trefin	117	④			✓		✓		✓	
Plas Alltyferin	Nantgaredig	110	⑬				✓		✓		
Preseli Venture	Mathry	109	⑤					✓		✓	
The River House Backpackers	Cardiff	101	㉔						✓	✓	✓
The Ship	Tresaith	117	⑨	✓		✓			✓		
Skomer Island	Skomer Island	113	①				✓	✓	✓		
The Start	Hay-on-Wye	104	㉖		✓				✓		✓
Trericket Mill	Erwood	103	㉒				✓		✓	✓	✓
Ty Newydd	Llanfrynach	105	㉑				✓	✓			
Western House	Llangennith	108	⑪	✓				✓	✓		
YHA Port Eynon	Port Eynon	110	⑫			✓	✓	✓		✓	✓
YHA Pwll Deri	Trefasser	116	⑥				✓	✓		✓	
YHA St David's	St David's	114	②			✓	✓	✓		✓	
Yr Hafod	Aberystwyth	100	⑭						✓		✓

From left *Bridge Café* (see p.100); *The Ship* (see p.117); *YHA St David's* (see p.114) **Previous page**: Tenby, Pembrokeshire

Yr Hafod

The brown swirly carpet in the hall promises another dated holiday B&B. But by the time you leave, you'll wonder why all seaside stays can't be like this. Set behind the beach at the quiet southern end of Aberystwyth's promenade, with a medieval castle and harbour for neighbours, *Yr Hafod* is by far the best budget stay on a seafront that is awash with them. There's nothing flash or cutting-edge about it. Rather, like its soft-spoken owner (Aberystwyth-born and bred, gently humorous, endlessly helpful), it is understated. Beyond that hall carpet, the accommodation turns out to be comfortable and spacious. Sure, the pine furnishings are simple and the pastel colour scheme rather bland, but the carpets are thick, the towels fluffy and surfaces are spotless under the close scrutiny of light that pours through the bay windows of front rooms which overlook the sea. Extras such as flatscreen TVs and DVD players or the bottled water and chocolates laid out on arrival impress, but not nearly as much as the wetroom-style marble bathrooms. At first they seem an extravagance for a budget stay, but then you realize they sum up the secret of *Yr Hafod*'s success; this is a B&B that ticks all boxes in the basics then exceeds expectations where it matters.

Yr Hafod, 1 South Marine Terrace, Aberystwyth, Ceredigion, SY23 1JX ☎01970 617579, ⓦyrhafod.co.uk.
Price 2 singles £31, 2 doubles £62, 2 en-suite doubles £78. Breakfast included.
Facilities Internet. TVs in rooms.
Open Year-round. Check in: flexible. Check out: 10am.
Getting there Follow the A487 to central Aberystwyth then signs to the seafront. Turn left onto the one-way seafront and continue until you reach the ruined castle on the left; the B&B is on the corner opposite. Direct rail services to Aberystwyth from Birmingham and Wolverhampton.

Bridge Café

You'll need to be quick to bag a spot at the *Bridge Café*; with only three rooms, the biggest bargain in Brecon fills up quickly. If its central location is one reason why, another is Carole and Jon Paish. The young owners possess the easy friendliness of seasoned travellers and in their cottagey town house they have created the sort of place in which they'd like to spend a break, meaning TVs and primly ironed sheets are out, while relaxed vibe and character is in. The style is eclectic and homely, with the owners' own furniture and watercolours by a local artist decorating cosy rooms painted in earthy colours, while throughout are wonky floors and whitewashed stone walls. When closed, the couple's excellent bistro beneath (late March–Oct Thurs–Sat from 6.30pm & Sun 9am–noon) doubles as a lounge, with squishy leather sofas and a woodburner. The Paishs will gladly proffer OS maps and advice over sensational home-made, cooked breakfasts (£3). If you feel more friend than guest at such times it is because Carole and Jon – unlike some grumpy B&B owners you may have encountered elsewhere – actually enjoy their visitors. It's a refreshing feeling, and just one of the many reasons to return.

Bridge Café, 7 Bridge Street, Brecon, Powys, LD3 8AH ☎01874 622024, ⓦbridgecafe.co.uk.
Price 1 en-suite double £65, 2 doubles with shared bathroom £55. Breakfast included.
Facilities Internet. Café. Garden.
Open Year-round. 2 night minimum stay during weekends. Check in: flexible. Check out: 11am.
Getting there Take the A40 Brecon Bypass and exit where it joins the A470 in a roundabout onto B4601; Brecon Golf Club is on your left. Across the river, continue past the *Three Horseshoes Inn*; the B&B is just before the bridge on your left. Buses from Abergavenny and Cardiff.

Beacons Backpackers

Rhys Champion put a lot of thought into what kind of hostel he wanted to buy. As an experienced backpacker, he knew the ideal budget stay had to be steps from the hiking trails but accessible by public transport. It also had to be small enough to be intimate but not cramped. And it had to be attached to a quiet pub – after all, who wants to travel for a pint after a hard day in the hills? He eventually found the *New Inn* in Bwlch village, wedged between the Brecon Beacons and the Black Mountains in the beautiful Usk Valley, and the result is a mountain backpackers' haven with mellow nightlife. With only 26 beds in five dorms – small and simple but with modern bunks and all en suite – there's a friendly community feel here. Guests pile into the pub for cook-in nights and the quiz; indie-folk band Mumford & Sons appeared on one occasion then sang into the wee hours. A quieter private lounge is also available, as is the pub kitchen on request. It's all good fun, but the focus here is without, not within. That's why Rhys has printed walk leaflets that guide you from front door to hilltop, and door-code entry means no more keys lost in the hills – Rhys thought about that, too.

Beacons Backpackers, The New Inn, Brecon Road, Bwlch, Powys, LD3 7RQ ☎01874 730215, ⊕beaconsbackpackers .co.uk.
Price Dorms (all en suite): 5x4, 1x6 £21. Breakfast (tea or coffee & toast) included.
Facilities Internet. On-site parking. Bar. Games/common room. Tours. Dinner available.
Open Year-round. Check in: flexible. Check out: 10am.
Getting there Bwlch is on the A40, almost midway between Brecon and Abergavenny. The hostel is on the main road in the village centre; on the right if coming from Brecon. Bus #X43 from Cardiff to Abergavenny drops you at the front door.

The River House Backpackers

Among the brochures and flyers on the noticeboard of this central Cardiff hostel are postcards from recent guests, all of which have the same two words on them: "Thank you!" It's not often that backpackers thank just one more hostel on the road. But then *The River House* is not just another hostel; between 2008 and 2010, it bagged the Best UK Hostel award consecutively and was ranked in the world's top 10 twice at the Hoscars, the hostel world's Oscars. The restored town house probably had a lot to do with it: stylish communal areas, a well-equipped home-style kitchen and daily cleaning of dorms (cosy but modern, with Room 6 and Room 10 the pick). As important and appealing is the easygoing, community vibe, which young sibling owners Charles and Abi Prothero encourage. It's why they offer free dinners several times a week, on top of the best hostel breakfast in Wales. It's also why *The River House* feels less a backpackers' place than a relaxed home from home in a city where most hostels are boozy riots of stag and hen parties. And that is something to be thankful about.

The River House Backpackers, 59 Fitzhamon Embankment, Cardiff, CF11 6AN ☎02920 399810, ⊕riverhouse backpackers.com.
Price 2 doubles with shared bathroom £40. Dorms: 4x6, 5x4, plus 1x4 (single-sex), all from £17.50. Breakfast included.
Facilities Internet. Kitchen. Games/common room. Garden. Bike rental.
Restrictions Bed linen required.
Open Year-round. 2 night minimum stay during weekends. Check in: flexible. Check out: 11am.
Getting there Enter Cardiff on the A470 to the centre and follow the main road around the castle. Over the bridge turn left into Lower Cathedral Rd (A4119), then left at the mini-roundabout on Despenser Street to reach Fitzhamon Embankment.

Dolgoch Hostel

In 2006 the YHA panicked die-hard hostellers with a selling spree of its least used hostels and *Dolgoch*, a 17th-century former farmhouse in the heart of the Cambrian Mountains, was among the first to receive notice. Cue a heroic local fund-raising effort that put *Dolgoch* under the stewardship of the Elenydd Wilderness Hostels Trust. A change of ownership did not entail a change of style, however. So, first the negatives. Despite modest updates such as solar power, *Dolgoch* remains a hostel of the old generation: a mite musty, with basic bunkrooms and furnishings of the granny's armchair variety. To complain about this, however, is to miss the point. No hostel in South Wales is as remote as *Dolgoch*

Dolgoch Hostel, Dolgoch, Tregaron, Ceredigion, SY25 6NR ☎01974 298680, ⊛elenydd-hostels.co.uk.
Price Dorms: 1x4, 1x6, 1x11, all £12.
Facilities Internet. On-site parking. Games/common room. Garden. Lockers.
Open April–Oct. Check in: call for time. Check out: 10am.
Getting there At Llanwrtyd Wells on the A483, follow signs to Aberwesyn, then turn left towards Tregaron. Continue through the valley for three miles, pass the left turn to Ystradffin and Rhandirmyn, and the hostel road is a half-mile further on the left over a cattlegrid.

and its sense of isolation will bring a quiet thrill to any outdoors purist: to walkers and cyclists on the Cambrian Way footpath and Lôn Las Cymru respectively, or perhaps to bog-snorkellers practising for the world championship in nearby wacky festival centre Llanwrtyd Wells. Isolation also preserves *Dolgoch* in aspic. Lighting is by gas in the flagstoned kitchen-common room, while heat is from a chunky old woodburner. There are modest creature comforts, too, such as cafetieres and even a stove-top espresso maker. Yet as YHA hostels go ever-more IKEA, it's reassuring to know there remain places such as *Dolgoch*, places where you can revel in the simple purity of going wild.

Clockwise from top left The two-person bunk room at *Trericket Mill*; the comfortable bunkhouse; the red-brick guest house; *Dolgoch Hostel* occupies a remote seventeenth-century farmhouse in the Cambrian Mountains

Trericket Mill

Half B&B and half bunkhouse, *Trericket Mill* feels a world apart from the reality of day-to-day life. Kids splash in a brook in the garden, walkers chat around a communal campfire pit and things tick over at a relaxed pace. Life revolves around the listed red-brick mill, a labour of love that the owners rescued from ruin. Guests eat among the old milling machinery at its heart, tucking into breakfasts of hot croissants, home-made jams and fresh-laid duck eggs, or delicious veggie meals that are chalked up each day for dinner. A snug lounge with a woodburner is an ideal spot to curl up with a book afterwards, while upstairs are the bedrooms, all en suite and all prettily decorated with pine furnishings; the pick of the rooms, Tom's and Annie's, are ideal for couples, leaving families and groups to the stone bunkhouse. It's a credit to its name, with wood floors, solid bunks (each with a reading light) and a covered kitchen outdoors. You're close to the River Wye, so pick up the footpath to Glasbury then paddle a canoe for a magical day-trip to the tourist hot spot of Hay-on-Wye. Just don't be surprised when you're glad to be back at *Trericket* again.

Trericket Mill, Erwood, Powys, LD2 3TQ ☎01982 560312, ✆www.trericket .co.uk.
Price 3 en-suite doubles £70; includes breakfast. Bunkrooms: 1x2 en suite £18 for single occupancy, £30 for room; 2x4, used as double £32, as triple £42, whole room £52.
Facilities Internet. Kitchen. On-site parking. Café. Games/common room. Garden. TVs in rooms. Breakfast and dinner available.
Open Closed New Year to Feb half-term. Check in: 4pm. Check out: 11am.
Getting there Take the A470 north of Brecon towards Builth Wells. Trericket is signposted "Mill" midway between Llyswen and Erwood, on the left. Buses (Mon–Sat) from Brecon to Llandrindod Wells and the T4 from Cardiff drop outside the door on request.

Hay Stables

This is a real find among the more la-di-da accommodation in Hay-on-Wye, where prices are often Way-on-High. Affordable and easy-going, it's a refuge for the post-backpacker market as much as young families and walkers. Where other B&Bs set the sort of early breakfast times no holidaymaker should have to see, *Hay Stables* is a home from home. Here, you have an open-plan kitchen (with a fully stocked fridge) to prepare the full works whenever it takes your fancy. Guests on weekend breaks often retire back to bed with a mug of tea, rousing themselves later for a late breakfast before a lazy afternoon's book-buying or a stroll in the hills. The modern lounge also makes a fine place to hang out, which is handy since the rooms, though crisply modern and neutral, are also fairly compact (blame the king-size beds in all); Room 1 is the largest and like both ground-floor rooms has a small terrace. All are serviced daily, which lends *Hay Stables* the feeling of a hotel-stay without any of the formalities.

Hay Stables, Oxford Road, Hay-on-Wye, Herefordshire, HR3 5AJ ☎01497 820008, ✆haystables.co.uk.
Price 3 en-suite doubles May–Oct £60, Nov–April £50. Breakfast included.
Facilities Internet. Kitchen. On-site parking. Games/common room. TVs in rooms.
Open Year-round. 2 night minimum stay during weekends and high season. Check in: flexible. Check out: 11am.
Getting there Arriving in Hay from the south, on A438, follow signs to the parking and tourist information centre on Oxford Road. Continue past it (on the right) and the B&B is on the left after 100m. Regular buses from Hereford and Brecon.

The Start

Nicely located on the edge of Hay-on-Wye in a spacious garden by the river, this eighteenth-century cottage offers a warm and homely welcome. You walk straight into the flagstone-floored dining room, with a wood-burning stove and ceiling beams; beyond that the lounge has a Welsh oak spinning wheel and views onto the impressive veg garden – the chickens and ducks outside provide eggs for breakfast. The industrious owners also supply their own jam and cider, and free packets of seeds for guests. Upstairs, there's a pleasant cottage-like feel to the rooms, which are fairly plain but comfortable and quiet, with handsome wooden furniture and coloured throws on the beds. Hay-on-Wye itself, which straddles the border between England and Wales, is best known for its umpteen second hand bookshops, and early summer festival, when the literary world descends for ten days of talks and readings: Bill Clinton described it as "the Woodstock of the mind". If you want to visit during this time, book accommodation way in advance. But Hay has plenty to offer out of season, not least verdant walks along the river, and trips to the hills, valleys and castles of the Brecon Beacons. Back in town, there's good pub food at the *Three Tuns* and the *Old Black Lion*, which serve's its own Black Lion bitter.

> **The Start, Hay-on-Wye, Herefordshire, HR3 5RS** ☎01497 821391, 🖥the-start.net.
> **Price** 2 en-suite doubles, 1 en-suite twin £70. Breakfast included.
> **Facilities** Internet available. Games or common room. Garden. TVs in rooms.
> **Open** Open year-round. Check in: flexible. Check out: 10am.
> **Getting there** The A40 passes Gloucester and heads on to Ross-on-Wye. At the Wilton roundabout outside Ross take the A49 to Hereford. Take the left turning for Hay-on-Wye (B4348). *The Start* is situated on the B4351 just over Hay Bridge – do not follow GPS.

The Cawdor

For residents of South Wales' cities, hilltop Llandeilo – with its parade of multicoloured houses where craftshops, galleries and hardware shops jostle for space – makes a fine weekend break. For walkers, it makes an excellent launchpad for the bare hills ahead. And while escaping urbanites usually want their country life in magazine format, hikers seek the real deal. Thanks goodness, then, for *The Cawdor*, which gets due credit for satisfying both groups. This grand eighteenth-century coaching inn brings boutique to the Black Mountain at rates to suit all budgets, making it a good compromise for groups of any type. Don't let on but the cheaper rooms, though far smaller, feature much the same hip boutique style, with padded headboards, goosedown duvets and Welsh woollen throws on beds, along with flatscreen TVs and the same DVD library to browse, while all the bathrooms also have wetroom showers and fluffy dressing gowns; ask for a rear room, as traffic noise is noticeable during the week. Downstairs areas are spacious and grand, finished in a palette of dusty heather and charcoal. Over breakfast – relaxed, delicious and locally sourced where possible – you can look across to a smart gallery and pick the day's purchase or examine a map, plotting the day's hike.

> **The Cawdor, Rhosmaen Street, Llandeilo, Carmarthenshire, SA19 6EN** ☎01558 823500, 🖥thecawdor.com.
> **Price** 2 doubles £65, 4 doubles £85, 1 double £100, 5 doubles £110, 7 doubles £125, 2 doubles £150, 2 suites £200; all en suite. Breakfast included.
> **Facilities** Internet. On-site parking available. Bar. Café. Games/common room. TVs in rooms.
> **Open** Year-round. Check in: flexible. Check out: 11am.
> **Getting there** The hotel is in centre of Llandeilo directly on the main throughfare (A483). Trains to Llandeilo station.

Clockwise from left Rich reds dominate *The Cawdor*'s Egremont room; the spacious Dinefwr room is on the hotel's top floor; the Grade II listed Georgian-style *Cawdor* is in the heart of lovely Llandeilo

Ty Newydd

Buried deep in the tranquility and scenery of the Brecon Beacons National Park, *Ty Newydd* is one of the loveliest budget stays in the Brecon area. Young couple Sid and Rachel Griffiths – the epitome of hospitality – have refreshed the family B&B without sacrificing its historic character, giving it a stylish country-modern makeover of soft colours, contemporary fabrics and discreet flatscreen TVs alongside old beams and the occasional traditional Welsh blanket. Rooms in the eaves have the most space, and number two appeals for its wood floorboards and view to the mountains. All have a freshness and charm, not to mention a small but swish modern en-suite bathroom. As effortlessly relaxed are the breakfasts; full Welsh, of course, and showcasing fine local produce. Guests tend to linger after filling their bellies, drifting into the adjacent conservatory with a cup of coffee to pore over maps and plot a route to Pen-y-Fan, the national park's literal highpoint, five hours away on foot, or to Brecon via a canal towpath that runs at the bottom of the garden. So wonderful are the views and so relaxing is the atmosphere, don't be surprised if you never get beyond the planning stage.

Ty Newydd, Llanfrynach, Powys, LD3 7LJ
☎01874 665797, ⓦtynewyddbandb.com.
Price 3 en-suite doubles £65. Breakfast included.
Facilities Internet. On-site parking. Garden.
Open Year-round, except at Christmas. 2 night minimum during bank holidays and local festivals. Check in: flexible. Check out: 10am.
Getting there From Brecon on the A40 towards Abergavenny take the first exit signposted B4558 (Llanfrynach). Turn left, go over a single lane bridge and continue for a mile. Just before a canal bridge turn left; the B&B is beyond the narrowboat marina on the left.

Mandinam

Caught between the holiday playgrounds of the north Brecon Beacons National Park and Pembrokeshire, Carmarthenshire is the forgotten region of South Wales. And that's just one reason to come to *Mandinam*. It is a place for space and silence among patchworked hills that have all the perfection of a child's storybook. The clue is in the title. The Welsh word "mandinam" translates roughly as "A holy place without blemish", which perfectly describes this hilltop farm estate; 450 acres of lush fields and natural woodland, wildflower meadows and rivers teeming with trout, with beautiful views across valleys to the west Brecon Beacons peaks a short drive away. The map insists that you're just two miles from Llangadog village and its award-winning pub *The Red Lion*, but it feels like a million miles. No wonder Prince Charles recently bought a holiday hideaway up the road near Myddfai as a retreat from the pomp of office.

> **Mandinam, Llangadog, Carmarthenshire, SA19 9LA** ☎01550 777368, ⓦmandinam.co.uk.
>
> **Price** 2 en-suite doubles: 1 £70, 1 £80; breakfast included. Self-contained gypsy van and shepherd's hut £70.
>
> **Facilities** Internet. On-site parking. Games/common room. Garden. Dinner available.
>
> **Open** Year-round, though Coach House closed from Nov to late March; call ahead to check. 2 night minimum stay. Check in: flexible. Check out: 11am.
>
> **Getting there** In Llangadog (off A40), leave the Black Lion on your left to turn right towards Myddfai. Go past the cemetery, then take the first right turn towards Llanddeusant; the entrance is on the left after a mile. Free transfers from Llangadog train station.

How you experience this isolated place depends on which of *Mandinam*'s four accommodation options you select. The most comfortable is the New Room, a smartly renovated barn with a four-poster bed, a mezzanine lounge, a roll-top bath and underfloor heating. The Coach House is a little more removed, a little more rustic, with little in its simple open-plan interior to detract from the wonderful view outside. It's a short walk from either across the courtyard to the main farmhouse for breakfasts of home-made bread, jam, honey, home-grown fruit and farm sausages. Artistic and charming, Marcus and Danielle Lampard are the perfect hosts, able to discuss everything from the eco-ethics behind their farming to modern art (Marcus trained at the Chelsea School of Art and his work furnishes the handsome farmhouse); they also have a knack for being on hand to help when it's required and leaving you alone when you simply want peace.

The latter is available in spades in a gypsy van and shepherd's hut. Prettily decorated in powder pastels and furnished with mini-kitchenettes and wood-burning stoves, these self-

contained options are arguably the gems of *Mandinam*. Offering a sort of glamping-lite experience, they are snug bolt holes in which to drop off the radar, spaces for romance and reflection hidden away in quiet corners of the estate, with gorgeous views everywhere. Days are spent exploring the estate's paths, with lambs and red kites for company, while nights are best appreciated from the outdoor hot-tub beneath vast skies boiling with stars. Magic.

Clockwise from top A quiet place to contemplate at *Mandinam*; the Coach House room; the lounge; Llyn y Fan Fach, a remote lake in the nearby Brecon Beacons National Park

Western House

Within a mile of Wales's most reliable surf beach, Rhossili, and 200m from the legendary pub *The King's Head*, *Western House* is everything you secretly want a surfer house to be: definitely easy-going and enjoyably eclectic. From the first glimpse of a magnolia-print surfboard-style worksurface or crazy porcelain chandelier resembling a Quentin Blake illustration in the kitchen, you just know this will be fun. Owners Pippa and Steve Poulton treat their guests as instant friends, proffering mugs of coffee and surfboards to rent, and their family home has the same instant appeal. There's no bland beige haze here, thank

> **Western House, Llangennith, Swansea, SA3 1HU** ☎01792 386620,
> Ⓦwesternhousebandb.co.uk.
> **Price** 3 en-suite doubles £60. Breakfast included.
> **Facilities** Internet. Garden. TVs in rooms.
> **Open** Christmas Day. Check in: flexible. Check out: 11am.
> **Getting there** Take Junction 47 off the M4 and follow signs to Gower via the B4295. Beyond Bury Green in Llangennith village, go past the *King's Head*; the B&B is on the left, just before the mini-roundabout.

you very much. Instead, *Western House* is a kaleidoscope of colour, tone and texture; a mix-and-match of vintage furnishings, artwork, Pippa's patchwork wallhangings and proper beach-cool (love those driftwood bedside tables). Bathrooms are as fun, whether the roll-top tub in Room 3, which overlooks a pretty garden, or the colour explosion of that for the loft room, which has wonderful views seaward. In less confident hands this would be a mess – a hippie refuge at best, student digs at worst. Yet *Western House* has been created with such flair and artistic panache that it probably has more genuine style than any other B&B in Llangennith.

Llanthony Priory

If history, a wildly romantic setting or just utter escapism is your thing, the idiosyncratic *Llanthony Priory Hotel* may be your sort of stay. Although built in the 1700s as a hunting lodge, it incorporates the ruins of a medieval Augustinian priory. Rooms are in the twelfth-century tower, the upper two reached via a staircase whose tight spiral explains the warnings against bringing large bags. Plumbing back then was as much of a mystery as suitcases, which means you're limited to a simple shared bathroom on the first floor, where you'll find the other two rooms; opt for Room 2, with its extra space and views over the ruins. Rooms have half-tester or four-poster beds. To suit a quirky historic style the owners refuse to compromise with TVs or even washbasins. Revel instead in an antique bowl and pitcher; remember, you're paying for character, plus a location in the magical Vale of Ewyas

> **Llanthony Priory, Llanthony, Abergavenny, NP7 7NN** ☎01873 890487,
> Ⓦllanthonyprioryhotel.co.uk.
> **Price** 2 doubles, 2 twins, all with shared bathrooms £80. Breakfast included.
> **Facilities** On-site parking. Bar. Restaurant. Games/common room. Garden.
> **Restrictions** No children under 10.
> **Open** Nov–Apr closed Mon–Thurs; May–June & Sept–Oct closed Mon. 2 night minimum stay during weekends. Check in: flexible. Check out: 10am.
> **Getting there** Go north of Abergavenny on the A465 for about five miles. Turn left into the village of Llanvihangle Crucorney, and turn left just after the Skirrid Mountain Inn. Follow the road for about five miles; Llanthony Priory is on the right.

that begs for exploration. There are horses to ride from an adjacent farm and Offa's Dyke to march on the hills above. End your action-filled days by sipping real ales in the confines of what was once the prior's cellar, or enjoying home-made meals in the vaulted-celing dining room – without the monastic silence, of course.

Preseli Venture

Come here for life on the edge in every sense. Located at the tip of Wales, *Preseli Venture* activity centre lets you delegate the nitty-gritty of organization and focus instead on the thrill of getting in, on and frequently under the water of the most spectacular coastline in the country. The bulk of a day here is spent out of doors with an instructor, coasteering, sea kayaking or surfing. It's an exhilarating blast of cold water and endorphins before you return to the only five-star-graded eco lodge in Pembrokeshire. Evenings are spent in a modern bar and lounge, where young staff keep things lively and fun. There's pool to shoot, beer to sink or chat to be had around the woodburner in between excellent home-cooked food served in generous portions; full board and B&B deals are available. Simple rooms are a sort of Welsh take on ski chalet-style: think mezzanine beds propped on oak beams and, in most, slate floors with underfloor heating. *Preseli* is hugely popular with weekend groups but the real surprise is that it's also a popular mid-week destination for couples and families seeking a gentle nudge to test their boundaries – and perhaps turn them into full-fledged adrenaline junkies. Consider yourself warned.

Preseli Venture, Parynole Fach, Mathry, Pembrokeshire, SA62 5HN ☎01348 837709, ⓦpreseliventure.co.uk.
Price 2 doubles £78, 1 family room £78. Dorms: 2x2, 1x3, 3x4, 1x6, 1x9; all £39 per person B&B or £50 per person full-board. Breakfast included.
Facilities On-site parking. Bar. Games/common room. Garden. Tours. Bike rental.
Open Year-round. Adults only at weekends. Check in: flexible. Check out: 11am.
Getting there Turn off the A487 to Mathry, then immediately right onto a single-track lane. Preseli Venture is the pink house on the left after two-thirds of a mile. Free transfer from Haverfordwest train station on Friday evening and weekends.

Clockwise from left Porthgain Harbour at low tide; *Preseli Venture*'s eco lodge; the lodge's bar, where you can sample local beers after a hard day of coastal thrillseeking

Plas Alltyferin

Come to *Plas Alltyferin* if you have forgotten how to relax. Pillowed in countryside that's far nearer a gastropub than the narrow lanes suggest, it is a de-stress experience par excellence. Never mind the National Botanic and Aberglasney gardens nearby; on this 270-acre estate alone there are footpaths to follow, a stream to fish or just views across the Tywi Valley to drink in. Once inside the wisteria-clad Georgian manor, it takes just five minutes to realize this is no standard B&B. Gerard and Charlotte Dent are wonderful hosts for a start, as generous and relaxed with guests as with old friends. Their house possesses a similar easy charm, its every inch lived-in yet quietly grand, too, with flagstone floors, wonky door jambs, creaky staircases, antiques and bookcases crammed with titles on walls covered in art. The two twin rooms – former children's bedrooms – are an equally eclectic mix-and-match of antiques pieced together over the decades. Uncharitably, you could call them dated; even Gerard and Charlotte admit the bathrooms are far from designer. But that misses the point. Staying at *Plas Alltyferin* is like entering a summer holiday from an Enid Blyton story, with all the escapism and faint touch of eccentricity that suggests. A wi-fi connection? God forbid and amen to that.

Plas Alltyferin, Nantgaredig, Carmarthenshire, SA32 7PF ☎01267 290662, ⓦalltyferin.co.uk.
Price 2 twin rooms (1 en suite, 1 private bathroom) £70 for 1 night, or £60 for 2 nights. Breakfast included.
Facilities Internet. On-site parking. Garden.
Restrictions No children under 10.
Open Year-round, except over Christmas and New Year. Check in: flexible. Check out: 11am.
Getting there Go to Nantgaredig on the A40 east of Carmarthen. Just before the bridge turn left then continue ahead, keeping the hedge on your right; you will cross another small bridge and bend right at a left turn by a farm. The entrance is on the right after two miles.

YHA Port Eynon

If there is a better family holiday on the Gower than this former lifeboat station it's being kept quiet. Sea and sky spread across a wall of windows in the small modern lounge, while outside the air is heady with salt and seaweed. With no busy road within half a kilometre, no keys to manage (it's key-code entry only) plus lifeguards in high season, parents can let kids roam free, whether to poke into the nearby rockpools or splash in the shallows with a hired hostel bodyboard and wetsuit. Evenings can be spent on the beach, grilling up dinner on a rented barbecue. The holiday vibe is maintained indoors by a breezy white-and-blue colour scheme in small, simple bunkrooms, while cafetieres and wineglasses are as plentiful in the kitchen as toys and games are in the lounge. There's even a pub and chippie at the end of the beach; after all – whisper it – this is a holiday for mum and dad, too.

YHA Port Eynon, Old Lifeboat House, Port Eynon, Swansea, SA3 1NN ☎0845 371 9135, ⓦyha.org.uk.
Price 3x2, 2x4 (1 en suite), 1x5 (1 double, 3 singles), 1x8; all £20.40 per person. Couples in two-bed £51, family room (2 adults, 2 children) £66.
Facilities Internet. On-site parking. Games/common room. Bike rental.
Open April–Oct. Private-hire only from Nov to March. Check in: 5pm. Check out: 10am.
Getting there Exit the M4 at J42 in Swansea and follow the brown signs for Gower, then the A4118 for Port Eynon. Follow the road across the seafront roundabout and turn left down a track before the beach carpark (parking at hostel Easter–Sept 5pm–10am). Bus #118 from Swansea to Port Eynon.

Port Enyon's coast has all the required ingredients for family holiday perfection: sea, sky and plenty of seaweed

Beili Neuadd

The most memorable stays are always the most personal. They are not the product of a star-grading checklist but of their owners' vision of an ideal night's rest. One such is mid-Wales smallholding *Beili Neuadd* (pronounced "bailey niath"). B&B accommodation in the farmhouse is enchanting: think antique beds with wool throws, soft natural colours and views into a garden overflowing with plants and wildlife. Factor in the home-made cakes presented on arrival plus the superb breakfasts and you have a stay that is stylish yet still rates high for cottagey romance. The surprise, however, lies in the sixteenth-century barn. If this is a bunkhouse, Harrods is a corner store. Original vintage film-posters decorate exposed stone walls and Chesterfield sofas sit among the old beams of a mezzanine level. Little extras such as free stock cubes make the kitchen faultless. Brownie points, too, for sturdy bunks and thick duvets in dorms, all of which are en suite. Fabulous for groups, it seems overly luxurious for passing walkers and cyclists – the Radnor Forest and Elan Valley trails, plus long-distance footpaths the Wye Valley Walk and Glyndwr's Way are nearby – yet owners Alison and David Parker explain simply that this is what they would want. Return the favour: purchase farm produce for breakfast.

Beili Neuadd, Rhayader, Powys, LD6 5NS
☎ 01597 810211, Ⓦ midwalesfarmstay. co.uk.
Price 2 en-suite doubles £70 (breakfast included). Four-bed self-catering chalet £80. Dorms: 1x4, 2x6, all en suite, all £16.
Facilities Kitchen. On-site parking. Games/ common room. Garden. TVs in rooms. Dinner available.
Open Year-round. Check in: flexible. Check out: 11am.
Getting there Take the A44 east from Rhayader town centre; after half a mile turn on to a road signposted "Abbey Cwm-Hir" and watch for a brown sign to Beili Neuadd. After a mile and a half turn left at the next sign to Beili Neuadd and go for another half-mile up the lane to the second house on the right.

Aberporth Express

Swing through the picket gate tangled with dogrose and you can't help but feel like the Famous Five on an adventure. You're here to stay with "Wendy", one of the most unusual properties on the books of niche Welsh holiday lets agency Under The Thatch – Wendy is an Edwardian Great Western Railway carriage. Dressed in oak, she's a simple old girl, but for bygone charm she has no equal on the Ceredigion coast. Travel posters of the golden age of rail decorate a narrow passageway that you keep expecting to sway, and an old trunk serves as a coffee table in the snug sitting room with a woodburner. In the cosy and romantic bedrooms you'll find delightful trinkets such as a leather-bound shaving kit on the old luggage rack. Other thoughtful touches, including a vase of wild flowers on the dining room table, help add to the charm. Mercifully, the bathroom has a modern shower and the kitchen is entirely recognizable from home. Just as you never quite get over the escapism of your stay, you never really tire of the empty panorama of sea and sky spread beyond the veranda. Expect to do little except potter to the beach, read books or sit with a mug of tea spotting dolphins. Ace, as the Five might say. Note that, while Wendy sits on the outskirts of Aberporth, which is where our directions take you, the booking office is in nearby Rhydlewis.

Aberporth Express, Felin Brithdir, Rhydlewis, Ceredigion, SA44 5SN
☎0844 500 5101, ⓦunderthethatch.co.uk/wendy.
Price 2 doubles (1 with child's bunk), £292 for both rooms for 2 nights.
Facilities Kitchen. Garden.
Open Year-round. 2 night minimum stay. Check in: flexible. Check out: 10am.
Getting there Turn to Aberporth in Tan-y-Groes on the A487 and follow the road into the village. Go through a mini-roundabout (a post office is on the right), then turn right to a free public car park. Pick up the coast path and walk north for 300m; Wendy is on the right. Buses from Cardigan to Aberporth.

Clockwise from left *Ffynnon Fendigaid*'s farmhouse; the B&B's country-style double room; overnight visitors to *Skomer Island* bed down behind the thick stone walls of a renovated former farm building

Ffynnon Fendigaid

Although the highlights of the Cambrian seaside for which everyone comes – National Trust-listed Penbryn beach, Dylan Thomas's New Quay or colourful Georgian Aberaeron – are just a few miles distant, at *Ffynnon Fendigaid*, buried deep in the tranquility of the remotest Ceredigion countryside, they feel a world away. Your stay on the eighteenth-century farmhouse is more style than slurry, however. Look about as owner Huw Davies chats over fresh coffee and home-made cake and you'll see vintage Italian glassware and modern art pieces, while breakfast (don't pass on the local cheeses) is served on a chic slate-topped table. The bedrooms provide something for all tastes: there's country romance in one powder-blue room furnished with pretty wallpaper and antiques; cool boutique style in the other. The beds are big and soft, the modern bathrooms luxurious. The mood throughout is so utterly relaxed it's a struggle to leave. You can lose a morning – even a whole lazy day – in the gorgeously overgrown garden that spills down beneath the house; with paths to potter, clearings to discover and (armed with a good book) sunshine to sit in, you may just never feel the urge to join the crowds on the coast.

Ffynnon Fendigaid, Rhydlewis, Ceredigion, SA44 5SR ☎01239 851361, ⓦffynnonf.co.uk.
Price 2 en-suite doubles £77 (£72 second night). Breakfast included.
Facilities Internet. On-site parking. Games/common room. Garden. Dinner available.
Open Year-round, except for Christmas and New Year's Eve. 2 night minimum stay during bank holidays. Check in: 4pm. Check out: 10am.
Getting there Take the A487 north of Cardigan to Brynhoffant. In the village centre turn right onto the B4334, continuing for a mile to where a lane joins on the right; the drive is on the left.

Skomer Island

Within five minutes of embarking in a tubby ferry from the tip of St Brides Bay you are in open sea, gannets circling overhead. In front loom the cliffs of your own treaure island – Skomer. This nature reserve is famously a breeding colony for puffins from May to July, but for over half the year it also accommodates thirty human visitors per night, split between researchers and guests. The latter stay in upmarket hostel-style accommodation on a former farm, with simple double rooms, a shared kitchen, a lounge and shower rooms. There's no heating and only four electricity sockets, but thick stone walls add character and attentive wardens help keep things comfy, while also lending wildlife guides and binoculars. Most guests are out from dawn to dusk to spot wildlife: the puffins, plus seals, porpoises, peregrine falcons, the world's largest colony of Manx Shearwaters (June–Aug) and short-eared owls. You don't have to come for the birdwatching, of course – anyone whose soul sings at wild places will thrill to the castaway romance of overnighting on Skomer.

Skomer Island, Pembrokeshire, ☎01239 621600, ⓦwelshwildlife.org.
Price 2 doubles, 1 triple, 1 four-bed room, 1 five-bed room. Prices per adult: April £30, May–July £50, August £30, Sept & Oct £20.
Facilities Internet. Games/common room. Garden. Tours.
Restrictions Bed linen required.
Open April–Oct. No boats on Monday. 2 night minimum for Sunday arrivals. Check in: 9am. Check out: 10am.
Getting there Take the B4327 from Haverfordwest towards Marloes and follow brown signs for Skomer Island; there's a car park above the ferry quay at Martin's Haven. Up to 5 ferry trips daily in peak season; 9am boat reserved for overnight visitors. The "Puffin Shuttle" bus between St David's and Milford Haven stops at the car park from May to Sept.

The Coach House

ST DAVID'S

Celebrity endorsement came shortly after Steve and Kim Lawton took on this Georgian house. Rolf Harris stayed for a week in August 2010 and enthused about a "lovely week with great breakfasts". He was right on both counts. The well-travelled couple have transformed what was a rundown B&B into a splendid stay in the heart of Britain's smallest and prettiest city. Though still designated a B&B, *The Coach House* has the atmosphere of a small, personal hotel; a marriage of the former's charm and the latter's service. Take the breakfasts. A former private executive chef for the Jordanian royal family, Steve offers restaurant-quality cuisine in the morning: local crab with cockle and lavabread potato cake; porridge with berry compote; poached haddock; or the full Welsh, with stuffed roast peppers available in place of Pembrokeshire bacon for vegetarians. The decor is a cut above, too. Changing exhibitions of modern art (most of which is for sale) are on the walls, while modern cottagey rooms, though small, have a bright and breezy seaside feel thanks to snowy white linen and pops of fresh aqua. All this means it's as much a pleasure to return after a day's walk as it is to sally forth after a sustaining breakfast.

The Coach House, 15 High Street, St David's, Pembrokeshire, SA62 6SB ☎01437 720632, ⊛thecoachhouse.biz.
Price 1 en-suite single £50, 2 en-suite doubles £80. Family rooms: 1x3 (double/twin, plus single) £105; 1x4 (double or twin, plus 1 single & 1 pull-out) £130; family suite (double & single, plus single in adjoining room) £130. Self-contained five-bed cottage £40 per person. Breakfast included for rooms only.
Facilities Internet. Games/common room.
Restrictions No children under 8.
Open Year-round. Check in: flexible. Check out: 10am.
Getting there Enter St Davids on the A487 from Haverfordwest; the B&B is on the right, 100m past the information centre. Bus#411 from Haverfordwest to Fishguard.

YHA St David's

ST DAVID'S

Fans of walks, wildlife, surfing and kayaking delight in this hostel. You can see St David's cathedral across the fields, but this tranquil and friendly place feels cut adrift, far further than a thirty-minute walk from west Pembrokeshire's most popular tourist destination. The surroundings help. The former farmhouse is impeccably sited beneath Carn Lidli mountain on St David's Head, magical walking country that's a highlight of the Pembrokeshire Coast Path for many hikers. Yet the hostel is also the stuff of which seaside holidays are made, and families will love it. You'll find no beds closer to the waves and sandcastles of Whitesands beach than those in the pleasingly simple rooms. The best are in the renovated Old Dairy, whose cottagey modern kitchen is flagstone floored and comes equipped with proper teapots. A simpler, large dorm is in the former granary while a self-contained bunkhouse is great for small groups. Facilities include a heated drying room, plus a large equipment store. Deserted by day, the hostel assumes a friendly vibe at dusk and is filled with soft chatter as the night takes over – a refreshing change from the happy hordes in St David's.

YHA St David's, Llaethdy, Whitesands, St David's, Pembrokeshire, SA62 6PR ☎0845 371 9141, ⊛yha.org.uk.
Price Dorms: 5x2 (£46 as double), 2x4 (£60 as family room), 1x7; all £21.40. Self-contained four-bed bunkhouse £75.
Facilities Kitchen. On-site parking. Shop. Games/common room. Garden.
Open Year-round. Check in: flexible. Check out: 10am.
Getting there Take the B4538 to Whitesands beach off the A487 towards Fishguard. The hostel is signposted on a right turn after one mile, then again on a turn immediately left. Bus #403 (mid-April to Sept) from St David's.

The Crescent

In a city besieged by identikit chains and tired old guesthouses, Dena Cartwright and Andy Hall's home is the sort of place that gives B&Bs a good name. In the quiet hillside residential area of Uplands, about fifteen minutes' walk from the centre, the seven-bed house makes for a peaceful stay – and a proper one, too. There's something reassuringly traditional about its spacious Edwardian proportions, about how your bags are carried to your room and advice and information is proffered over cups of tea on arrival. Yet *The Crescent*'s style is as modern as its rooms. There's no dispiriting faux-historical decor here; instead, rooms are bright, airy, crisply and individually decorated with fresh colours and all en suite. For everyone's benefit, a family suite is at the opposite end of the house from the more glamorous accommodation at the front, where large bay windows command views to the bay and valleys beyond. The contemporary feeling is enhanced by a laidback atmosphere; there are no formalities or guest curfews – just the freedom to come and go as you please, or enjoy a lie-in before a late breakfast at weekends.

> **The Crescent, 132 Eaton Crescent, Swansea, SA1 4QR** ☎**01792 465782,** ☺**thecrescentswansea.co.uk.**
> **Price** 7 doubles £65 (£75 with superking bed), 1 family suite £110. Breakfast included.
> **Facilities** Internet. On-site parking. Games/ common room. TVs in rooms.
> **Open** Year-round.
> **Getting there** Enter Swansea on the A483 and continue ahead on Kingsway then St Helen's (beyond the church). At traffic lights turn right into Bryn-y-Mor Road and go up a steep hill to Eaton Crescent on the left; the B&B is 50m beyond, on the corner. Major train links to Swansea; city buses #29, #20, #21 and #90 stop at Belgrave Court at the top of Bryn-y-Mor Road.

Bay House

The trouble with traditional seaside resorts is too often their traditional seaside budget decor: too many net curtains, too much chintz. Which is where Tenby's first five-star residence comes in. Occupying a handsome Victorian home moments from South Beach, *Bay House* is proof that budget and boutique are not mutually exclusive. The lounge sets the tone: a symphony of off-whites and cream, its sofas scattered with cashmere and cushions, its table stacked with local-interest books, it is luxurious yet blissfully relaxed. The three bedrooms maintain the grown-up vibe and add toys such as iPod docks, plus fluffy bathrobes and fine toiletries; the Manorbier Room is the most popular for its marriage of historic features with interior style. However, what raises *Bay House* above being a boutique B&B is the five-star welcome from charming owner Debbie Rogers. She may casually dismiss that her guests return each day to fresh home-baked cakes, and is as modest about a spectacular breakfast, yet it's thanks to her that this is as relaxed a stay as it is stylish. And isn't that what a grown-up holiday is all about?

> **Bay House, 5 Picton Road, Tenby, Pembrokeshire, SA70 7DP** ☎**01834 849015,** ☺**tenbybandb.co.uk.**
> **Price** 3 en-suite doubles April, May & Oct £75, June–Sept £85. Breakfast included.
> **Facilities** Internet. Garden. TVs in rooms.
> **Open** April–Oct. 2 night minimum stay during peak season; 3 nights during bank holidays. Check in: flexible. Check out: 11am.
> **Getting there** Entering on the A478, turn right on White Lion Street before the high street, then left onto South Parade to the seafront Esplanade. Picton Road is the second on the right, and *Bay House* is towards its far end on the left. Direct trains to Tenby from Swansea.

YHA Pwll Deri

Search as long as you like, you won't find a Pembrokeshire sea view more perfect than that from *Pwll Deri.* "Perfect" is a big word for a humble hostel, but a cliff-edge location on Strumble Head, a remote rocky knobble that juts into the Irish Sea west of Fishguard, affords this cottage a million-dollar outlook: a wraparound panorama of ragged cliffs and empty silver-grey sea. Gulls and buzzards cruise the updraught at head-height, porpoises occasionally dip past the bay and sunsets are epic. A recent renovation has added an extension whose wall of glass makes the most of the view. The new layout also boasts a modern open-plan kitchen-diner and has improved the snug lounge area and small, simple rooms, all of which are en suite. The communal areas can struggle to accommodate a full house, especially the kitchen since there is no on-site catering and no pub within strolling distance. But *Pwll Deri* and its ever-shifting vistas are a de-stress par excellence. Sure, you could stride away on the spectacular Pembrokeshire Coast Path – which passes by the backdoor – after breakfast. But why not take some good books and linger for days?

YHA Pwll Deri, Pwll Deri, Castell Mawr, Trefasser, Pembrokeshire, SA64 0LR
☎0845 371 9536, ⊕yha.org.uk.
Price Dorms: 2x2 (£41 as double), 1x3 (£58 as family room), 1x4 (£61 as family room), 1x6, 1x8: all £19.40 per person. 1 separate family room £61.
Facilities Kitchen facilities. On-site parking. Games/common room.
Open April–Oct. Check in: 5pm. Check out: 10am.
Getting there Go west from Fishguard on the A487 through Manorowen and Panteg, then turn right at the next crossroads towards St Nicholas. Continue straight ahead for several miles – the hostel is signposted on the left. Bus #404 from St David's to Fishguard stops half a mile from the hostel.

From left *The Old School Hostel's* invitingly laidback lounge; the former YHA's rooms are filled with welcome splashes of colour

The Old School Hostel

A mid-life crisis isn't necessarily a bad thing. Because Chris Clements and Sue Whitmore got the jitters about the direction of their lives, they embarked on a tour around Britain as hostel managers. And because they wound up on this stretch of the north Pembrokeshire coastline, they rescued *The Old School Hostel* when it was cut adrift by the YHA in 2006. A hostel of the old school this is not, however. Out went the regimented style of YHAs past. In came a new kitchen and personal possessions to furnish the living room – no hostel in Wales can have such an interesting library for guests to browse. Ongoing refurbishment has introduced a flair no YHA hostel in Britain can match. Even the most basic rooms – all but one now en suite, incidentally – are packed with personality: funky wallpapers, perhaps, or artwork by a local painter and a bookshelf of reading material by the bed. Solar-power and discounts for guests who arrive by eco-friendly methods tick the green credentials box. The result is Chris and Sue writ large: laidback, environmentally aware, but also eclectic and, in the nicest possible way, a little eccentric. So a suggestion to the YHA: give them another hostel.

The Old School Hostel, Ffordd-yr-Afon, Trefin, Pembrokeshire, SA62 5AU ☎01348 831800, ⓦtheoldschoolhostel.co.uk.
Price 4 en-suite doubles (can be used as twins) £34, plus another en-suite double with kitchenette £44, 1 four-bed en-suite family room & 1 four-bed family room (shared facilities), both £17 per person. Dorms: 1x4 £17, 1x6 £15.
Facilities Internet. Kitchen. On-site parking. Games/common room. Breakfast and lunch available.
Open Year-round. Check in: 5pm. Check out: 10am.
Getting there From either direction on the A487, turn north to Trefin, 1 mile further on. The hostel is in Trefin, on the right, immediately after the pink house. Bus #550 from Cardigan and Fishguard.

The Ship

That Britain doesn't really do accommodation on its rural beaches is one reason why *The Ship* is such a discovery. Tucked beneath a steep hill, the inn sits behind some of the loveliest powder sands in the area. The rooms – all first-floor en suites – each command a view of beach and bay, and two come with the added bonus of a balcony. A refurbishment in 2009 has refreshed the decor in crisp and pleasingly unfussy style; prints of seascapes above kingsize beds lend shots of aqua zing to an otherwise neutral colour scheme and the modern wood furniture is of the proper solid variety. There's a private side-entrance for guests, though you can also ascend through the inn restaurant, which has an excellent reputation hereabouts for superb fresh seafood. All of this makes *The Ship* a dream for family holidays. With dinner on the doorstep, minimal traffic and lifeguards in high season, kids can scamper safely between room and beach while mum and dad lounge quietly on the terrace (now that is a dream). Were it in Cornwall, *The Ship* would be celebrated far and wide. Here in Ceredigion, though, it is a little haiku of holidaymaking; so simple, so pure, and all at a price little above that of a hostel.

The Ship, Tresaith, Cardigan, SA43 2JL ☎01239 811816, ⓦwww.shiptresaith.com.
Price 4 en-suite doubles £60. Breakfast included.
Facilities Internet. On-site parking. Lunch and dinner available. Bar. Café. TVs in rooms.
Open Year-round. Check in: flexible. Check out: 11am.
Getting there Take the A487 north of Cardigan and turn at Tan-y-groes to Tresaith. At a sharp left-hand turn at the furthest end of the village, take a right downhill (signposted "Dead End"); the inn is on the left. Bus #554 (Mon–Sat) from Cardigan.

NORTH WALES

The weather may be predictably unpredictable, but grand scenery is guaranteed in North Wales. If the south is the region of coastlines, the north is dominated by moors and mountains. It's home to the Rhinog mountains – pipsqueaks by local standards at under 800m but wonderfully remote – and impressive Cader Idris, both in the south of the region. To the northwest, and most celebrated of all, is Snowdonia National Park, whose eponymous mountain is not just the literal highpoint of Wales but, for well over a century, the biggest reason that many visitors come to the north at all. Rising from the moorland hills of central Wales, it's a landscape of glaciated valleys and clear tarns cupped in high wind-blown hills; a place where pretty stone villages hunker down beneath majestic peaks. More than anything, Snowdonia feels wilder than any other region in Wales. The possibilities for adventure seem limitless.

The thrill of the outdoors remains an essential element of the North Wales experience for most visitors. There's whitewater rafting at the National Whitewater Centre near Bala and superb mountain biking in dedicated parks like Coed y Brenin, between Machnylleth and Dolgellau. And there are great opportunities

for walking just about everywhere, from the much-tramped routes up Snowdon to the climbers' scrambles on nearby Tryfan and the barely visited ridges of the Clwydian Range, a bucolic area of villages and sheep hills that compares to the more famous Brecon Beacons in everything but visitor numbers.

So it's little surprise that hostel and bunkroom accommodation is central to the budget-stay experience in North Wales. Our selection lists the convenient as well as the outstanding, from a simple but clean bunkdown among like-minded enthusiasts at its most basic to a modern hostel possessing all the comforts of a mid-range hotel but with twice the personal charm.

But North Wales is not all about muddy boots and toughing it out. A new breed of farmstays and B&Bs provides a stylish getaway as much as a walking base. Sure, the best places will pack you off each morning with a freshly prepared homemade lunch and an OS map, welcoming you home each afternoon with cups of tea and cake. But you could just as well book in to remember how to relax, slowing down amid the deep calm of timeless countryside while experiencing some genuine luxury.

NORTH WALES

NAME	LOCATION	PAGE		REAL BARGAIN	TREAT YOURSELF	FAMILY-FRIENDLY	GREAT RURAL LOCATION	OUTDOOR ACTIVITIES	GREAT FOOD AND DRINK	DORMS	PUBLIC TRANSPORT
Bala Backpackers	Bala	122	⑩					✓		✓	✓
Bryn Tirion	Llanferres	128	⑮				✓	✓			
Brynwylfa	Montgomery	131	⑱				✓	✓			✓
Glasgwm	Llangollen	129	⑯					✓			✓
Gwaenynog	Welshpool	135	⑫			✓	✓				
Gwern Gof Uchaf	Capel Curig	124	③	✓			✓	✓		✓	✓
HyB Bunkhouse	Dolgellau	125	⑤						✓	✓	✓
Llandudno Hostel	Llandudno	127	⑧			✓				✓	✓
Llangollen Hostel	Llangollen	129	⑰			✓		✓		✓	✓
Morgans B&B	Holywell	126	⑭		✓	✓	✓				
Pen y Gwyrd	Nant Gwynant	132	②				✓	✓			✓
Pistyll Rhaeadr	Llanrhaeadr ym Mochnant	130	⑪				✓	✓			
Plas Efenechtyd	Ruthin	134	⑬	✓	✓	✓	✓				
Reditreks Bunkhouse	Machynlleth	130	⑥					✓		✓	✓
Talbontdrain	Uwchygarreg	134	⑦	✓	✓	✓	✓	✓	✓		
Totters	Caernarfon	123	①	✓						✓	✓
Tyddyn Mawr	Dolgellau	125	④			✓		✓	✓		
The Vagabond Bunkhouse	Betwys-y-Coed	123	⑨					✓		✓	✓

Clockwise from top left *Bala Backpackers* (see p.122); *Gwaenynog* (see p.135); *Plas Efenechtyd* (see p.134); *Glasgwm* (see p.129) **Previous page** Snowdon from Capel Curig

Bala Backpackers

It seems appropriate for a place that's popular with rafters and kayakers to be likened by its owner to "a tight ship that never sinks". That's one way to describe a backpackers hostel run by regulations. There are rules on how to make your bed (with demonstrations) and rules on deposits during your stay. Automated systems enforce the hostel's midnight curfew – woe betide anyone who tarries in the pub – then its lights-out policy (1.30am). And if that seems a throwback as even YHA hostels relax, the number of Gideon's bibles is bizarre. The reason why *Bala Backpackers* remains a popular weekend stay, nevertheless, is its location. At the heart of the solid little town of Bala, it is as convenient for pubs and food as it is for the National Whitewater Centre four miles away. And it is undeniably well run. A refurbishment in 2009 introduced bright colour throughout and upgraded the facilities: a smart new kitchen off the lounge, pristine bathrooms, a good drying room. Spotless dorms with single beds appeal, too. More appealing still are three budget doubles in a house opposite the hostel that provide a bargain base for couples. They have key-code door entry, so you can return as late as you please – though hopefully you'll be too tired from paddling for nightlife.

Bala Backpackers, 32 Tegid Street, Bala, Gwynedd, LL23 7EL ☎01678 521700, ⓦbala-backpackers.co.uk.
Price 2 doubles £45, 1 en-suite double £55, 1 family room £52.50. Dorms: 1x3, 3x4, 3x5, all £17.50 per bed.
Facilities Internet. Breakfast, lunch and dinner available. Kitchen. Games/common room.
Restrictions Midnight curfew.
Open Year-round. Check in: 5pm. Check out: 10am.
Getting there Enter Bala on the arterial A494. Turn into Tegid Road, opposite the White Heart pub in the town centre, and the hostel is on the right after 110yd. Bus #X94 from Chester and Llangollen.

Clockwise from left *Bala Backpackers*: a private twin room; the dining room; flying the flag for Wales; a dorm

The Vagabond Bunkhouse

Among the prim B&Bs of Betws-y-Coed, the *Vagabond* really stands out. Easygoing and fun, it's an independent hostel that prides itself on providing guests with a good dose of activity and some well-earned R&R, not chintz doillies and tea served in fine china. The climbing routes bolted onto the sidewall of the house and a power bike-wash tell you all you need to know about the clientele; outdoor adventure rules in this area of north Wales. With that focus, it's no surprise the clean rooms are more simple than stylish. That doesn't faze the core clientele of 30-something activities enthusiasts and young families, however, and extra marks are awarded for sturdy, high bunks with individual reading lights. But the *Vagabond* also scores highly because it offers more than just a comfy bunkdown. After a hard day in the hills, guests hang out at the small bar with a cold drink until dinner is served or the barbecue fires up. Some venture out on the town only to discover that this is the liveliest spot in it. Comfort and company at the edge of the Snowdonia mountains, all for the price of a tent pitch – now that's a bargain.

The Vagabond Bunkhouse, Craiglan Road, Betwys-y-Coed, Gwynedd, LL24 0AW ☎01690 710850, 🖰thevagabond .co.uk.
Price Dorms: 2x4 (1 can be used as family room), 2x6 (1 can be used as family room), 2x8; all £17 per bed Mon–Fri (no breakfast) and £22 Sat & Sun (including breakfast). Bed, breakfast & dinner £29.
Facilities Internet. Kitchen. On-site parking. Bar. Games/common room. Garden. Tours. Bike rental.
Open Year-round. Check in: 5pm. Check out: 10am.
Getting there Arrive in Betwys-y-Coed on the A5 from the south, pass the Best Western hotel on your left and 110yd beyond, beside the Rock Bottom and Costwolds outdoors stores, turn left; the hostel is uphill on the right. Trains to Betwys-y-Coed from Llandudno Junction.

Totters

Totters can seriously ruin your holiday. No matter where you travel in North Wales, nearly every hostel after this one will likely be a disappointment. Where so many establishments are tired or cramped, *Totters* is modern and bright; there's crisp IKEA-esque decor in the airy rooms of its two-hundred-year-old town house, and a smart kitchen-diner in a fifteenth-century basement, where you help yourself to breakfast beside a Gothic arch. Its young owners greet you with real warmth and reams of local tips. It is what they would want from a hostel, the well-travelled couple say – a personal input that explains the relaxed atmosphere and faultless cleanliness as much as the lack of wi-fi; a hostel should be a friendly community, not an internet café, they point out. Of course, there is privacy if you want it. The attic double room provides a lovely stay for a couple, while a self-contained six-bed house across the road is a bargain for groups. Both provide a good base and with so much to see – Anglesey across the water, Snowdon twenty minutes away – there's little incentive to hurry on.

Totters, 2 High Street, Caernarfon, Gwynedd, LL55 1RN ☎01286 672963, 🖰totters.co.uk.
Price 1 en-suite double £50. Dorms: 2x4 £19, 3x6 £17. Self-contained house for 6 £120. Breakfast included.
Facilities Internet. Kitchen. Games/ common room.
Open Year-round. Check in: flexible. Check out: 11am.
Getting there Enter Caernarfon on the A487 and circle around the back of the castle. Take the second right, Stryd y Castell, then the first left onto High Street (Stryd Fawr); the hostel is on the left at the end of the road. Buses to Caernarfon from Bangor and Chester.

Gwern Gof Uchaf

Tourists go to Snowdon, adventurers head to Tryfan. Unlike its big sister with a railway to the summit, this triple peaked spur in the Ogwen Valley is a mountaineer's mountain. In place of well-trod trails there are scrambles. Instead of the blue-rinse brigade, there are feral goats. No wonder the successful 1953 Everest expedition trained here. That Tryfan lies almost within touching distance makes this National Trust-listed sheep farm an essential destination for anyone who seeks adventure in Snowdonia's great outdoors. Accommodation is in two sleeping areas within a white-painted breezeblock converted barn, with separate toilets

Gwern Gof Uchaf, Nant y Benglog, Capel Curig, Gwynedd, LL24 0EU ☎01690 720294, ⓦtryfanwales.co.uk.
Price Dorms: 1x4, 1x10, both £10.
Facilities Kitchen. On-site parking. Garden.
Restrictions Bed linen required.
Open Year-round. Check in: call for time. Check out: 10am.
Getting there Take the A5 west through Betws-y-Coed, then Capel Curig. Go a mile past Gwern Gof Ichaf farm (on the left) and the entrance is on the left. The Sherpa bus (#S6) from Bangor to Caernarfon via Betws-y-Coed stops outside on request.

and showers you share with a campsite. And although this is a true walkers' and climbers' bunkhouse, littered with Gore-Tex and rope, it's nowhere near as basic as you might expect. It has a proper tiled floor and sturdy high bunks – no wobbles or banged heads here. There's also a heated drying room that tackles most wet clothes in an hour, and a well-equipped kitchen area (note that the farm sells its own meat) where like-minded enthusiasts gather around a long table to talk trails. The summit path is just outside the door, so check the Met Office report that's posted daily, lace up those boots and pretend you're heading for Everest.

Clockwise from top left *HyB Bunkhouse's* small and cosy four-bed bunkroom; interiors store Medi, aka the hostel's check-in; each room comes with a kitchenette

HyB Bunkhouse

The hiking and biking magazines in the lounge are the giveaway. Half hostel, half self-contained stay, this is an ideal option for groups who come to scale Cader Idris mountain or cycle Coed y Brenin bike park. Yet because all bunkrooms have a kitchenette, and because this seventeenth-century town house is among the pubs and shops of Dolgellau (a private car park allows you to avoid the nightmare of pay and display), *HyB* will appeal to young families who value the freedom of private accommodation over a traditional B&B. Sure, Dolgellau's only bunkhouse remains a hostel in feel. It has sturdy bunkbeds and low ceilings, and compared with other accommodation options in town it's basic – a mite tatty even. But with the right eyes there's a quirky shabby chic about the

> HyB Bunkhouse, 2–3 Heol y Bont, Dolgellau, Gwynedd, LL40 1AU ☎01341 421755, Ⓦmedi-gifts.com.
> **Price** 3x4 with shared bathroom, 1x4 en suite; all £18. Bed linen (if required) £4.50.
> **Facilities** Internet. Kitchen. On-site parking. Games/common room.
> **Restrictions** Bed linen required.
> **Open** Year-round. Check in: flexible. Check out: 10am.
> **Getting there** Enter Dolgellau from the A470 over the bridge and turn immediately right into the public car park. At the toilet block take a sharp left through the gates into the rear car park of Medi/HyB. Buses go hourly from Machynlleth to Dolgellau.

crisp white walls and palest grey woodwork that offsets the original oak floors. Certainly, French linen curtains and the pretty bathroom seem overly charming for this type of establishment. That's no accident, though, as owner Nia Medi is a former designer for TV series *Real Rooms* and operates Medi, the interiors store below. That she lives off-site (entry is by keycode) simply reinforces the private-stay feel, leaving you free to roam – or sleep until noon.

Tyddyn Mawr

There are many ways to experience Cader Idris mountain. You could camp on its summit then descend the next day either a poet or raving mad, if a Welsh folktale is to be believed. Or you could book into *Tyddyn Mawr* beneath Cader's spectacular northern ridge. If rural luxury in some of the grandest scenery in Wales is your thing, this is your place, with a wall-full of awards to prove it. In fact, the best B&B in Wales several times over feels more like a two-room traditional hotel than anything else. The welcome from Olwen Evans (1999 Landlady of the Year finalist) is full of Welsh warmth, the spacious, country-style rooms are a cut above the usual B&B and smartly

> Tyddyn Mawr, Islawrdref, Dolgellau, Gwynedd, LL40 1TL ☎01341 422331, Ⓦwales-guesthouse.co.uk.
> **Price** 2 doubles £76. Breakfast included.
> **Facilities** On-site parking. Garden. TVs in rooms.
> **Open** Feb–Nov. Check in: flexible. Check out: 11am.
> **Getting there** On Dolgellau main square follow a sign towards Tywyn then take a left after 110yd signposted Cader Idris. Continue for two miles and the entrance is on your right, a half-mile past pub-restaurant *Gwesty Gwernau*.

decorated – think half-tester oak beds, pretty floral fabrics and immaculate modern bathrooms – and the view from each is worth the price alone. You could lose hours simply watching the sun pick out detail in the crags of Cader, or clouds spin into wisps from its ridges. That scenery is one reason, perhaps, why *Tyddyn Mawr* is as popular a getaway for older guests as it is for outdoorsy 30-somethings; another is that it prepares what is officially one of Wales's finest breakfasts, an award-winning five-course extravaganza of home-made goodness. What better excuse could you have for forgoing that night on Cader?

Morgans B&B

Morgans is all about sybaritic escapism on a coastline better known for candyfloss and arcade slots. From its hilltop location you can gaze across a silver-grey sea to see the lights of Liverpool, and Blackpool Tower is visible on a clear day. Yet Llanasa village, a mile away, is a dead ringer for the Cotswolds. All it lacks is the crowds, even though there is excellent walking in the Clywdian Range hills nearby or the conclusion of Offa's Dyke path a few miles away. A stay here is as exquisite as it is rural. You arrive to be greeted with genuine warmth (and home-made nibbles), then wake to birdsong before a first-rate breakfast created from home or local produce. Drift into the garden afterwards and soak up the silence. If the ambience is remote countryside, their B&B – bright, modern and spacious – exudes genuine style and luxury that is softened with homespun craft. Immaculate rooms have bespoke modern furnishings, but are also decorated with co-owner Kate Morgan's home-made quilts and embroidery samplers. It's this blend of old and new that gives *Morgans* instant appeal; part country, part cool contemporary style, all charming home-from-home.

Morgans B&B, Penygraig, Axton, Holywell, Flintshire, CH8 9DH ☎01745 570981, ⓦmorgansbedandbreakfast .co.uk.

Price 1 en-suite double £70, 1 en-suite suite (1 double, 1 twin) £120. Breakfast included.

Facilities Internet. Games/common room. Garden. TVs in rooms.

Open Closed Christmas and New Year's Eve. 2 night minimum stay. Check in: flexible. Check out: 11am.

Getting there Exit the A55 at Junction 31, signposted to Prestatyn. Follow the A5151 for 3.5 miles; just past Jacksons Garden Centre and the Total garage on the left, turn sharply right for Axton onto Fford Trelogan Road. After 110yd, turn left at a crossroads into Axton Lane, then take a sharp left at a T-junction, then turn left again up a track opposite the post box. Pass a house on left, turn left up the track, then fork right for Pen y graig.

You'll awake to birdsong at *Morgans B&B*, which combines homespun charm and contemporary cool

The Grade II listed pier at Llandudno is the longest in Wales

Llandudno Hostel

For a traditional seaside resort that is awash with B&Bs, groups are left high and dry in Llandudno. The exception lies in this immaculately restored Victorian terrace house just ten minutes from the pier; half hostel, half budget B&B, and all good value. Just as modern crystal chandeliers throughout or the reproduction antiques on the landings suggest, this spacious stay is no ordinary hostel, so only two rooms are allocated as shared dorms for individual travellers. Most are intended for the groups or young families who form the majority of Llandudno's budget visitors. Decor is also more B&B than hostel; while the bunkbeds in most rooms are familiar (family rooms have a double bed, plus bunks), the floral linen, embroided duvet covers and soft colour schemes lend a traditional atmosphere, and sinks and tea- and coffee-making facilities in all make for a pleasant surprise. Of course, such allowances for a B&B clientele have their downsides; the self-catering kitchen, for instance, amounts to a microwave in the dining room, and there is little of the usual hostel community vibe here. Shower pressure can be iffy at peak times, too. Yet for young families and groups on a tight budget this is a real find, giving you a chance to save on accommodation and spend more on Llandudno's traditional resort fun.

Llandudno Hostel, 14 Charlton Street, Llandudno, Conwy, LL30 2AA ☎01492 877430, ⓦllandudnohostel.co.uk.
Price 2 twins £48, 2 en-suite twins £52, 2x6 £90 for 4 or £132 for 6, 1 en-suite family room (sleeps six) £120. Dorms: 1x8 (mixed), 1x8 (female-only), both £20. Breakfast included.
Facilities Internet. Games/common room.
Open Year-round. Check in: flexible. Check out: 10am.
Getting there Take the A470 into Llandudno town centre, going straight ahead at all roundabouts. Pass Asda and two sets of traffic lights, then turn left into Vaughan Street (signed for the train station) and take the first right into Charlton Street; the hostel is 100yd down, on the left. The train station is 220yd away.

Bryn Tirion

Even after you have made the journey, *Bryn Tirion* seems like a fantasy. Just half an hour earlier you were fighting the traffic on the M53 south of Liverpool. Now you're nibbling on a home-made scone in front of a cottage, gazing out to empty hills from a pretty garden that bursts with blooms. It is the country idyll writ large. *Period Living* magazine thought so when it named *Bryn Tirion* the best traditional B&B in Britain in 2006. This, then, is not a place for sleek minimalism – uncharitably you could even call it twee. For a traditional cottage stay, however, it is a marvel. Wherever you look is layer upon layer of detail: floral bedspreads on an antique bed, embroidery samplers on the walls, old candlesticks and hat boxes, dried flowers, pretty china cups by your silver tea set, a grandfather clock that ticks soporifically in a lounge hung with Toby jugs. In less confident hands it would look forced at best, chintzy at worst. Yet interiors stylist Sylvia Hughes finishes her home with such flair and confidence that *Bryn Tirion* has the romance of a vintage storybook. Factor in a fine pub just up the lane and walks everywhere and you have the city decompression par excellence.

Bryn Tirion, Llanferres, Denbighshire, CH7 5LU ☎01352 810444, ⓦbryn-tirion .com.
Price 1 double £70 (£65 for 2 nights), breakfast included. 1 double holiday apartment £70, or £335 per week.
Facilities Internet. On-site parking. Games /common room. Garden. TVs in rooms.
Open Year-round. Check in: flexible. Check out: 11am.
Getting there From the A494, approximately 3 miles from Mold, turn left for Maeshafn village past the Rainbow Inn and follow winding road for a mile to the village. At a left-hand bend by a mini-roundabout, turn right, pass the *Miners Arms* on the left and a phone box on the right, then continue downhill for 200yd and fork right at the Llanferres sign, onto a track; the B&B is past the cottages on the right.

Clockwise from left *Glasgwm*, a Victorian town house with real character; *Glasgwm's* welcoming lounge mixes soft blues and comfy sofas; *Bryn Tirion* has the romance of a vintage storybook

Glasgwm

There's huge attention to home comforts at *Glasgwm*, and real character too. Owners John Spicer and Heather Petrie clearly enjoy sharing their central Victorian town house, pushing tea and fresh Welsh cakes into your hand as soon as you arrive. The lounge is equally welcoming, its mix of soft blues and comfy sofas draped with Indian fabrics hinting at the decor of the bedrooms above, all of which feel slightly different and are crammed with things the couple have accumulated over the decades: splendid beds of brass or walnut, soft armchairs, old prints and books and long floral curtains that pile grandly on the floor. The front rooms are brightest and most spacious, while a ruby-red backroom is furnished with Indian and southeast Asian finds, a canopied bed adding to the romance. The watchword is eclectic, but without sacrificing traditional B&B comforts such as tea- and coffee-making facilities in all rooms. Former restauranteurs, John and Heather provide fine home cooking with a little notice – a good option after a hard day in the hills or after rides with the kids on the Llangollen steam train.

Glasgwm, Abbey Road, Llangollen, Denbighshire, LL20 8SN ☎**01978 861975,** **Ⓦglasgwm-llangollen.co.uk.**
Price 1 en-suite single £37.50. 2 en-suite doubles, 1 £55 (normal), 1 £65 (kingsize).1 en-suite twin £65. Breakfast included.
Facilities Internet. On-site parking. Games/common room. Lunch and dinner available.
Open Year-round. Check in: flexible. Check out: 11am.
Getting there Head into Llangollen on the A5 and turn down Castle Street (towards the tourist information centre). Across the bridge, turn left and Glasgwm is about 75yd down, on the right. Bus #5 from Wrexham.

Llangollen Hostel

LLANGOLLEN

Even before the front door there's a hint of what makes this a credit to the new breed of independent hostel: "Creoso" (welcome) reads a plaque in the slate forecourt. Family-owned, it is the antithesis to the draughty rule-bound hostels of old, and just as its central town house looks like a home, so too does the decor after a top-to-bottom renovation in 2009. There's an excellent modern kitchen and dining area, and an informal lounge with an eclectic mix of furnishings, plus a woodburner to keep things cosy. Rooms – most of which are en suite – are all excellent, with individual spotlights for dorm beds and homely doubles that could shame many budget hotels; Room 7 is the pick for its views. As important are the friendly staff who keep the place spotless, but also go out of their way to help you settle in. Where other hostels set breakfast times that no holidaymaker should have to see, breakfasts here are DIY – have them as late as you like (or as early). Mention plans for a walk and staff proffer OS maps or offer to arrange myriad outdoor adventures available hereabouts. The vibe is more homestay than hostel – and praise doesn't come much higher than that.

Llangollen Hostel, Berwyn Street, Llangollen, Denbighshire, LL20 8NB ☎**01978 861773,** **Ⓦllangollenhostel.co.uk.**
Price 3 en-suite doubles/family room (double, plus 1–3 singles) £45 as doubles or £46–66 as family rooms; 1 twin £40. Dorms: 2x4, 1x6 (both en suite), plus 1x6 (shared bathroom); all £18. Breakfast included.
Facilities Internet. Kitchen. Games/common room. Tours. Lunch available.
Open Year-round. 2 night minimum stay during school holidays and weekends. Check in: flexible. Check out: 10am.
Getting there The hostel is in the centre on the main A5 through-road. Approaching from the east off the A483, it's on the right, 55yd past the town centre traffic lights at Castle Street, where you'll find a car park. Buses from Ruabon or Wrexham train stations, plus National Express coaches from London to Llangollen.

Pistyll Rhaeadr

Owner Phill Facey insists the showman's caravan he offers as part of the *Retreat Campsite* is not just a budget stay, but a chance to drop off the radar; it is "a retreat or a quietening cell", a place for reflection in one of the most magical locations in Wales. There are trails by the mile to explore, but first you have to bring yourself to stray from the pea-green caravan. Built in the 1940s to house the Wild West act of a travelling circus, its interior is enchanting. Painted floral designs on varnished woodwork, original etched glass and pretty curtains lend a cosy vintage atmosphere, while an old woodburner keeps things toasty and boils up the enamel coffeepot. Actually, while simple, most cons are reassuringly mod, including the gas hob, a fridge and electric radiators. A café at the waterfall also serves breakfast and lunch. Sleeping is either on a double daybed or in the bunks of a wee cabin-sized bedroom. It's basic, of course (the bathroom is a public toilet block you share with campers and there are no showers), but what magic to wake in the meditative stillness of this landscape; to open the door with a morning cuppa and hear nothing but wind and water.

Pistyll Rhaeadr, Retreat Campsite, Waterfall Lane, Llanrhaeadr ym Mochnant, Powys, SY10 0BZ ☎01691 780392, ⊕pistyllrhaeadr.co.uk.
Price 1 double or twin £60.
Facilities On-site parking. Café. Garden. Lunch available.
Open Year-round. 3 night minimum stay. Check in: flexible. Check out: 10am.
Getting there Take the A495 off the A483 south of Oswestry, then the B4396 to Llanrhaeadr. In the village centre follow a sign to "Waterfall" beside Greatorex Village Store. The road ends at the waterfall three miles away, where the café serves as the reception.

Reditreks Bunkhouse

Mountain-bikers take note: though everyone raves about the rollercoaster rides of Coed y Brenin Mountain Bike Centre, you don't really need to stray from Machynlleth. That the trails start less than half a mile away is what inspired The Holey Trail bikeshop (where you check in) to open this smart, modern bunkhouse. A former bakery, it now features bright rooms with bunkbeds in a large dorm or singles in two smaller dorms/family rooms. All are spotless and spacious. They're also rather spartan, but no matter – you'll probably spend most of your time in the excellent lounge-kitchen. Other facilities include a storage and workshop area, plus a bike-wash and kit-drying room. Guests aren't exclusively bike-mad though; indeed, so central is *Reditreks* it makes an excellent budget stay for anyone visiting Machynlleth, and both types of visitor will find that this feels more a guesthouse or homestay than hostel. Perhaps that's because the managers are off site. Or maybe it's explained by the way the patio doors are thrown open on summer weekends, guests spilling into the yard for a barbecue before heading off to the pub. Either way, *Reditreks* is doing something right.

Reditreks Bunkhouse, 31 Maengwyn Street, Machynlleth, Powys, SY20 8EB ☎01654 702184, ⊕reditreks.com.
Price Dorms: 2x4, 1x8; Mon–Thurs £15, Fri–Sun £17.50. Bed linen (if required) £5.
Facilities Kitchen. On-site parking. Games/common room. Garden. Lockers. Bike rental.
Restrictions Bed linen required.
Open Year-round. Check in: 2pm. Check out: noon.
Getting there The Holey Trail bikeshop is beside the *Rendezvous Café*, on the A489 (Maengwyn Street). To find the bunkhouse turn right off Maengwyn Street onto New Street (opposite the White Horse pub) then take the first left into Heol Powys; the bunkhouse is on the left corner at the end of the street. Direct trains from Birmingham, Shrewsbury and Aberystwyth.

Clockwise from left *Brynwylfa's* sun-streaked conservatory, scene of many a good long chat; the B&B's cosy and very comfortable double room; breakfast a la *Brynwylfa*

Brynwylfa

MONTGOMERY

Here's a halfway treat at the most impressive section of Offa's Dyke footpath. With prior notice, owners Hugo and Jill Jones will scoop you off the long-distance trail then drive you to their handsome Georgian town house. Within ten minutes, you're through the gardens and sitting, boots off, in a bright conservatory with tea and home-made cake. The wild uplands feel far, far away. Although nearly all guests come straight from the trail, the Jones's relaxed B&B provides a fine stay for anyone visiting this idyllic small town draped over a hill. The two pretty, modern rooms – one twin, one double, both en suite, both hugely comfortable – are in the old stables in a separate section of the house. Well-travelled Hugo and Jill may pop in for a chat and to check you have all you need, otherwise the place has the feel of a self-contained stay, complete with guests' private entrance. Why watch TV in your room when you can settle into that glass-roofed conservatory by the garden, whiling away the hours with chat around a long oak table or plucking at Hugo's acoustic guitar? There's no need to travel for a night out either: a pub is ten paces away, while fine food is around the corner at *The Checkers*. Good luck with getting back on the trail.

Brynwylfa, 4 Castle Street, Montgomery, Powys, SY15 6PW ☎01686 668555, ⓦbrynwylfa.co.uk.
Price 1 en-suite double, 1 en-suite twin, both £60. Breakfast included.
Facilities Internet. Games/common room. Garden. TVs in rooms.
Open Closed Christmas and New Year's Eve. Check in: flexible. Check out: 11am.
Getting there Follow signs off the A483 into Montgomery, then continue uphill on the through-road; the B&B is on the right, just past the town square (Broad Street) at the top of the hill. Bus #71 goes to Montgomery from Welshpool.

Pen y Gwyrd

There is no better base for Snowdon than this. From outside, *Pen y Gwyrd* seems unremarkable except for its superb location beneath Wales's highest mountain. Indeed, the former coaching inn on Llanberis Pass looks rather tired. Yet within lies mountaineering history. A haunt of rock-hoppers since the mid 1800s, *Pen y Gwyrd* was the training headquarters for the successful Everest expedition of 1953 and it positively creaks with its own heritage. The mountaineers (alongside famous names such as Chris Bonington) signed the ceiling downstairs and mementos of the expedition decorate a wood-panelled bar that begs for whisky and chill nights. That battered enamel cup on display is the same one in the black and white photo of Sir Edmund Hillary drinking near Everest's summit.

The inn must have been a period piece even in his day. It has been in the hands of the Pullee family since 1947 and retains the Edwardian decor from its time as a base for gentleman climbers. In fact, *Pen y Gwyrd* is so defiantly old-fashioned in an age tyrannized by design trends that it seems rather hip. Reached by a creaky staircase are snug rooms (no locks, incidentally) with tassled light cords above proper oak beds and traditional Welsh blankets; Room 9 is the brightest. There are no plastic kettles or telephones and certainly no flatscreen TVs. All you get is a porcelain sink in a wooden surround and a bar of Imperial Leather soap. Shared bathrooms are splendidly old-fashioned – one has a fabulous roll-top babth, another a Victorian shower and a Thunderbox toilet – and the swimming pool is distinctly bygone, a small stream-fed lake in the bosom of the mountains. There are three modern en suites in an annexe, but contemporary accommodation is hardly the point of *Pen y Gwyrd*.

Nor is the throwback limited to looks. At 8.30am sharp a Nepalese gong presented by the Everest team summons guests to porridge, kippers, silver cutlery and napkins in rings. Sleep in till 9am and you'll miss it. It's an anachronism, of course, but just the sort of detail that makes *Pen y Gwyrd* so much fun. The story goes that when news of Hillary and Tenzing

Norgay's triumph reached the inn, the landlord roused his guests at 1am to demand they drink a toast in the bar within ten minutes or be thrown out the next morning. Something of that "King and Country" eccentricity lingers on and the scenery is as fabulous as it was in 1953.

Pen y Gwyrd, Pen-y-Pass, Nant Gwynant, Gwynedd, LL55 4NT ☎01286 870211, ⓦpyg.co.uk.
Price 11 doubles £80, 2 en-suite doubles £96, 3 "modern" en-suite doubles £100. Breakfast included.
Facilities Internet. On-site parking. Bar. Games/common room. Garden. Lunch and dinner available.
Open Jan–Oct. 2 night minimum stay during weekends. Check in: noon. Check out: 11am.
Getting there The hotel is at the junction of the A498 and A4086. All Snowdon Sherpa buses go to to Pen-y-Pass near the hotel. Those from gateway destinations are the #S1 from Llanberis; the #S2 and #S97 from Betws-y-Coed; and the #S4 from Caernarfon.

Clockwise from top The nearby Llynnau Mymbyr lakes; rooms are named after local peaks; the hotel's interior is littered with climbing memorabilia; Sir Edmund Hillary presented a rock from Mt Everest's summit to the inn, now on display in the bar; the traditional rooms have an Edwardian character, right down to the tassled light cords

Plas Efenechtyd

RUTHIN

Draped in wisteria, with a menagerie of chickens in the orchard and lazy cats in the sunshine, this pristine farmhouse makes an instant impression, and is as charming as owners Dave Jones and Marilyn Jeffery. Their welcome is wholehearted, their house one of informal style: a marriage of soft powdery paint colours, old beams and southeast Asian wall-hangings collected on travels. While rooms are individually styled – there's modern-country minimalism in a snug room at the rear (which has the best shower), modestly bling boutique or an antique brass bed in a traditional room – all have the same uncluttered, easy feel. You'll wake to nothing louder than birdsong then descend to a superb breakfast: delicious home-made jams made from garden fruits, fresh home-made breads and yoghurt, the full fry-up made from local produce, and even salmon fishcakes. Fortified, there's stupendous scenery to discover, including medieval Ruthin or Offa's Dyke as it marches over the Clwydian Range, a Brecon Beacons nobody knows. Order a packed lunch and head to the hills.

Plas Efenechtyd, Efenechtyd, Ruthin, Denbighshire, LL15 2LP ☎01824 704008, ⓦplas-efenechtyd-cottage.co.uk.
Price 3 en-suite doubles £65. Breakfast included.
Facilities Internet. On-site parking. Garden. Lunch available.
Open Year-round. 2 night minimum stay during high season weekends. Check in: flexible. Check out: 11am.
Getting there In Ruthin, follow signs to Bala then pick up the B5105. Go through Llanfrwog with the Cross Keys on your left, then uphill and around some bends for a mile. At some railings on the left, take a lane on the left to a T-junction. Turn right and the house is 55yd ahead on the right.

Talbontdrain

UWCHYGARREG

The lane narrows until you're hemmed in by hedgerows. The last house was way back. Just when you've given up hope, the route darts uphill and you're at a white-painted farmhouse. Even in a Welsh mist it hints at Arcadia, while in sunshine, with silence and views to the Cambrian Mountains, it is bliss. Notwithstanding the cockerel for an alarm clock, peace reigns supreme at *Talbontdrain*. Personality does, too, thanks to charming, child-friendly Hilary Matthews. She greets guests like old friends and has the same informality as her decor: a mix-and-match of antique armchairs and pretty watercolours. The loveliest room (en suite) retains original Arts and Crafts furniture. This feels more relaxed home-from-home than B&B, especially so at meals, when guests linger to swap stories over the home cooking. A pretty cottage garden segues into rural hills and Hilary can pack you a lunch then direct you onto the many walking tracks hereabouts. Many first-timers treat *Talbontdrain* as an overnight stop en route to somewhere else, then beg to extend their stay when they realize what they're leaving behind – too late, though, as rooms are invariably booked. So here's a tip: slow down, stay two days. Better still, stay three.

Talbontdrain, Uwchygarreg, Powys, SY20 8RR ☎01654 702192, ⓦtalbontdrain.co.uk.
Price 1 single £32, 1 double £66, 2 en-suite doubles £74. Breakfast included.
Facilities Internet. On-site parking. Games/common room. Garden. Lunch and dinner available.
Open Year-round. Check in: flexible. Check out: 11am.
Getting there From central Machynlleth, take the Newtown road (A489) to find the right-hand turn to Forge. Take a right turn to Uwchygarreg (signposted "Dead End") and continue for two miles until you pass a phone box, then ascend a steep hill; the entrance is on the right at the top of the hill.

Gwaenynog

It took 25,000 miles and eighteen months' searching for bubbly owner Fiona Potts to find the wrong farmhouse. A missed turn during house-hunting accidentally led her to a 'For Sale' sign and soon she was in a stone-floored kitchen, smitten by the views and peace of the house that would become her B&B. It's not hard to see why. Within ten minutes of arrival at this remote mid-Wales stay you are in the garden with a cup of tea. Sheep bleat. Red kites, which nest in the garden, wobble overhead. Bonnie and Beau, *Gwaenynog*'s affectionate sheepdogs, sit at your side in companiable silence. It is an instant de-stress and just as relaxing inside. Contemporary country are the watchwords, with horsebrasses above the fireplace, carved oak furniture and floral curtains in the lounge, soft colours and pine or rattan furnishings in the three rooms, with a four-poster and daybed in "Owl". Of course, this air of effortless ease is something of a false impression. For all the genuine warmth from Fiona and her husband Norman, and for all its home-from-home feel, *Gwaenynog* is a tight ship. Fiona keeps everything immaculate and works hard to provide small hotel-style luxuries such as fine toiletries and good breakfasts. That you may never realize it may be exactly why this is such a lovely place to stay.

Gwaenynog, Dolanog, Welshpool, Powys, SL21 0LJ ☎01938 810236, ⓦwww .gwaenynog.com.
Price 2 en-suite doubles £70, 1 large en-suite double £80 (used as a family room £90). Breakfast included.
Facilities Internet. On-site parking. Games/ common room. Garden. Dinner available.
Open Year-round. Check in: flexible. Check out: 11am.
Getting there Go west of Welshpool on the A458, go through Cyfronydd and after two miles turn right onto the B4382 to Dolanog. Go across the A495 and after a couple of miles turn left and continue to a crossroads. Turn left and the entrance is on the left after 330yd.

Clockwise from left The peaceful surroundings at *Talbontdrain*; the *Gwaenynog* grounds; idyllic *Plas Efenechtyd*

NORTHWEST ENGLAND

The Northwest is an established getaway for Brits, with Blackpool a time-honoured target and the Isle of Man offering a surprisingly rural and beautiful island escape. The area has somewhat fallen out of favour in recent times, with many visitors either heading north to the Lakes or east to the Peak District. But this can be a plus if you're looking for a less obvious holiday destination – the big cities offer some of the best nightlife and galleries in Britain, there are some little-known but interesting historic towns, and the Forest of Bowland is an unexpected pocket of wild moorland. Affordable accommodation is more achievable here than in more obviously touristy regions and we've sought out city-centre hostels for party weekends as well as coastal B&Bs and remote rural options.

   High summer aside, you're unlikely to have to book very far in advance in the Northwest, though Liverpool and Manchester see plenty of visitors for football, concerts and the like. Towns such as Blackpool have been making tourists welcome for over a century, and there's a plethora of sometimes startlingly cheap B&Bs. Quality is harder to come by, though, so we've tried to identify the very best budget choices either in town-centre locations or with countryside on the doorstep. All

are well run, welcoming and will set you up with an excellent and filling breakfast. There are plenty of hostels, some rather sylish: while Slaidburn's YHA is attractive but spartan, its Manchester equivalent shows the organization at its most modern, with funky decor and a great canalside location.

This compact corner of England is hugely varied. The great centres of Liverpool and Manchester have excellent art scenes, a wealth of fine architecture from their industrial heydays, and immigrant communities that have contributed to a strong culture of eating well on a budget. South of Liverpool, Chester is a well-preserved and very attractive little town with spectacular city walls, and Lancaster, to the north of the region, is similarly handsome. Lancashire contains some tracts of untamed countryside, most dramatically in the Forest of Bowland. The coast is traditional British holidayland – while Morecambe is rather sedate, albeit with stunning views across the water to the Lake District – Blackpool is gaudy, brash and on an epic scale. If donkeys, buckets and spades, fairground thrills and kiss-me-quick hats appeal, it's well worth a look. And, for an island adventure, take a ferry to the Isle of Man, with its sandy beaches and mountainscapes.

NORTHWEST ENGLAND

NAME	LOCATION	PAGE		REAL BARGAIN	TREAT YOURSELF	FAMILY-FRIENDLY	GREAT RURAL LOCATION	OUTDOOR ACTIVITIES	GREAT FOOD AND DRINK	DORMS	PUBLIC TRANSPORT
Aaron House	Isle of Man	142	①		✓			✓			
Ashley Hotel	Morecambe	148	②								✓
Etap	Manchester	145	⑧	✓							✓
Hark to Bounty	Slaidburn	148	④				✓	✓			
Hatter's	Liverpool	144	⑩						✓	✓	✓
International Inn	Liverpool	145	⑪							✓	✓
Middle Beardshaw Head Farm	Colne	141	⑦	✓			✓	✓		✓	
Recorder House	Chester	141	⑫								✓
Seabreeze	Blackpool	140	⑥			✓					✓
The Shakespeare Bed and Breakfast	Lancaster	143	③								✓
YHA Manchester	Manchester	146	⑨				✓			✓	✓
YHA Slaidburn	Slaidburn	149	⑤				✓	✓		✓	

Clockwise from top left Blackpool, home to *Seabreeze* (see p.140); *Aaron House* (see p.142), *YHA Slaidburn* (see p.149)
Previous page Salthouse Dock, Liverpool

Seabreeze

BLACKPOOL

Blackpool is the home of huge and generally pricey hotels, serried ranks of which line the promenade. But one street back from the seafront beyond the north pier you'll find this friendly place, a B&B in an Edwardian villa efficiently run by Mark and Corrie Norris, who live on the top floor. It's a homely option rather than a chic one, with a long breakfast menu that takes in the Full English, Danish pastries, cereals, porridge, smoked salmon and kippers as well as options for kids; the B&B is very popular with families, who can be easily accommodated in the larger rooms.

The street is quiet, lined with more sedate B&Bs, but it's a stroll away from the epic 7-mile promenade and its jaw-droppingly tacky candyfloss, rock and bucket'n'spade stalls, bingo halls, fortune tellers and tram and donkey rides. You're also within walking distance of the rowdy but rather beautiful North Pier, a cast-iron walkway crammed with arcades and amusements. Umpteen rides and attractions lure in the summer holiday crowds, while from September to early November the famous Illuminations bedeck the promenade with half a million lightbulbs. And of course the iconic late nineteenth-century Blackpool Tower dominates the whole gaudy panorama. When you need some respite, retire to the quieter comfort of *Seabreeze*.

Seabreeze, 1 Gynn Avenue, Blackpool, Lancashire, FY1 2LD ☎01253 351427, Ⓦvbreezy.co.uk.
Price 1 single £30, 1 small double £55, 1 double £60, 1 twin £60, 1 triple £70, 1 family room for 4 £80. All rooms are en suite. Breakfast included.
Facilities Internet. On-site parking. TVs in rooms.
Open Open year-round. Check in: 1pm. Check out: 11am.
Getting there The main train station is Blackpool North, around 1km from *Seabreeze*; there are car parks throughout town, and the B&B has its own small car parking area. The B&B is one street back from the seafront, at North Shore.

From left A homely room at *Seabreeze*; Blackpool's historic seafront and pier

Recorder House

CHESTER

Recorder House, 19 City Walls, Chester, Cheshire, CH1 1SB Ⓣ01244 326580, Ⓦrecorderhotel.co.uk.
Price 4 rear doubles £70, 1 rear four-poster double £80, 2 river-view doubles £80, 2 river-view four-poster doubles £90, 1 river-view king-size double £100. All rooms are en suite. Breakfast included.
Facilities Internet. TVs in rooms.
Open Open year-round. Minimum 2-night stay at weekends. Check in: 2pm. Check out: 10am.
Getting there The train station is at the northeast end of town – either take a taxi to Recorder House, or walk down City Road and Foregate Street, turning left at The Cross. Head down towards the river, taking a left on Duke Street. There's off-street parking.

This imposing Georgian house sits by the magnificent medieval and Roman walls of Chester, its elevated position allowing sweeping views of the River Dee and giving a feel of the unique layout of this stunning little city. Set on a quiet residential street on the south side of town, *Recorder House*'s ten rooms are run more like a small hotel than a homely B&B. But the welcome is warm, the staff are efficient, and rooms are attractively decked out with carved wooden four-posters, antique-style wallpaper and embroidered bedspreads. The cheaper rooms at the back look out over the compact courtyard garden rather than the river. Three of the rooms have an additional single bed, though they're not designed as family options – children under 14 aren't allowed. From the B&B you can walk round the walls to access The Rows, unusual raised shopping streets that mix Tudor buildings and Victorian imitations. There's plenty to do: as well as Chester Zoo, the city hosts extensive gardens, an impressive cathedral and the excellent Grosvenor Museum, which has a large collection of Roman artefacts.

Middle Beardshaw Head Farm

COLNE

Middle Beardshaw Head Farm, Burnley Road, Trawden, Colne, Lancashire, BB8 8PP Ⓣ01282 865257, Ⓦa1tourism.com/uk/midbeard.html.
Price B&B £25 per person. Barn £8 per person, plus contribution to energy use. Barn only available for groups (of up to 20) at weekends. Breakfast included for B&B.
Facilities Dinner available. Kitchen facilities. On-site parking. Games/common room. Garden.
Open Open year-round. The barn accepts group bookings only at weekends. Check in: flexible. Check out: flexible.
Getting there From the A6068, just northeast of Burnley, take the B6250 to Trawden. Follow the narrow lane with the church on your left and continue uphill. *Middle Beardshaw Head Farm* is signposted on the right-hand side of the road.

With a secluded rural setting in Brontë country, this delightful barn and B&B makes for an intriguing stop. The 300-year-old house has log fires, mullion windows, oak beams and suitably antique furnishings throughout, including a set of armour. There are three cosy rooms inside – two singles and one en-suite double/family room with a four-poster – while the beautifully restored eighteenth-century barn offers a cheap, atmospheric alternative. The barn is on a grand scale, with high whitewashed stone walls adorned with a stag's horns, and has a woodburning stove for cooler nights, six bunk beds and forty foam mattresses. You can cook in the well-equipped kitchen, or book in advance for dinner – which at £10 for three courses and a glass of wine is a tremendous bargain, and also allows you to take in the atmosphere of the house. The conservatory has a pool table, dart board and table tennis, and by day, you can ramble on the moors, where you might see golden plover and red grouse. A fifteen-minute walk takes you to the little village of Trawden, home to a pub and a good daytime café, and you can also walk to Haworth and visit the parsonage where the Brontës lived their short, remarkable lives.

Aaron House

The cliff-edged Isle of Man, accessed by ferry or "fastcraft" from Heysham or Liverpool, is for most of the year a picturesque tourist backwater – though it roars into life in late May for the TT motorbike races. Sitting on the bay of the attractive little southern town of Port St Mary, *Aaron House* is a very engaging and slightly eccentric option that's a must for lovers of Victorian kitsch. The hosts dress in mob caps and pinnies to serve lavish organic breakfasts and, aside from the incongruous inclusion of TVs, the seven double rooms fit the theme, with pretty floral wallpaper, polished wooden dressers, gleaming brass beds, clawfoot baths and chamber pots putting this at the luxury end of the budget B&B spectrum. In a further indulgent touch, home-made scones and jam are served in the parlour. Port St Mary can be enjoyably accessed by steam train from the island's captial, Douglas; from town, you can walk to the absorbing folk museum at Cregneash, with its thatched cottages and costumed spinners, weavers and smiths. A footpath continues to the sheer Manx slate cliffs of Spanish Head, taking you to the very southern tip of this lovely island.

Aaron House, The Promenade, Port St Mary, Isle of Man, IM9 5DE ☎01624 835702, Ⓦaaronhouse.co.uk.

Price 7 en-suite doubles, £70–108. More expensive rooms have sea views. Breakfast included.

Facilities On-site parking. Breakfast available. TVs in rooms.

Restrictions No stag or hen groups. No children under 12.

Open Open year-round. Minimum stay 2 days at busy times. Check in: 2pm. Check out: 10am.

Getting there Contact the Isle of Man Steam Packet Company (☎01871 222 1333, steam-packet.com) for details of ferries and fast craft to Douglas, the island's capital. From Douglas, regular buses and a steam train (Ⓦiombusandrail.info) head to Port St Mary – or it's an easy 20min drive.

Clockwise from left *Aaron House*'s smart exterior; the ornate Victorian dining room; one of the double rooms

From left Lancaster's Norman castle; *The Shakespeare Bed and Breakfast* has an old-world feel

The Shakespeare Bed and Breakfast

LANCASTER

This tall, centrally located town house is a good-value base from which to explore Lancaster. It's cosy and extremely welcoming – the hosts are a great source of local knowledge – and floral decor gives the place an old-world feel. There's plenty of choice in the morning, including fresh fruit as well as a cooked Lancashire breakfast, and usually a cuppa provided on arrival.

The B&B was one of the last taverns on ancient St Leonard's Gate, and once fed and watered travellers through the city and workers in the nearby shipyards. The name is thought to relate to the proximity of the beautiful Grand Theatre across the road; it's the third-oldest working theatre in Britain and is said to house the ghost of Shakespearean actress Sarah Siddons. Otherwise, St Leonard's Gate is now mainly quiet and residential, but it's just a short stroll from the centre, with its fine collection of Georgian buildings – a reminder of the town's role as a major slave-trade port. Lancaster's focus is its castle, built by the Normans and added to throughout the medieval period, and while there are few other standout sights, the leafy town is a lovely place for some gentle exploration, particularly if you hire a bike to pedal down the canal towpaths and riverside tracks.

The Shakespeare Bed and Breakfast, 96 St Leonard's Gate, Lancaster, Lancashire, LA1 1NN ☎01524 841041, ✉theshakespeare lancaster@talktalk.net.
Price 7 en-suite doubles £66. Breakfast included.
Facilities Internet. On-site parking. TVs in rooms.
Open Closed Aug and Christmas holidays. Check in: 11am. Check out: 1pm.
Getting there The train station is on Meeting House Lane, around a 10min walk from the B&B. Follow signs for the tourist information centre before heading down Market Street and through the shopping arcade, bearing left for St Leonard's Gate. One parking space is provided for guests on a first-come-first-served basis; if it's taken, the owners will advise on the best options.

Hatter's

Hatter's is housed in an ornate red-brick Victorian building, which until recently was home to the first purpose-built YMCA in the world, founded in the mid-nineteenth century. It's a big place, with five floors and space for 300 guests, and while it tends to accommodate a quieter backpacker crew midweek, at weekends, especially during the football season, it's party central, with large groups of guys and girls making the most of the nearby pubs and clubs.

The atmosphere is upbeat and welcoming, and the place staffed round the clock with young, well-informed staff who can book city and Beatles tours and advise on the best places to visit as well as onward travel. The garden/yard is a nice social space in summer – there's also a well-equipped kitchen, a huge common room with pool tables, a TV lounge, a pub that's open for special events and a games room with darts and board games.

Hatter's, Mount Pleasant, Liverpool, L3 5SH ⓣ0151 709 5570, ⓦhattersgroup.com.
Price £16–19 for a dorm bed and £45–70 for a double; the higher prices are for weekend rates. Dorms sleep 4–12, and there are also triples, doubles, twins and singles. Most are en suite. Light breakfast (tea, coffee, juice and toast) included.
Facilities Internet. Kitchen facilities. Games/common room. Tours on offer.
Open Open year-round. Check in: 2pm. Check out: 11am.
Getting there The hostel is a 15min walk from the city centre; from Lime Street station turn left and keep walking on the left-hand side until you see Mount Pleasant Road. Turn left here and follow the road until you see the hostel on the right. Drivers should follow signs to Lime Street station and then the instructions above.

From left *Hatter's* Victorian building housed the world's first YMCA; the hostel's games room

International Inn

This grandly titled place provides great budget accommodation in the heart of the city, either in basic dorms and doubles or the marginally more expensive "cocoon pod rooms". These are billed as "a conceptualised, stylish, compact space", although the International Inn is recommended more for its reasonable prices and cracking location than for any chic extras. The pod rooms are well but minimally fitted out with en-suite bathrooms, TVs and tea- and coffee-making facilities, but are fairly simple and none have windows as they're below ground level – fresh air pumped in from the outside stops them feeling too claustrophobic. In the hostel area, meanwhile, rooms are plain but have decent en-suite bathrooms, and the games/TV lounge has a pool table. There's wi-fi throughout, and computers in the adjoining café, lively *Sam and Joe's*, which provides a good all-day breakfast, and you're within strolling distance of Chinatown with its multitude of bargain restaurants, as well as one of the most lively nightlife scenes in the northwest. Culture vultures won't be disappointed either – in addition to the revitalized Albert Dock area, you're close to the Walker Gallery and its fine collection of Pre-Raphaelite paintings, plus contemporary attractions including the FACT arts centre and cinema on Wood Street.

International Inn, 4 South Hunter Street, Liverpool, L1 9JG ☎0151 709 8135, Ⓦinternationalinn.co.uk.
Price Dorm beds £15–20, twins and doubles £36–45; higher rates listed are for the weekends. The 32 double/twin cocoon rooms cost £43, £53 at weekends.
Facilities Internet. Breakfast available. Café. Games/common room. TVs in rooms.
Open Open year-round. Check in: 3pm. Check out: 11am.
Getting there The hostel is located near the town centre on South Hunter Street, a 15min walk from Lime Street Station. By car, follow signs to Liverpool Central station, then head up Renshaw Street and fork left on Hardman Street, turning left for South Hunter Street.

Etap

Etap couldn't be described as beautiful – part of a French budget chain, it's located in a monolithic block in glitzy Salford Quays and has 210 bedrooms. But the room rates are remarkably low, and the no-frills ethos is employed to good effect, with minimal but bright decor. Breakfast isn't included in the price but only costs £3.75; there's a little café on the ground floor as well as a bar. Rooms are plain and functional with TVs and en-suite bathrooms; all but 25 of them have a bunk bed as well as a double, making this a bargain for families. Best of all, you can walk to the attractions of Salford Quays, notably The Lowry, a gleaming arts centre which showcases the poignant paintings of L. S. Lowry, and the dramatic new Imperial War Museum North, designed by Daniel Libeskind. Very much concerned with the social impact of war as well as its hardware, it's a thought-provoking stop. You could continue your journey for a mile or so to Old Trafford, hallowed ground of Manchester United, before returning for a distinctly budget night's sleep in a city that, apart from the showcase YHA (see p.146), is low on bargains.

Etap, 19 Trafford Road, Salford, Manchester, M5 3AW ☎01618 480898, Ⓦetaphotel.com.
Price 180 doubles with extra bunk bed, 25 standard doubles. £25–65 per room; rates vary according to online discounts.
Facilities Internet. On-site parking. Breakfast available. Bar. Café. TVs in rooms.
Restrictions Dogs allowed. Good disabled access.
Open Open year-round. Check in: noon. Check out: noon.
Getting there The hotel is on Trafford Road, 100 yards from the Salford Quays tram stop. From the centre of Manchester, the follow signs for Salford Quay, taking the A5063 to join Trafford Road.

YHA Manchester

Manchester's YHA is the city's best hostel and a flagship property for the charity, purpose-built in 1995 with all the mod cons of modern hostelling, plus a dash of style that's all its own. It's located on the Bridgewater Canal in the Castlefield area of Manchester, around fifteen minutes' walk from the revamped and lively city centre.

The warehouse-style building has 32 pristine four- and five-bed dorms, plus three "premium rooms" for two people. There's wi-fi throughout (though beware the YHA's high charges), plus good disabled access, a wet room, TV lounge, bike store and laundry. The large number of four-bed dorms makes the hostel a good choice for families: kids are welcome and cots are available. There's no curfew, but quiet is requested after 11pm, meaning there isn't the rackety party feel you sometimes find in independent hostels. Social activities focus around the games room with its pool table and table football, as well as a spacious café/dining room with canal views. Breakfast costs an extra £4.95, and bar meals including decent pizzas are also on offer.

> **YHA Manchester, Potato Wharf, Castlefield, Manchester, M3 4NB ☎0845 371 9647, ⓦyha.org.uk.**
> **Price** Prices vary according to availability, and weekend stays are more expensive. Dorms: 2x5 £17.65–28.15, 30x4 £21.25–30.50. 3 doubles £44–70.
> **Facilities** Internet. Dinner available. Kitchen facilities. Lunch available. Breakfast available. Bar. Café. Games/common room. Lockers.
> **Restrictions** Good disabled access.
> **Open** Open year-round. Check in: flexible. Check out: noon.
> **Getting there** The hostel is 1 mile from Manchester city centre. Follow signs to Castlefield or the Museum Science and Industry on Liverpool Road: the hostel is on Potato Wharf just off Liverpool Road.

Throughout the building, from the open and inviting reception with its world map graphics and monochrome decor to the bright green games room, specially commissioned art works brighten the walls, some symbolizing the resurgent city. Bold and colourful furniture and funky signage further enhance the hostel's credentials as Manchester's hippest budget stay.

Indeed, the whole canal area, once almost derelict, has a buzzy and revitalized air, with the YHA sitting among swish cafés and enticing waterside towpaths; the hostel has details of routes, which include a 4.5-mile circular walk via the Rochdale Canal and Duke's Lock. Just across the road from the hostel sits the popular Museum of Science and Industry, featuring

a hall crammed with original steam engines as well as a working replica of a Stephenson train, which transports visitors to the world's oldest passenger railway station. The museum is appropriately sited: the Bridgewater Canal was the country's first man-made waterway and was integral to the industrialization of the north. Between the museum and the hostel is a dramatic line of high Victorian viaducts, whose arches provide a dramatic entrance way to the YHA, as well as a reminder of the city's proud engineering heritage.

Clockwise from top left The revitalized Bridgewater Canal; *YHA Manchester* sits on the waterfront; the reception area; a footbridge stretches over calm waters to Potato Wharf and the YHA

Ashley Hotel

Sitting on the picturesque sweep of Morecambe Bay, this traditional family-run hotel enjoys fine views that extend from the sands and sea to the mountains and valleys of the Lake District. Located on four floors, its comfy rooms feature king-sized beds, TV and wi-fi, and with picture windows looking out onto the bay, you're in a prime position for Morecambe's famous sunsets. Big breakfasts including Lancashire bacon are cooked to order, and there's freshly brewed tea, pancakes and crumpets. Twitchers should bring binoculars, as the town is a wintering stopoff for waders and wildfowl, the sandflats providing a feeding ground for a quarter of a million wading birds, ducks and geese. Be sure to check out the restored *Midland Hotel*, a Deco classic built in 1933 and featuring sculptures by Eric Gill; opposite is the Victoria Pavilion, known as Morecambe Winter Gardens. There are few other formal sights, once you've taken in the seafront statue of local boy Eric Morecambe, but cycle paths lead north to Lancaster, just 5 miles away, or 3 miles south to Heysham Village. Here lovely seventeenth-century cottages sit by the sea, the Saxon church has a Viking hogback tomb and the tearooms serve local speciality nettle beer.

> **Ashley Hotel, 371 Marine Road East, Morecambe, Lancashire, LA4 5AH**
> ☎01524 412034, ⓦashleyhotel.co.uk.
> **Price** 10 en-suite doubles £58. Breakfast included.
> **Facilities** Internet. On-site parking. TVs in rooms.
> **Open** Open year-round. Check in: 3pm. Check out: 11am.
> **Getting there** Morecambe is 5 miles west of Lancaster on the A589 and then the A683, and can be accessed by train from Lancaster. The B&B is near the centre of the small town, near the town hall and on the bay.

Hark to Bounty

This traditional stone-built inn is thought to have acquired its quaint name from a local squire calling out to his favourite hound, Bounty, who was baying outside the pub. As you might expect, it's a historic place: there was an inn here in the fourteenth century, and the extremely picturesque current building dates back to the sixteenth century. It's a quintessential country pub, with real ales on tap, roaring fires, shiny brasses and a rugged stone exterior, and upstairs there's an architectural curiosity – a medieval "moot" court, which was used for trials until as recently as the 1930s. Bedrooms are modestly but comfortably furnished, with cosy floral decor. The substantial bar food includes big breakfasts for guests, plus pies, grills, Lancashire sausages, roasts and lighter meals, and the English puds are home made. Staying here you're in the centre of Slaidburn, a wonderfully well-preserved village; don't miss the church with its Jacobean screen and Georgian pulpit. The inn is ideally placed for hiking and off-road cycling in the Forest of Bowland, whose wild rolling moorland stretches over 312 square miles of Lancashire and Yorkshire.

> **Hark to Bounty, Slaidburn, Lancashire, BB7 3EP** ☎01200 446246, ⓦharktobounty.co.uk.
> **Price** 3 en-suite twins £65, 4 doubles £75–85 and 1 single £42.50. 1 double and 1 twin can accommodate an extra bed. Breakfast included.
> **Facilities** Dinner available. Breakfast available. Bar. Garden. TVs in rooms.
> **Restrictions** Dogs allowed.
> **Open** Open year-round. Check in: 1pm. Check out: 1pm.
> **Getting there** Slaidburn is on the B6478 between Clitheroe and Long Preston. The infrequent #B10 bus from Clitheroe or Settle stops outside the village store.

Clockwise from left Heading into the Hodder Valley, the Forest of Bowland; *YHA Slaidburn*; *Hark to Bounty*

YHA Slaidburn

SLAIDBURN

This is not the most luxurious YHA you will ever stay in, but it is one of the most characterful, located in a restored eighteenth-century inn in the heart of the Lancashire village of Slaidburn. This tiny settlement has a genuine feel of the past: in an archaic feudal touch most of it has been owned by the King-Wilkinson family for 200 years. The hostel is a great base for walking and cycling in the Forest of Bowland, a great stretch of heather-clad hills which was once reserved for royal hunting. The protection of the peat moorland, gritstone fells and valleys continues in the area's designation as an Area of Outstanding Natural Beauty, and a network of lanes and paths radiate out from the village; try the 11-mile circular route round Stocks Reservoir, over fells and farmland.

YHA Slaidburn, King's House, Slaidburn, Lancashire, BB7 3ER ☎0845 371 9343, ⓦyha.org.uk.
Price Dorms: 1x6, 1x5, 4x4, 1x3 £19.40. Breakfast included.
Facilities Kitchen facilities. On-site parking. Games/common room. Bike hire available.
Restrictions Curfew 11pm.
Open Open year-round. Check in: flexible. Check out: 10am.
Getting there Slaidburn is on the B6478 between Clitheroe and Long Preston. The #B10 bus from Ciltheroe or Settle stops outside the village store.

The hostel itself, hugely popular with walkers, has retained original features such as beamed ceilings and open fires in the common rooms. Dorms are plain but comfortable and there's a decent kitchen for self-catering. Breakfast isn't provided here: if you haven't brought your own supplies, head across the road to the handily located village store. Otherwise, you're a very short stroll from the *Hark to Bounty* (see opposite).

YORKSHIRE

For a measure of Yorkshire – England's largest county – you only need to turn up in York – its most fascinating, historic city – and start the hunt for accommodation. There are B&Bs by the score, of course, not to mention the usual budget chains, tourist hotels and backpacker joints. But York, like the rest of Yorkshire, has stay-the-night tricks up its sleeve, from a unique art-design hostel to beds in a historic convent. It's this variety that sets the region apart – nothing new to canny Yorkshire folk, of course, who wouldn't dream of spending the night anywhere other than in "God's own country".

York aside, the major Yorkshire cities – Sheffield, Leeds and Hull – each have a thriving city-break trade these days, which may surprise those still wedded to "grim-up-north" stereotypes. Imaginative economic and cultural regeneration has transformed these post-industrial centres into vibrant places to live, work and visit, whether you're into shops, clubs, galleries, museums or restaurants. Budget city-centre accommodation might be heavily weighted towards the low-cost chains, but there's always an alternative, from bargain boutique hotel to cosy canal-boat. There are age-old reasons to visit the smaller towns and historic market centres, like Beverley's minster or Richmond's castle, and there's generally a local B&B or hostel to hand – and sometimes

something quirkier, like the Buddhist retreat in the rolling Wolds beyond Beverley.

Even in the bad old days of mills, mines and factories it was never very hard to escape to the country, with the celebrated Yorkshire moors and dales crowding to the very edges of the biggest conurbations. These are still among the most emblematic of British landscapes, from the rolling hills, valleys and picturesque villages of the Yorkshire Dales to the bluff, bleak, heather-scuffed North York Moors. These two national park areas contain the bulk of the region's traditional – and not-so-traditional – hostel and bunkhouse accommodation, and dedicated Pennine Way walkers and coast-to-coast hikers and bikers are certainly not short of lodgings as they pass through the wilder parts of North Yorkshire.

To the east, meanwhile, generations of families have decamped to the long Yorkshire coast for traditional seaside fun, from Bridlington in the south to Whitby in the north. Scarborough, bang in the middle, even lays claim to be the oldest resort in the country, the eighteenth-century "Queen" of the east coast. Even here, if you look hard enough among the serried ranks of traditional seaside B&Bs, you'll turn up a budget gem or two that has "made in Yorkshire" stamped all over it.

YORKSHIRE

NAME	LOCATION	PAGE		REAL BARGAIN	TREAT YOURSELF	FAMILY-FRIENDLY	GREAT RURAL LOCATION	OUTDOOR ACTIVITIES	GREAT FOOD AND DRINK	DORMS	PUBLIC TRANSPORT
3 Peaks Bunkroom	Horton in Ribblesdale	161	❷				✓	✓		✓	✓
Bank House Farm Hostel	Glaisdale	156	⓮				✓	✓		✓	
The Bar Convent	York	168	⓬						✓		✓
Cosmopolitan Hotel	Leeds	162	❿		✓				✓		✓
Dales Bike Centre	Fremington	155	❼				✓	✓		✓	✓
Dalesbridge	Austwick	154	❶	✓		✓	✓	✓		✓	
The Fort	York	169	⓭		✓				✓	✓	✓
Hebden Bridge Hostel	Hebden Bridge	160	❺	✓		✓				✓	✓
Houseboat Hotels	Sheffield	166	⓫						✓		✓
Interludes	Scarborough	165	⓳	✓							✓
Mercure Royal Hotel Hull	Hull	161	㉑								✓
Shepherd's Purse	Whitby	167	⓱						✓		✓
Whashton Springs Farm	Richmond	164	❾				✓				
The Wolds Retreat	Pocklington	164	⓯		✓		✓				
YHA Beverley	Beverley	154	⓴				✓			✓	✓
YHA Grinton Lodge	Grinton	157	❽				✓	✓	✓	✓	✓
YHA Hawes	Hawes	157	❸				✓	✓	✓	✓	✓
YHA Haworth	Haworth	158	❻							✓	✓
YHA Lockton	Lockton	163	⓰				✓	✓		✓	✓
YHA Malham	Malham	163	❹				✓	✓	✓	✓	✓
YHA Whitby	Whitby	167	⓲		✓	✓	✓	✓	✓	✓	✓

From left York's skyline, seen from *The Fort* (p.169); *The Fort*'s stylish interior; *YHA Malham* (p.163) **Previous page** Swaledale, Yorkshire Dales

Dalesbridge

The Yorkshire Dales is full of B&Bs, campsites and bunkhouses, but at eager-to-please *Dalesbridge* you get all three on the same site, in a really convenient location between Settle and Ingleton. Once a convalescent home and hospital, it now offers comfortable B&B rooms with nice views in the Edwardian main house (formerly the nurses' home) and more budget-rated accommodation in the garden and grounds. Here, there's a line of well-used four- and six-bunk cabins, whose fairly spartan decor – ceiling strip lights, basic campground-style wet-room showers and loos – reflect the largely boots-and-bikes clientele. The four-bed cabins are pretty small, though you do get a kettle, toaster and microwave; the six-bed versions are much more spacious, with a proper kitchen area and a big picnic-style dining table. You can barbecue (and park) at the cabins, and there's a family friendly pub in the nearby village. The whole complex is much quieter during the week, when kids will have the run of the large tree-lined field out front that doubles as the campsite. There are loads of outdoor activities nearby, and *Dalesbridge* can put you in touch with local operators.

Dalesbridge, Austwick, North Yorkshire, LA2 8AZ ☎01524 251021, ⓦdalesbridge.co.uk.

Price Rooms: 1 single £39, 4 doubles £74, 1 family room (sleeps 4) £100; all en suite. Breakfast included. Bunkhouses: 4x4 £60 per night, 4x6 £90 per night; individual bed in bunkhouses (if available) £16 per person.

Facilities Internet. Kitchen. On-site parking. Bar. Shop. Games/common room. Garden. Tours.

Restrictions Bed linen required.

Open Year-round. Check in: 4pm. Check out: 11am.

Getting there Buses from Settle or Ingleton run to Austwick, a 10min walk away. The nearest train station is 1.5 miles away at Clapham.

YHA Beverley

The pretty, honeyed-stone-and-brick hostel in the elegant minster town of Beverley simply oozes history. In a neat piece of symmetry, it was originally the guest house for a medieval friary – mentioned, no less, in the "Canterbury Tales" – and it retains a huge amount of traditional character. The main portal, leaning with age, has a duck-your-head doorway, while inside are high beamed ceilings and massive antique fireplaces. Two kings have slept here (Edwards I and II), and there are seventeenth-century wall paintings in one room, and Georgian panelling in another, not to mention Boris, the presiding papier-mâché boar (a gift of the Richard III Society). The building has undergone various renovations and, at the time of writing, was in line for yet more major refurbishment; there's already a brand new kitchen (the hostel is self-catering only). But, worry not, the essential charm, loved by many over the years, will remain, from the little rugs laid by each bed to the sun-trap walled garden shaded by a spreading cherry tree.

YHA Beverley, Friar's Lane, Beverley, East Yorkshire, HU17 0DF ☎0845 371 9004, ⓦyha.org.uk.

Price Dorms: 2x2, 2x4, 2x6, 1x8 (single-sex, unless occupied by couples/family/groups) all with shared bathrooms £17.40.

Facilities Internet. Kitchen. On-site parking. Games/common room. Garden. Lockers.

Open Year-round, though only available for sole-use groups Nov–March. Check in: 5pm. Check out: 10am.

Getting there The hostel is less than a 5min walk from Beverley train station. It's 100yds from the Minster, down Friar's Lane, off Eastgate. Parking at the hostel is limited; drivers may only be able to drop off luggage.

Dales Bike Centre

Long may you wonder at the names of the bunk-rooms at *Dales Bike Centre* in deepest Swaledale – "Booze" and "Crackpot" among them. But keen mountain-bikers know them as local villages, as you'll doubtless be told in the funky little leather-armchair and espresso-machine café at the heart of the operation. There are also serious cycle facilities on site (bike shop, rental and guided tours, lock-up, repairs and bike wash), while the accommodation sits above both café and bike shop in the two adjacent, stone-built Dales barn buildings. Small bunk-rooms in pine, cream and peppermint green share high-quality, modern showers and toilets, and the above-café rooms also have a walk-in kitchenette. Everyone gets after-hours access to the café where there's free wi-fi and "24hr cake" – drop your money in an honesty box and tuck into yummy coffee and walnut cake, brownies and caramel shortbread.

Dales Bike Centre, Parks Barn, Fremington, Reeth, North Yorkshire, DL11 6AW ☎01748 884908, ⓦdalesbikecentre.co.uk.
Price Dorms: 3x2, 2x4, both £28 per person, both shared bathrooms; sole occupancy of room £38. Breakfast included.
Facilities Internet. Kitchen. On-site parking. Café . Garden. Tours. Bike rental. Lunch available.
Open Year-round, except at Christmas and New Year; also closed Tues Dec–Feb. Check in: 4pm. Check out: 11am.
Getting there Driving, take the B6270; it's 10 miles east of Richmond, on the left, just before you reach the village of Reeth. Buses (Mon–Sat) to Reeth run past the centre six times a day from Richmond.

Breakfast is cereal and a bacon sandwich or scrambled eggs, after which you're set up for a day's biking on Swaledale's old lead-mining trails and grouse-beater tracks. No question, the centre is aimed squarely at bikers (and a few coast-to-coast hikers), and you'll probably feel a bit of a spare wheel if you don't arrive expecting to hit the trails. But for a "bunk and breakfast" with a touch of class, this place can't be beat.

Bikes, trails and a classy "bunk and breakfast": *Dales Bike Centre*

Bank House Farm Hostel

The delightful valley of Glaisdale goes almost unnoticed in the eastern half of the North York Moors, with the nearby attractions of Goathland (*Heartbeat* country), the steam railway to Pickering and even Whitby soaking up most visitors. This relative isolation makes Bank House Farm even more of a gem, sitting in an elevated position on one side of the wide valley, with scintillating views to all sides. Emma and Chris Padmore farm organically here (sheep and cows), and welcome visitors to their converted lambing barn and "cart shed", which sleeps eleven upstairs under the beams in IKEA single beds on oatmeal carpets. Downstairs, the huge old doorways have been glassed in to throw light on a large open-plan communal space with a modern kitchen, bench tables and long sofas which can sleep three more. There's a smart two-shower washroom in snazzy red, and three "Goldilocks" loos – one big, one middle, one small – behind restored pine doors. It's all thoroughly up to date, and very well equipped, from spin-dryer to slow-cooker; breakfast fixings (to cook yourself) and organic meat from the farm are also available. Outdoors, there's a huge trampoline for panoramic bouncing, a stone-flagged barbecue and seating area, and walks right off the property, including the couple of miles down through ancient woodland to Glaisdale village and the nearest pub. One thing to note: at weekends, you usually have to book the whole hostel, though there may be flexibility at certain times of the year.

Bank House Farm Hostel, Glaisdale, North Yorkshire, YO21 2QA ☎01947 897297, ⓦbankhousefarmhostel.co.uk.
Price Dorms: 1x11 Sun–Thurs £18, under-16s £10, under-5s free; Fri & Sat whole-hostel, full-weekend bookings only, 2 nights for £400; shared bathrooms.
Facilities Internet. Kitchen. On-site parking. Games/common room. Garden.
Restrictions Bed linen required.
Open Year-round. 2-night minimum stay during weekends; 3 nights during bank holiday weekends. Check in: 3pm. Check out: 11am.
Getting there The farm is 12 miles from Whitby, and 2.5 miles from Glaisdale village; call for directions, don't rely on SatNav. The nearest train station is Glaisdale, on the Esk Valley (Whitby–Middlesbrough) line, with connections from Grosmont for the North York Moors Railway steam service from Pickering/Whitby.

Bank House Farm Hostel has views on all sides – you can enjoy them while bouncing on a trampoline

YHA Grinton Lodge

There are few more dramatic locations in the northern Dales than the YHA's *Grinton Lodge*, a two-hundred-year-old, castellated shooting lodge set amid purple heather on the moors above Swaledale. It's full of period appeal, from the main arched courtyard to the open fire and mounted antlers in the cosy lounge, and the interior has been smartly refurbished, with bunk-rooms ranged along deep-red panelled corridors. All the rooms have a view of some kind – straight across the moors and down the dale in some cases – and while there are no en suites, there are plenty of showers and loos. You can also camp in the grounds, though the locally made wooden camping pods are proving more popular, and come with a fire pit, barbecue and children's play area; you'll need to bring your own gear if staying in the pods. Good-value breakfasts and evening meals are served in the lodge, and although it seems like the middle of nowhere, the nearest pub is only a fifteen-minute walk downhill, while the wilds of Swaledale itself await adventurous bikers and hikers.

YHA Grinton Lodge, Grinton, Richmond, North Yorkshire, DL11 6HS ☎0845 371 9636, ⓦyha.org.uk.
Price Dorms: 71 beds in 16 rooms (all single-sex) sleeping 2–8 £19.40 per person; two-bed private room £47, four-bed family room £75; all rooms have shared bathrooms. Pods: 2x2 £30 per night, 3x4 £35 per night.
Facilities Internet. Kitchen. On-site parking. Bar. Shop. Games/common room. Garden. Lockers. Breakfast and dinner available.
Open Year-round. Check in: 5pm. Check out: 10am.
Getting there The hostel is off the B6270, 10 miles east of Richmond; at the Bridge Inn in Grinton, follow the minor road uphill (Leyburn direction) for half a mile; the lodge is on your left. A bus from Richmond runs 6 times daily (not Sun) to Grinton.

YHA Hawes

The hostel at Hawes sits at the highest point of Yorkshire's highest market town, and offers superb views. From the lounge of the large, stone-built house you can look across the central part of Wensleydale, while from the en-suite shower-room of "Room 13" you get what's billed as the "million-pound toilet seat view" across the valley. There are two bunk-bed en-suite rooms; otherwise accommodation is in standard dorms with cheerful yellow-painted brick walls and pine bunks and panelling. The hostel was purpose-built in the 1970s and there's something of a vintage feel, especially in the shared bathrooms which, while spotless, are decidedly old-fashioned. But there's plenty of space in the public areas, and a more up-to-date approach to facilities and services, including good bistro meals available nightly and a well-stocked bar. Being bang in the middle of one of the more well-trod Dales means it's walker-friendly, but families too will find it a really useful base. Not only is it just around the corner from the Wensleydale Creamery, makers of Yorkshire's most iconic cheese, but drive a few miles down the road and you're in the heart of Askrigg, with the tumbling Aysgarth Falls just beyond.

YHA Hawes, Lancaster Terrace, Hawes, North Yorkshire, DL8 3LQ ☎0845 371 9120, ⓦyha.org.uk.
Price Dorms: 52 beds in 14 rooms sleeping 2–8 (single-sex, unless occupied by couple/ family/ group) £19.40; private two-bed en-suite room £49, four-bed family room £63.
Facilities. Kitchen. On-site parking. Bar. Shop. Games/common room. Garden. Lockers. Breakfast and dinner available.
Open Year-round; groups only Nov–March. Check in: 5pm. Check out: 10am.
Getting there Hawes is on the A684; drive through Leyburn, past the Wensleydale Creamery turn-off, and turn left up B6255. There are daily buses from Leyburn, Masham and Richmond.

YHA Haworth

The West Yorkshire moorland village of Haworth is famous for one thing: being a source of inspiration for the novel-writing Brontë sisters, Charlotte, Emily and Anne, whose former parsonage home, now a museum, attracts hundreds of thousands of visitors a year.

But while the Brontës were busy scribbling, Haworth was quietly getting on with business as a typical Yorkshire weaving village. The many old weavers' cottages lining the cobbled lanes indicate the former scale of the industry, but naturally enough the wealthy mill-owners and manufacturers themselves had far grander aspirations, resulting in magnificently decorated mansions like the building that's now *YHA Haworth*, built originally in 1884 as a private home

It's set apart from the village – it wouldn't do to get too close to the workers – and impresses from the start, with the entrance through a grand stone portico, leading through stained-glass doors into a soaring lobby laid with oak and inlaid-ebony flooring. Above your head is a gilded, painted ceiling, while up the grand oak staircase is a carved upper gallery surmounted by an intricate plaster frieze.

YHA Haworth, Longlands Drive, Lees Lane, Haworth, West Yorkshire, BD22 8RT
☎ 0845 371 9520, ⊛ yha.org.uk.
Price Dorms: 90 beds in 18 rooms (single-sex, unless occupied by couples/families/groups) sleeping 1–8 £19.40 per person; private two-bed room £47, 4-bed family room £63.
Facilities Kitchen. On-site parking. Bar. Games/common room. Garden. Lockers. Breakfast and dinner available.
Restrictions Curfew 11pm.
Open Year-round. Group bookings only Nov–Feb. Check in: flexible. Check out: 10am.
Getting there Haworth is 8 miles northwest of Bradford on the B6144; the hostel is three-quarters of a mile from the village, signposted off the B6142. Keighley is the nearest train station, though the weekend-and-holidays Keighley & Worth Valley Railway runs steam trains between Keighley and Haworth.

This is seriously upmarket decor for a hostel and although you don't get the same level of luxury in the rooms – otherwise you'd be paying £200 a night – they still possess a certain faded grandeur. Decorated in cream, brown and blue, the rooms (singles to eight-bed dorms) have high ceilings and lots of space, and most retain a differently carved and tiled fireplace from the house's Victorian heyday. A ground-floor room has the hostel's only double bed, with bunk above, and a huge private disabled-access bathroom; otherwise the only en-suite room in the place is one of the six-bed dorms. An upper floor has more rooms in the old servants' quarters, which are far less spacious and have mind-your-head black beams, but there are views from these over the village and moors beyond.

Families enjoy the facilities and sense of space, from garden and self-catering kitchen to games room with pool and table football. Breakfast is served in the large dining room, overlooking the garden, and there are changing bistro meals offered nightly here, too, though it's worth a walk into Haworth to see how it's changed since the days of *Wuthering Heights* (many local walks and landmarks appeared in Emily Bronte's masterpiece). The steep cobbled street up and down which the sisters tramped is still cottagey and cute, but it's a different kind of industry on offer these days, with vintage clothes stores, antiquarian bookshops, cool cafés and classy B&Bs dominating the scene.

Clockwise from top *YHA Haworth*'s exterior; the lounge; the Brontë Parsonage Museum; the sisters; an airy dorm

Hebden Bridge Hostel

If you sat down to design a hostel for arty, eco-friendly, hippy-chic Hebden Bridge – a vibrant old mill town nestling in the Calder Valley – you'd almost certainly end up with something like Dave and Em Weirdigan's offbeat joint, carved out of the concert rooms of a 1930s Baptist chapel. Their outgoing personality is stamped all over the hostel (they also run a pop-up organic café at summer festivals) and although there are only a few rules, these help define the place's character, from quiet-after-10pm to veggie-food-only in the kitchen. It's a big, bright building with plenty of natural light, and wood and laminate floors throughout. All the bedrooms bar one are upstairs and are reminiscent of ship's cabins, with two single beds and then two more in an upper gallery, reached by a steep wooden ladder. One room squeezes in six beds and shaves a few quid off the regular price, but you'll need to bring a sleeping bag if you wind up here; all the other rooms come with bedding. There's also a double and a twin, while each room has a cupboard-style shower and loo – nothing fancy but perfectly serviceable. Once you've bonded with Kipper the hostel cat, or sat out on the patio for a while, then it's out on the trail of poetic star-crossed lovers, with Ted Hughes' birthplace only a couple of miles away in Mytholmroyd and the grave of his wife, Sylvia Plath, found in the next village of Heptonstall.

Hebden Bridge Hostel, The Birchcliffe Centre, Hebden Bridge, West Yorkshire, HX7 8DG ☎01422 843183, ⓦhebdenbridgehostel.co.uk.
Price 2 doubles £55, 6 four-bed bunk rooms £18.50 per person or £70 for private use, 1 six-bed bunk room (no bedding) £12.50; all rooms en suite. Light breakfast included.
Facilities Internet. Kitchen. On-site parking. Games/common room. Garden.
Open Closed to individuals (whole-hostel bookings only) from second week in Nov to the start of Easter holidays. Check in: 5pm. Check out: 10am.
Getting there The hostel is a 15min walk from Hebden Bridge station (on the Manchester–Leeds line). Driving up Birchcliffe Road, note the hostel is not on Chapel Avenue but is the next left, just after the Birchcliffe Centre sign; park in the top car park.

Hebden Bridge Hostel, sat in the shade of a 1930s chapel, is an offbeat, friendly place to hole up

3 Peaks Bunkroom

The peaks in question are the Yorkshire Dales' iconic triumvirate of Pen-y-Ghent, Ingleborough and Whernside, the latter topping out as Yorkshire's highest at 2416 feet. A circuit of them all – the "Three Peaks Walk" – is a classic 12-hour, 25-mile gut-buster, with hikers all setting off from the tiny hamlet of Horton in Ribblesdale. The bunkroom – a modern barn-like construction of weathered Dales stone – aims its sights squarely at hardcore hikers who want a bed for the night, a hot shower, a drying room and somewhere to make a filling meal. There are just two barrack-like, bring-your-own bedding dorms, both with twenty bunk-beds, and while it's undeniably frill-free, it is kept clean, warm and spotless. Individuals are welcome as long as there's already a group booked in (otherwise you need a minimum of five people) and keen walkers won't be at all surprised to learn that most weekends between March and October are really busy on this most famous of English long-distance hiking challenges. The *Golden Lion* pub next door is on hand for a restorative beer and chips-with-everything meals.

3 Peaks Bunkroom, Horton in Ribblesdale, North Yorkshire, BD24 0HB ☎01729 860380, ⓦ3peaksbunkroom.co.uk.
Price Dorms: 2x20 (shared bathrooms) £15 per person; discounts for midweek bookings and Nov–Jan. Sole-use bookings: 1 dorm £300, whole building £600.
Facilities Kitchen. On-site parking. Garden. TVs in rooms.
Restrictions Bed linen required.
Open Year-round. Check in: flexible. Check out: flexible.
Getting there Horton is 6 miles north of Settle (follow the signs off the A65); the bunkhouse is at the southern end, near the church and next to the Golden Lion pub. There are regular trains to Horton on the Settle to Carlisle Railway (connections from Skipton and Leeds).

Mercure Royal Hotel Hull

Hull's original railway hotel first opened in 1851, and just three years later Queen Victoria – pioneering the city break – came by train and stayed for the night, waving at the crowds from her room (now the "Prince Albert Suite"). Like Hull itself, the hotel has seen major refurbishment; only the facade is original, but it retains its grand Victorian dimensions, red carpeted steps and rather dramatic lobby lounge, while decently sized, good-value rooms have springy beds and up-to-date bathrooms. Decor is contemporary–corporate with matching carpets and curtains, and faux leather armchairs. Free wi-fi, parking and good weekend deals give an even bigger budget boost. There's still railway romance here, too, with access directly off the station concourse and platform announcements wafting in on the air over breakfast. Invigorated by a hearty feed, it is now only a few minutes' stroll into the centre of Hull; with a marina, award-winning museums and a restaurant strip off Princes Avenue, it's rather a lively place these days.

Mercure Royal Hotel Hull, 170 Ferensway, Hull, East Yorkshire, HU1 3UF ☎01482 325087, ⓦmercure.com.
Price 155 en-suite doubles and twins £70; advance website rates from as low as £49.
Facilities Internet. On-site parking. Bar. TVs in rooms. Breakfast, lunch and dinner available.
Open Year-round. Check in: flexible. Check out: flexible.
Getting there The hotel is right by Hull railway station, with direct access from the platform. Drivers should follow signs for Hull station, park in the car park and then arrange free parking with the hotel.

Cosmopolitan Hotel

LEEDS

It's not long since people would have laughed at the idea of weekend city breaks in Leeds – incredulous Yorkshire folk among them – but arguably the north's most improved city now does a roaring trade in glitzy shopping and clubbing trips. Whether your scene is Harvey Nicks, Opera North, the renowned West Yorkshire Playhouse or dusk-to-dawn DJ bars, Leeds is a happening place with some classy accommodation to match, not all of it stratospherically priced. *The Cosmopolitan* is a case in point, a boutique refit of an old Victorian red-brick hotel (formerly *The Golden Lion*), the tone set by the racks of *Vogue* and *Harpers Bazaar* in the fashionably dimly lit lobby. There's an

Cosmopolitan Hotel, 2 Lower Briggate, Leeds, West Yorkshire, LS1 4AE ☎0113 243 6454, Ⓦpeelhotels.co.uk.
Price 31 en-suite singles £69, 53 en-suite doubles £89, 5 en-suite family rooms £99; website prices £5–15 cheaper; special offers for certain dates from £59 for doubles.
Facilities Internet. Bar. TVs in rooms. Breakfast, lunch and dinner available.
Open Year-round. Check in: 2pm. Check out: noon.
Getting there The hotel is a 5min walk from Leeds train station. There's discounted parking in a nearby car park (call the hotel).

open-plan bar and bistro on site, and a vintage cast-iron staircase that runs up through the building to bold, colour-splashed corridors lined with decently appointed rooms. Everything's as you'd expect – earth tones, gleaming bathrooms, a touch of designer style – with only the very reasonable prices a surprise, even more so if you book online well in advance. This leaves you with cash in hand to head up Briggate to Leeds' glam Victorian shopping arcades, notably the glass-roofed Victoria Quarter, home to designer labels and flashy names galore. Day or night, dine in style in the nearby revamped Corn Exchange, whose ground-floor restaurant is set under twinkling lights under a gargantuan dome.

The Cosmopolitan Hotel in Leeds is a slice of boutique style without the astronomical pricetag

YHA Lockton

The long-serving manager at *YHA Lockton* feels a real affinity for the cosy, red-brick hostel in this small North York Moors village, right next door to the churchyard. It used to be the old village school and she and her parents were once pupils here – there's still a line of antique coat-hooks in the lobby. Everything else, though, has been revamped on modern, eco-friendly lines, as Lockton was the first YHA "green beacon" hostel; from the solar-heated showers to the insulating grass cover on the living room roof, Lockton is entirely dedicated to cutting its carbon footprint. Three smart little bunk rooms have decent carpets and matching curtains, and share bathrooms down the hall. A snug fourth room (sleeps three, but is great for couples) has an en-suite wetroom designed for disabled access.

YHA Lockton, Old School, Lockton, Pickering, North Yorkshire, YO18 7PY
☎0845 371 9128, ⓦyha.org.uk.
Price Dorms: 1x3, 1x4, 1x6, 1x8 £21.40; 2 adults in three-bed room £57, four-bed room £69.
Facilities Kitchen. On-site parking. Games/common room. Lockers.
Open Year-round; only whole-hostel group bookings from mid-Sept to Easter. Check in: 5pm. Check out: 10am.
Getting there Driving on the A169 from Pickering, after a couple of miles look for the sign on the left to Lockton. Lockton is a stop on the daily Leeds–Pickering–Whitby bus service.

There's a spotless stainless-steel kitchen and otherwise facilities are limited. But, frankly, why laze about when there are remote moorland walks and age-old villages to all sides?

YHA Malham

The hostel at Malham provides budget beds in one of the Yorkshire Dales' prettiest and most dramatically sited villages, a short walk from soaring Malham Cove and its stupendous limestone pavement. Purpose-built in the late 1930s – and designed by one of Britain's national park pioneers, John Dower – the rather unlovely pebble-dash house improves markedly inside, where cheery long-time managers Christine and Martin Peryer keep things decidedly bright and bubbly. A refurbishment programme has smartened up showers and added double-glazing, while simple rooms in shades of green have uninterrupted views across the dale. There's one tiny but much sought-after two-bunk room and a separate annexe, which is a bit more utilitarian, but contains the only en-suite room in the hostel, plus a good drying room and a self-catering kitchen. Breakfast gets

YHA Malham, North Yorkshire, BD23 4DB
☎0845 371 9529, ⓦyha.org.uk.
Price Dorms: 82 beds in 15 rooms sleeping 2–8 (single-sex, unless occupied by couple/family/group) £21.40; private twin room £52, four-bed family room £69.
Facilities Kitchen. On-site parking. Bar. Shop. Games/common room. Garden. Lockers. Breakfast and dinner available.
Open Year-round. Check in: 5pm. Check out: 10am.
Getting there Malham is 12 miles northwest of Skipton, off the A65; the hostel is signposted in the village, just beyond the Lister Arms pub. The bus from Skipton (trains from Leeds and Bradford) to Malham runs daily in summer, otherwise weekdays only (schoolbus) in winter.

good reviews, cakes and scones are baked daily and there are bistro meals and even takeaway pizzas available, with picnic benches outside under the walnut trees and flowering cherry. The *Lister Arms*, right next door, is known for its food, while the *Buck Inn*, over the bridge, has a back-bar where you can swap hiking and biking tales over a pint or two of real ale.

The Wolds Retreat

It's billed as "North Yorkshire's most tranquil B&B", and you really do have to take them at their word – voices are barely raised above a whisper in the serene surroundings of the Madhyamaka Buddhist Centre, beautifully located in an imposing nineteenth-century country mansion on the outskirts of the market town of Pocklington. Five light-and-bright guest rooms are set in the former stable block; think "contemporary country", with handmade pine furniture, oak floors and snazzy bathrooms with all-natural soaps and lotions. Outside are forty acres of lovely grounds with lawns and a lake, a walled garden and an old Norman church and a stable-block café with log fire. The Buddhist aspect impinges only in incidental ways: a tray for outdoor shoes (and no alcohol allowed) in your room, and a cooked or continental veggie-only breakfast in the morning is delivered by saffron-robed residents. The welcome, though, is all-encompassing, whether it's day visitors come to walk dogs or take a meditation class, or anyone looking just to "stop the world" for a night or two of peaceful relaxation in the gorgeous, rolling Yorkshire Wolds.

The Wolds Retreat, Kilnwick Percy Hall, Pocklington, North Yorkshire, YO42 1UF ☎0800 028 3104 or 01759 305968, ⊛thewoldsretreat.co.uk.
Price 3 en-suite doubles £65, 2 singles with a shared bathroom £35. Breakfast included.
Facilities On-site parking. Café. Garden.
Open Year-round; café closed Mon and Tues. Check in: 3pm. Check out: 10am.
Getting there Kilnwick Percy Hall is around a mile from Pocklington, off the B1246 (follow the signs); the hall driveway is opposite Kilnwick Percy Golf Club.

Whashton Springs Farm

There's a gracious air at *Whashton Springs Farm*, just three miles from the lovely market town of Richmond in the northern Yorkshire Dales. The farm is of the same Georgian pedigree as Richmond itself, with elegant bay windows overlooking a garden and rolling fields beyond, while three very spacious en-suite rooms inside the main house sport antique chairs, floral wallpaper and lovely old beds, including one swagged four-poster. The style is more contemporary in the courtyard annexe, where another five rooms occupy converted farm buildings. Less spacious but modern and light, with country pine furniture, pale carpets and handmade bedspreads, the family suite comprises two adjoining rooms sharing a neat little bathroom. Breakfast is a big old Yorkshire farm fry-up, served with home-made preserves and local honey from the heather-clad moors. Nearby country pubs – all horse-brasses, beer gardens and bistro meals – offer good rural dining, or it's only a short drive to Richmond's restaurants, Georgian theatre and medieval castle.

Whashton Springs Farm, Richmond, North Yorkshire, DL11 7JS ☎01748 822884, ⊛www.whashtonsprings.co.uk.
Price Main house: 3 en-suite doubles £85 first night and £80 thereafter. Courtyard: 4 en-suite doubles £75 first night and £70 thereafter. Family suite (2 adults, 2 children) £112 first night and £105 thereafter. Single occupancy of any double room £50 first night and £45 thereafter. Breakfast included.
Facilities Internet. On-site parking. Games/common room. Garden. TVs in rooms.
Restrictions No children under 2.
Open Closed Christmas and New Year. Check in: flexible. Check out: 11am.
Getting there There are regular bus services to Richmond from Darlington, 10 miles to the northeast; it's a 10min taxi ride to the house from Richmond. Driving, follow the Ravensworth road out of Richmond for 3 miles and look for the signposted farm entrance on your left; don't rely on SatNav.

Interludes

Pretty Georgian *Interludes* has been a fixture in bucket-and-spade Scarborough for two decades and it's fair to say there isn't another guesthouse in town quite like it. It's set two blocks back from the seaside bustle, up a cobbled hill on a quiet eighteenth-century street, and while you can be on the beach or in the fish-and-chip shops and amusement arcades within minutes, *Interludes* looks to the theatre for its inspiration – principally Scarborough's Stephen Joseph Theatre, home of celebrated local playwright Alan Ayckbourn. Playbills, posters and photographs line every wall of the genteel town house, while spacious, pastel-coloured rooms with an old-fashioned elegance take their names from famous theatres; one of them – "Hippodrome" – comes with a pine four-poster. The views are better the higher you go, and from "Wyndhams" there's a fabulous panorama of the coast. Owners Bob Harris and Ian Grundy keep the house serene and sparkling, while finding time to offer pre-theatre meals and arrange seats at the Stephen Joseph. It's a hit with actors and theatre folk, who stay here regularly, and while it's gay and lesbian friendly, *Interludes* is certainly not exclusive. Bob and Ian would rather guests are *Interludes*-friendly and, accordingly, welcome anyone looking for some seaside peace and quiet – rare qualities, it has to be said, in a full-blown traditional resort like Scarborough.

Interludes, 32 Princess Street, Scarborough, North Yorkshire YO11 1QR ☎01723 360513, ⓦinterludeshotel.co.uk.

Price 4 en-suite twins/doubles £66, single-occupancy £36; 1 twin/double (no sea view) with private bathroom £54, single-occupancy £30; reductions for stays of 4-plus nights. Breakfast included. Pre-theatre dinner by arrangement £14.

Facilities Internet. Games/common room. TVs in rooms. Dinner available.

Restrictions No children under 16.

Open Closed during owners' annual holiday; call for dates. 2-night minimum stay during bank holiday weekends. Check in: flexible. Check out: 10am.

Getting there Regular direct trains go to Scarborough from Manchester, Leeds and York; the B&B is a 15min downhill walk from the station. Drivers can unload on Princess Street (parking restrictions apply), but guests get a parking disc or scratchcard that allows them to park nearby.

Interludes is a quiet retreat in bustling seaside Scarborough

Houseboat Hotels

Waking up to the gentle lap of water on the cobbled quayside with the prospect of a fresh croissant for breakfast – it can only be a night on a canal boat, but in Sheffield city centre? Ex-sub-postmistress Kathryn Marsh changed her life completely when she took charge of *Lily May, Ruby* and *Mallard,* three traditional narrow boats permanently moored in the regenerated Victoria Quays, just five minutes' walk from the shops, markets and galleries of bustling Sheffield. *Lily May* is the biggest, at fifty feet long, and sleeps a family or two couples "who know each other very well" in two head-to-foot double beds. Both *Ruby* and *Mallard* just have the one double bed, and on all three everything is laid out – necessarily – in a line, from galley kitchenette and lounge area with wood burner to partitioned-off bedroom and squeeze-yourself-in wetroom shower. *Mallard* is perhaps the smartest of the three, though they all have their individual attractions – not least a decanter of port, biscuits, tea and coffee for new arrivals. Breakfast can be delivered, either continental or cook-your-own, and there's a quayside café or two for cappuccinos and meals. With traffic noise and post-industrial urban views it's no rustic idyll, but it is really quite pleasant down by the canal basin; you're very close to Sheffield's bars and restaurants, and there's discounted entry to the nearby Hilton's health club and pool.

Houseboat Hotels, Victoria Quays, Sheffield, South Yorkshire, S2 5SY ☎ 01909 569393, ⊕ houseboathotels .com.

Price *Ruby* and *Mallard* (sleep 2): Mon–Thurs £75, Fri £79, Sat £86, Sun £65; Mon–Thurs last-minute discounts down to £59. *Lily May* (sleeps 4): Mon–Thurs £86, Fri £89, Sat £95, Sun £75; Mon–Thurs last-minute discounts £65. Continental breakfast £8, cooked breakfast £10.

Facilities Kitchen. TVs in rooms.

Open Year-round. Check in: 4pm. Check out: 11am.

Getting there Victoria Quays is a 10min walk from Sheffield train station. Nearby parking can be arranged; call for directions.

Clockwise from left *Shepherd's Purse* courtyard; a room at *Shepherd's Purse*; the romantic ruins of Whitby Abbey

Shepherd's Purse

Whitby's Georgian old town is an appealing tangle of cobbled alleys, courtyards and cute shops, and the *Shepherd's Purse* cunningly manages to combine all three. The wholefood deli and dress shop on Church Street has long been a town stalwart, and if you like its hippy-dippy style you'll love the gorgeous galleried courtyard accommodation around the back. The decor is country-chic but not cottagey, so the small - but - pretty rooms come with furniture collected by the family over the years, plus found and vintage rugs, bedspreads and decorative items, from cane cabinets to wind chimes. The two ground-floor rooms open directly onto the pebbled courtyard, where there's a romantic pergola and space to sit. Other rooms are ranged around the gallery, and are all differently styled; "Room 3", with its antique brass captain's bed, is draped in tulip lights, while "Room 5" has a lace-swagged four-poster and a private balcony. You'll find breakfast in several cafés a short walk away, including one sharing the same alley and courtyard. Be warned that parking is notoriously difficult, and Church Street is local-access only.

> Shepherd's Purse, 95 Church Street, Whitby, North Yorkshire, YO22 4BH ☎01947 820228, ⊕theshepherdspurse .com.
> **Price** 5 en-suite doubles £60–70, 2 doubles with a shared bathroom £55.
> **Facilities** Shop.
> **Open** Year-round. Check in: 2pm. Check out: 10am.
> **Getting there** Whitby is on a regular bus service from Leeds, York and Scarborough, and there are trains from Middlesbrough. The *Shepherd's Purse* is a 5min walk from the adjacent stations. Use the signposted car parks in Whitby.

YHA Whitby

Backing on to the romantic clifftop ruins of Whitby Abbey, the YHA's home in this up-and-coming coastal port and resort is one of its grandest addresses. An historic mansion dating back in part to the twelfth century, Abbey House was once home to the all-powerful abbots of Whitby and, later, a Georgian home of great refinement. A classy refurbishment has left reminders of this long past everywhere, from preserved wattle-and-daub walls and leaded windows to a magnificent stained-glass clerestory, while the excellent rooms go way beyond simple hostel standard accommodation. Most have bunks, it's true, but there are three with decent double beds and all with smart wetroom showers and separate toilets, plus high ceilings, abbey views from some ("Room 11" is a real favourite) or Georgian panelling, window seats and garden and river views from others. The self-catering kitchen retains its original medieval fireplace, while the lounge and conservatory open out onto manicured eighteenth-century gardens. All in all, it makes a super base for a family holiday, as guests get free entry to the adjacent abbey, and Whitby itself is accessed directly down the famous 199 Steps.

> YHA Whitby, Abbey House, East Cliff, Whitby, North Yorkshire, YO22 4JT ☎0845 371 9049, ⊕yha.org.uk.
> **Price** 100 beds in 22 rooms sleeping 2–10 (single-sex, unless occupied by a couple/ family/group) £23.40; twin room £57, four-bed family room £75.
> **Facilities** Internet. Kitchen. On-site parking. Bar. Café. Shop. Games/common room. Garden. Lockers. Breakfast, lunch and dinner available.
> **Open** Year-round. Check in: flexible. Check out: 10am.
> **Getting there** Whitby is on a regular bus service from Leeds, York and Scarborough, and there are trains from Middlesbrough. Abbey House is a 15min walk from the adjacent stations, along Church Street and up the very steep 199 Steps.

The Bar Convent

In a city with York's long and colourful history – early Christian centre, Viking capital, birthplace of Guy Fawkes, pioneering railway town – certain quirks and surprises are inevitable, and so it seems entirely in keeping that the oldest living convent in England (founded originally in 1686) should offer up rooms for visitors. These are housed in monumental red-brick Georgian premises that also contain a convent museum and a skylight-courtyard café, where breakfast can be taken at tables on a beautiful Victorian tiled floor. Room style is largely country pine -and -cream, and while only three are en suite (including a sleeps three-plus-one family room), there are plenty of shared bathrooms, loos and showers to go round. Nine small-but-smart single rooms also mean solo travellers get a good deal, while a book-lined sitting room, galley kitchen and top-floor recreation room with rooftop views make for a comfortable self-catering base. *The Bar Convent* is still home to the nuns of the Congregation of Jesus and all the rooms are named after saints, but there's a warm welcome to those of any or no faith and a generally hospitable air all round. Indeed, there's probably not another convent in England where you can lounge in a leather sofa or play a game of pool.

The Bar Convent, 17 Blossom Street, York, North Yorkshire, YO24 1AQ ☎01904 643238, ✆bar-convent.org.uk.
Price 2 en-suite twins/doubles £82, weekends £92; 5 doubles with shared bathrooms from £66; 2 family rooms, 1 en suite, from £105; 9 singles with shared bathrooms from £35, depending on size, weekends £40 or £45. Continental breakfast included; full breakfast £4.50.
Facilities Internet. Kitchen. Café. Shop. Games/common room. Garden. TVs in rooms. Lunch and dinner available.
Open Closed Christmas, New Year, the first 2 weeks in Jan, and Easter week. Check in: 1pm. Check out: 10am.
Getting there York is on the East Coast main line, and the convent is a 5min walk from the station. By road, the building is just outside Micklegate Bar (not a pub, but an historic city gate) – follow A1036 from the ring road. There's a pay-and-display car park opposite the convent on Nunnery Lane and another at the nearby train station.

The internal courtyard and facade of *The Bar Convent*, the oldest living convent in Britain

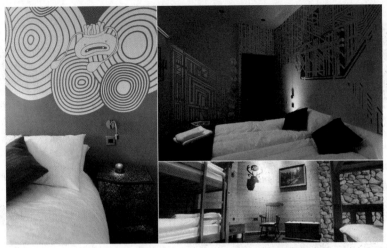

Funky decor at *The Fort*, which combines urban graphics and a historic location

The Fort

If anyone is ever sniffy about your choice of hostel over hotel, point them firmly towards *The Fort*, a glam budget town house based in the heart of historic York. Associated with a contemporary bar-restaurant, *Kennedy's*, that sits just off one of York's most photographed medieval streets (Stonegate), the next-door accommodation elicits oohs and wows every time from those expecting deadly dull dorms. Banksy-style urban graphics jump off the walls, while young artists and designers have been given free rein in the five rooms and have come up with an exotic range of experiences, from log-cabin dorm to turquoise, marine-swirl "Ocean Room", all with en-suite wetrooms, cool art and designer bedding. A further "superior de luxe" dorm is basically a chic, purple-and-black one-bedroom apartment in an adjacent building, with big sofas, bare floorboards and its own classy lounge and kitchen. There's tea, coffee and juice provided, and you can either cater for yourself or get a discount off breakfast at *Kennedy's*.

The Fort, 1 Little Stonegate, York, North Yorkshire, YO1 8AX ☎01904 620222, ⓦthefortyork.co.uk.
Price Rooms: 4 en-suite doubles £54, weekends £70. Dorms: 1x6 £24, weekends £26.50; 1x6 de luxe dorm £27, weekends £32; both dorms mixed-sex and en suite.
Facilities Internet. Kitchen. Bar. TVs in rooms. Lockers. Breakfast, lunch and dinner available.
Restrictions No children under 18.
Open Year-round. 2-night minimum stay during weekends. Check in: 1pm. Check out: 11am.
Getting there York is on the East Coast main line; The Fort is a 10min walk from the train station. Driving and parking is severely restricted in York city centre; follow the signs into town and use a signposted pay-and-display car park (the nearest to the hostel are at Monkgate and Marygate).

The feel throughout is young and hip, and with the late-opening bar, and plenty more bars and restaurants just a few steps away, this is not a place for anyone after total peace and quiet – the jar of ear -plugs in the lobby kitchenette rather gives the game away. But it's very definitely a cool space for city-savvy travellers and tourists, with a style that's all its own.

CUMBRIA AND THE LAKES

The Lake District is one of the most popular holiday destinations in England – millions visit each year for its famous lakes and mountains, picturesque villages and alpine landscapes, and there's no shortage of accommodation to cater for them. In fact, for such a small region, there's an amazing amount of variety, from farmhouse B&Bs to boutique charmers, lakeside hotels to mountainside hostels, country-house mansions to age-old rustic inns.

But demand for the best places is high, especially in school holidays, while prices are higher in the Lakes than in many other British regions (and some local hotels, frankly, seem to think they're in London or New York). You can do something about the first – if you find a great place to stay, make a booking as early as you can. And, actually, you can beat the second problem too, by thinking a bit more creatively about your visit.

Given the rural, outdoors nature of the region, there's a big weighting towards hostels and hiker-friendly places – the YHA alone has around twenty hostels in the Lakes, while independent backpackers, bunkhouses and farms with bunk-barns are a growing part of the market. And you don't have to be planning a walking tour to use these budget stalwarts – most are in magnificent locations, and virtually all hostels

have private rooms for couples and families, not to mention self-catering kitchens to help keep costs down.

On the other hand, if you are intending to knock off mountains and tramp around lakes, then paying a bit (and sometimes a lot) more than usual for a B&B looks like better value once you consider that you won't spend anything else that day. Fresh air, exercise and glorious views – all free. And a good Lake District B&B can be worth its weight in gold, offering local tips and walking advice, a cheap packed lunch, a hot bath and a place to dry wet clothes.

The central lakes of Windermere, Grasmere and Coniston Water see the biggest crowds and have the most varied attractions, from literary haunts to lake cruises, while the highest mountains and toughest hikes are found to the north and west, around Keswick Water, Ullswater, Buttermere and Wast Water. But don't forget that the national park makes up only a small part of the wider county of Cumbria. There are some great budget finds – from castle accommodation to shepherds' lodgings – in under-visited and off-the-beaten-track areas, like the western Cumbrian coast, the Eden Valley to the east, and Carlisle and around Hadrian's Wall to the north.

CUMBRIA AND THE LAKES

NAME	LOCATION	PAGE		REAL BARGAIN	TREAT YOURSELF	FAMILY-FRIENDLY	GREAT RURAL LOCATION	OUTDOOR ACTIVITIES	GREAT FOOD AND DRINK	DORMS	PUBLIC TRANSPORT
Ann Tysons	Hawkshead	182	20				✓				✓
The Archway	Windermere	189	19								✓
Burnthwaite Farm	Wasdale	187	12	✓			✓	✓			
Coachman's Quarters	Muncaster	185	21	✓	✓	✓	✓				
Dalegarth Guest House	Buttermere	176	8	✓			✓	✓			✓
Derby Arms	Witherslack	189	23						✓		
Ellergill	Keswick	183	4				✓	✓			✓
Grasmere Independent Hostel	Grasmere	181	13		✓	✓	✓	✓	✓	✓	✓
How Foot Lodge	Grasmere	182	15			✓		✓	✓		✓
Kirkby Stephen Hostel	Kirkby Stephen	184	14							✓	
Langleigh Guest House	Carlisle	177	1								✓
Mardale Inn	Bampton	174	6		✓		✓		✓		
Rainors Farm	Wasdale	188	16				✓	✓			
Rookhow	Ulverston	187	22			✓	✓	✓		✓	
Shepherd's Hut	Eden Valley	178	10		✓		✓				
Six Castlegate	Cockermouth	177	2		✓				✓		✓
Skiddaw House	Skiddaw	186	3	✓			✓	✓		✓	
Woolpack Inn	Eskdale	180	18				✓	✓	✓		
YHA Ambleside	Ambleside	174	17			✓	✓	✓	✓	✓	✓
YHA Black Sail	Ennerdale	180	11	✓			✓	✓		✓	
YHA Borrowdale	Borrowdale	175	9			✓	✓	✓		✓	✓
YHA Buttermere	Buttermere	175	7			✓	✓	✓		✓	✓
YHA Keswick	Keswick	183	5			✓	✓	✓	✓	✓	✓

From left *Ann Tysons* (see p.182); *Langleigh Guest House* (see p.177) **Previous page** Boats on Derwentwater, The Lake District

YHA Ambleside

AMBLESIDE

Best lake view on Windermere? A host of glamorous hotels make the claim, but in-the-know budgeteers plump for the Ambleside YHA every time. Never mind on the lake, it's almost in it, with only a narrow driveway and a thin patch of grass between the front entrance and private jetty. Most rooms have a water view, and the wooden deck of the "Lakeside" café-bar lives up to its name. As a hostel, *Ambleside* has always been a cut above – its 65 rooms and 260 beds occupy what was once a straight-up, stone-built Lakeland holiday hotel, so room sizes and public areas don't feel squeezed. The rooms themselves are plain but serviceable, with sinks and central heating, and toilets and showers down the corridors. Bunkrooms sleep two to six, but there are also two rooms with double beds and a couple more with a double bed and bunk on top. Facilities include wi-fi throughout, bistro meals, a bar with real ales, tours and rental – from bikes to kayaks. What better way to celebrate saving over a hundred quid a night than paddling about on Windermere, looking back on your cut-price room with a big-ticket view?

YHA Ambleside, Waterhead, Ambleside, Cumbria, LA22 0EU ☎0845 371 9620, ⓦyha.org.uk.
Price 260 beds in 65 rooms sleeping 2–6 people. Dorm beds £18, double room £56, twin room £54, 4-bed family room £70.
Facilities Internet. Kitchen. On-site parking. Bar. Café. Games/common room. Garden. Tours on offer. Lockers. Bike hire. Breakfast, lunch and dinner available.
Open Open year-round. Check in: flexible. Check out: 10am.
Getting there The hostel is 1 mile south of Ambleside, at Waterhead (top of the lake), on the bus route between Windermere town and Keswick. Ferries from Waterhead run to Bowness and Lakeside.

Mardale Inn

BAMPTON

"We've gone on holiday by mistake", bleats Richard E. Grant in cult classic *Withnail & I*, while enduring a disastrous stay in a rain-lashed cottage not far from Haweswater in the eastern Lakes. The owner of the beautifully refurbished *Mardale Inn* at nearby Bampton is a fan of the film, much of which was shot on location hereabouts – the secluded hamlet's old red phone box even pops up in one scene. Comforts at the inn are a decided cut above those on offer at lecherous Uncle Monty's cottage in the movie, with stone-flagged floors, handcrafted wooden tables, open fireplaces, stripped-back ancient beams and a tranquil green interior. Four snug rooms upstairs feature more rustic-chic wooden furniture and spick-and-span bathrooms, while tottering down to the bar presents you with a good-value pub-bistro menu hot on local produce, from Cumbrian lamb burgers to Eden Valley ice cream, plus a wide range of regional ales and bottled beer from three dozen countries – anyone still standing can track down more *Withnail* locations or take a steamer ride on nearby Ullswater.

Mardale Inn, Bampton, Cumbria, CA10 2RQ ☎01931 713244, ⓦmardaleinn.co.uk.
Price 4 en-suite doubles £80, breakfast included.
Facilities Internet. On-site parking. Bar. TVs in rooms. Lunch and dinner available.
Restrictions Dogs allowed.
Open Open year-round. Check in: flexible. Check out: flexible.
Getting there Bampton is 9 miles south of Penrith (M6 and west coast train line) and 4 miles northwest of Shap (A6). In Bampton, cross the bridge (by the post office) and the inn is on the right-hand side (Haweswater Road).

YHA Borrowdale

Borrowdale is all about its mountains, with the peaks at the head of the valley among the highest (the Scafells) and best-looking (Great Gable) in the Lakes. No surprise, then, that most of the local accommodation is geared towards hikers, including *YHA Borrowdale*, an Alpine-style lodge that was one of the first purpose-built hostels in the country. It sits in a riverside clearing – the main valley footpath runs right past the door – where the only sounds are the tumbling waters of the beck and the sheep on the hillside. The warm-toned interior is clad in its original Swedish pine, and there's a coal fire in the welcoming lounge. You'll sleep well in trim rooms with powder-blue carpets, simple pine bunks and sinks, and the eight twin-bedded rooms mean the hostel is as popular with couples as families. There are two hotels with bars a mile away, but Borrowdale serves good, home-cooked bistro meals – from veggie couscous to fish and chips, plus wine and local ales.

YHA Borrowdale, Longthwaite, Borrowdale, Cumbria, CA12 5XE ☎0845 371 9624, ⓦyha.org.uk.
Price 86 beds in 22 rooms, sleeping 2–8 people. Dorms £23.40, twin room £57, family room £75.
Facilities Kitchen. On-site. Bar. Shop. Games/common room. Garden. Lockers. Breakfast and dinner available.
Restrictions Curfew 11pm.
Open Closed Jan and first 2 weeks of Feb. Check in: 1pm. Check out: 10am.
Getting there The hostel is 7 miles south of Keswick and 1 mile south of Rosthwaite on the B5289, signposted on the right. Buses run from Kendal, Windermere, Ambleside, Grasmere and Carlisle; the #78 from Keswick through Borrowdale is roughly hourly; ask the driver to drop you by the hostel.

YHA Buttermere

The YHA has another beauty on its hands at Buttermere, the quiet western lake ringed by crags and peaks with resonant names – High Stile, Haystacks and Red Pike. The sturdy, slate-built hostel occupies a former hotel with amazing views just above the lake road, and while there's no internet, mobile reception or TV, watching the mountains turn pink in the setting sun is worth a thousand episodes of *The Apprentice*. Only a few original features survive – like the carved wooden porch out front and some antique tiling – and beds and decor are a little tired, though a refurbishment is planned. Shared facilities, on the other hand, are really good. There are lots of modern showers – so no waiting around in the morning – and the ground floor has had a smart facelift, from hotel-like reception to slick dining room and bar. Families, in particular, enjoy what's on offer here, from the good-value meals to the huge pile of games available. Low-level walks start straight from the door; peak-baggers won't want to miss the climb up Haystacks, the favourite mountain of Alfred Wainwright, whose ashes are scattered on the top.

YHA Buttermere, Cumbria, CA13 9XA ☎0845 371 9508, ⓦyha.org.uk.
Price 70 beds in 14 rooms, sleeping 2–8 people. Dorms £23.40, twin room £57, family room £75.
Facilities Kitchen. On-site parking. Bar. Shop. Games/common room. Garden. Lockers. Breakfast and dinner available.
Restrictions Curfew 11pm.
Open Open year-round. Check in: 5pm. Check out: 10am.
Getting there The hostel is 300 yards southeast of Buttermere village on the B5289. Buses head to Keswick from Kendal, Windermere, Ambleside, Grasmere and Carlisle; bus #77 runs here several times daily from Keswick (Easter–Oct), a 45min ride.

Dalegarth Guest House

A picture by the door of a manic John Cleese as Basil Fawlty might give pause for thought at some B&Bs, but it's an insight into the general good humour of James and Kelly Gillings, who run *Dalegarth* with a light and cheery touch. Set amid woods on a private estate at the foot of Buttermere, the house's steeply pitched roof and weathered timbers wouldn't look out of place on a Swiss lakeside, but inside it's not chintz and cuckoo clocks that prevail but stripped pine floors, apple-green and cream panelling, tumbling houseplants and a splash of bold colour here and there. Basil aside, the walls are hung with African masks, Indian prints, lakeland scenes and vintage pop photos, while twenty help-yourself teas are available in the welcoming fire-lit lounge. Rooms are rather more straightforward, but spruce, comfortable and incredibly good value for the Lakes, and although only four are en suite, the others share two good shower rooms and a cosy bathroom with a deep bath. They are well used to walkers here (there's a drying room for wet gear), and a campsite in the grounds adds to the general communal feel without impinging on the house itself. Breakfast is truly excellent; the nearest pub is a twenty-minute walk away, while a stroll through the grounds puts you right on Buttermere lake shore.

Dalegarth Guest House, Hassness Estate, Buttermere, Cumbria, CA13 9XA ☎017687 70233, ⓦdalegarthguest house.co.uk.
Price 4 en-suite doubles £60, 5 doubles with shared bathroom £50. Breakfast included.
Facilities Internet. On-site parking. Games/common room. Garden.
Restrictions Dogs allowed.
Open Closed 1 Nov to 28 Feb (dates are weather dependent). Check in: 2pm. Check out: 10am.
Getting there Take the B5289 from Keswick or Cockermouth to Buttermere; the house is around 10 miles from either, signposted about 1.25 miles south of Buttermere village. Buses from Keswick stop on the road near the main gate.

Comfortable, cheery *Dalegarth Guest House* sits at the foot of Buttermere

Langleigh Guest House

Cumbria's capital, and its only city, Carlisle makes much of its two-thousand-year-old history, not least its mighty medieval castle and cathedral and nearby Roman-era Hadrian's Wall. But it's the later Victorian period that defines much of the city centre, especially the trim, red-brick conservation area off Warwick Road, where the *Langleigh* makes for an elegant overnight stay. The restored house reflects its period magnificently, with original Victorian features, antiques, oils and prints at every turn. Rooms are fairly spacious – some have three single beds – and have lace-trimmed bedding and cushions, deep red carpets, heavy curtains, solid carved furniture, and marble-and-tile fireplaces. It comes as no surprise to find a cherub mirror and an antique chamber pot in your bathroom, while other nice touches include a china teapot and cups, and fresh milk brought to the room on arrival. The *Langleigh* has more accommodation four doors down, in a similarly restored Victorian property – guests have the use of this house's kitchen and Aga, and dinner cooked by the chef-proprietor is available in the main house, though Carlisle's best restaurants (Greek to Thai) are just five minutes' walk away down Warwick Road.

> **Langleigh Guest House, 6 Howard Place, Carlisle, Cumbria, CA1 1HR** ☎01228 530440, **W**langleighhouse.co.uk.
> **Price** 10 en-suite doubles £72, 5 en-suite singles £40. Breakfast included.
> **Facilities** Internet. Kitchen. On-site parking. TVs in rooms. Dinner available.
> **Open** Open year-round. Check in: 3pm. Check out: 10am.
> **Getting there** *Langleigh* is less than. 10min walk from Carlisle train station.

Six Castlegate

Riverside Cockermouth is a quiet Georgian gem of a town on the western side of the Lakes – a handy base for exploring the lesser-visited lakes of Loweswater, Buttermere and Ennerdale Water. It's also the birthplace of William Wordsworth (his house is open for visits), and has an elegant main street of restored facades, hidden courtyards, traditional pubs and independent shops – the perfect backdrop for a superior B&B like *Six Castlegate*. The nigh-on three-hundred-year-old house has been sympathetically refurbished and sensibly decluttered, leaving its clean lines and open spaces to speak for themselves. A magnificent oak staircase leads up to five bright rooms, all in muted cream and fawn colours and with sparkling en-suite bathrooms. They're named after the local mountains – "Melbreak" has a country brass bedstead and exposed beams, while light and airy "Blencathra" has hill views from its two windows. You'll save money in the two standard rooms – tighter on space, it's true, though a soak in the deep bath in "Scafell" is some compensation. Cafés and restaurants are only a few steps away, while Cockermouth has one big brewery (Jennings) and one small brew-pub (*The Bitter End*), making nights out a thoroughly local affair.

> **Six Castlegate, 6 Castlegate, Cockermouth, Cumbria, CA13 9EU** ☎01900 826786, **W**sixcastlegate.co.uk.
> **Price** 2 standard en-suite doubles £65, 3 premium en-suite doubles £75, 1 en-suite single £42–48. Breakfast included.
> **Facilities** Internet. TVs in rooms.
> **Restrictions** No children under 5.
> **Open** Closed 23–28 Dec. Check in: flexible. Check out: 10am.
> **Getting there** Buses from Keswick and Carlisle stop on Main Street, a few mins' walk from *Six Castlegate*. Driving, the A66 (from Keswick) bypasses the town to the south.

Shepherd's Hut at Crake Trees Manor

EDEN VALLEY

There are super-stylish B&B available in the boutique barn conversion that is *Crake Trees Manor* in the bucolic Eden Valley, but bargain-hunters looking for an offbeat night or two in the country can also stay in the farm's wonderful Shepherd's Hut – a romantic bolt-hole for two that resembles a sort of tin prairie cabin. Designed to be mobile – the nineteenth-century originals were dragged on to the fields in spring for the shepherds to live in – Ruth and Mike Tuer's specially designed contemporary version is given pride of place in summer, overlooking the farm pond, grass meadows and barley fields (in winter, it can be moved closer to the farmhouse, where there's a shower and other facilities).

Clad in galvanized steel, it looks fiercely utilitarian from the outside and anything but inside, where there's a lovely, hand-built wooden double bed, pristine white bedding with a vintage crochet throw and a floor made of local oak. Open the door, and you step out onto a little wooden veranda, perfect for star-gazing or an early morning cuppa. It's small, certainly,

Shepherd's Hut at Crake Trees Manor, Crake Trees Manor, Crosby Ravensworth, Penrith, Cumbria, CA10 3JG ☏01931 715205, ⓦcraketreesmanor.co.uk.
Price Shepherd's Hut (sleeps 2) £70 for 1 night, £60 thereafter (July & August £80/70), breakfast included. Extra guests can pitch a tent outside the hut if required (£5 per person without breakfast, under-16s can get breakfast included for £10). B&B rooms in the house £95.
Facilities On-site parking. Garden. Dinner available.
Open Open year-round. Minimum stay for B&B (not Shepherd's Hut), two nights at weekends. Check in: 3pm. Check out: 10am.
Getting there Crosby Ravensworth is a 10min drive from Shap (A6), or leave the M6 at junction 38 and approach via Orton. Drive through Crosby Ravensworth towards Maulds Meaburn; *Crake Trees Manor* is 200 yards on the left after the village school and then 500 yards up a rough lane.

with just about enough room for your bags and possessions, but it's also incredibly cosy – insulated with sheep's wool, clad in pine, and with a tiny (and very effective) woodburner for those nights when there's a chill. Indeed, the hut can be used year-round.

Although there's no electricity, and lighting is by candles and lanterns, a couple of minutes' walk away in the farm courtyard you get plenty more space in the shape of your own high-spec, slate-floored lounge and shower room, complete with TV, fridge and kettle, and more handmade oak furniture. Food and service is equally top-notch, with home-made biscuits for each guest and a terrific breakfast that incorporates (among other things) a seasonal fruit platter, Cumberland sausage with apple, Aga-roast tomatoes, home-made granola and home-cured bacon.

Walk it all off with a stroll in the rolling countryside (maps and guides provided), drive to the nearby market town of Penrith for some honest-to-goodness Cumbrian shopping, or head to Ullswater for steamer rides and lakeside walks. When you get back, supper trays (cheese, ham, quiche and the like) are available for anyone who doesn't want to head down to the local, community-owned pub in the yester-year hamlet of Crosby Ravensworth. This all makes for a pretty gracious heart-of-the-countryside experience – shepherds, surely, never had it so good – and there should be more idiosyncratic accommodation available at *Crake Trees Manor* once a converted roadmenders' hut gets the same imaginative treatment.

Clockwise from top *Shepherd's Hut*'s steel exterior; plus its woodburner, hand-built bed and small veranda

YHA Black Sail

The atmospheric walkers' refuge at *Black Sail* – high up the Ennerdale valley in the western Lakes – has an almost legendary status. Generations of outdoors enthusiasts have hiked up the trail (and hiking is the only way to get there) to the old stone shepherds' bothy, set in isolated grandeur among some of the Lake District's most dramatic mountain surroundings. It's open all day – weary hikers are welcome to drop in, make a cup of tea and warm themselves by the fire – but it's only by staying the night that you fully buy into the *Black Sail* experience. This won't be for everyone. Although refurbishments are planned, the accommodation is almost entirely frill-free – the three small bunkrooms have bare floors and rough plastered walls, and whatever the weather you have to go outside to use the basic shower and toilet. Yet a middle-of-the-night loo visit might show you more stars than you ever imagined existed, while a day on the hills ends with a hearty one-pot communal dinner served at timeworn wooden tables, as boots get an airing on the rafters above. On balmy summer evenings, glass of wine or beer in hand, you can see why *Black Sail* devotees wouldn't change a thing.

YHA Black Sail, Black Sail Hut, Ennerdale, Cumbria, CA23 3AY ☎0845 371 9680, ⊕yha.org.uk.
Price Dorms: 1x8, 2x4 £19.40, weekends £21.40.
Facilities Kitchen. Bar. Breakfast and dinner available.
Open Closed for winter from 1 Nov, reopens 2 weeks before Easter. Check in: 5pm. Check out: flexible.
Getting there *Black Sail* is only accessible on foot. The easiest parking is 6 miles away at Bowness Knott, Ennerdale – a 12-mile drive south of Cockermouth (A5086). This is also the easiest walk in, up a gentle valley, though there are shorter, tougher hikes to the hostel from Honister or Buttermere, both on a bus route from Keswick.

Woolpack Inn

From the outside, the *Woolpack* in upper Eskdale looks like a standard-issue Lake District inn – a black-and-white country pub with a beer garden and a rather splendid mountain backdrop. Inside, though, changes are afoot, starting with a knocked-through public bar with a real urban sheen – leather sofas, fancy wood-burner, back-lit bar and wood-fired pizza oven. A quirky shop sells games, kites, local produce and bottles of wine, making it a handy place to stock up for a lazy day out. The rooms currently play second fiddle to this rustic-pub reboot, though smart grey-and-white carpets from the local Herdwick flocks are creeping through the building, while decor, curtains and bathrooms are being freshened up. Some rooms are a bit short on space, but "Room 8" manages to fit in a red-draped four-poster and a massive jacuzzi in a palatial bathroom. There's also one family room with a private, deep-blue bathroom – this, and a few of the other rooms, is billed as "just a place to sleep", though with crispy pizzas and award-winning ales downstairs, and majestic mountains beyond, that's probably all you'll have time for.

Woolpack Inn, Eskdale, Cumbria, CA19 1TF ☎019467 23230, ⊕woolpack.co.uk.
Price 8 en-suite doubles £80. Breakfast included.
Facilities Internet. On-site parking. Bar. Shop. Garden. TVs in rooms. Lunch and dinner available.
Restrictions Dogs allowed.
Open Closed for 3 weeks in Dec. 2 nights min stay at the weekend, 3 nights on bank hols. Check in: flexible. Check out: 10am.
Getting there It's a 9-mile drive from Gosforth and the A595 to the *Woolpack*. Trains on the narrow-gauge Ravenglass and Eskdale Railway run from Ravenglass (Cumbrian coastal line) to Dalegarth station, Boot; the inn is another 1.5 miles from there.

Grasmere Independent Hostel

The Lake District's finest independent hostel is sited in a converted barn with views a ten-minute walk outside the invariably crowded tourist village of Grasmere – point one in its favour, if you're a fresh air and mountains kind of person. Point two, frankly, is everything else about the place, which knocks most other Lakeland hostels into a cocked hat. There's only so much you can do with small pine-bedded bunk rooms, but they do it well, with bedside lights, en-suite shower rooms, carpets underfoot, and cheery matching quilt covers and curtains throughout. Four rooms sleep four to six people each, but the top attic room, Helvellyn, sleeps just three and has its own private bathroom – great for couples if available. There are mountain views out of each bedroom (to be fair, they're hard to avoid around here), and more from the cosy lounge which frames the local peaks through a super, circular, slate-trimmed window. On ground level is a professionally equipped self-catering kitchen, and not just more showers and toilets for muddy hikers and bikers but also a coin-op sauna. Oh yes, point three – after a soak and a steam, the local pub is only four hundred yards down the road, very handy for a celebratory pint after you've completed the Grasmere and Rydal Water circuit or one of the tougher local mountain hikes.

Grasmere Independent Hostel,
Broadrayne Farm, Grasmere, Cumbria,
LA22 9RU ☎015394 35055,
🌐grasmerehostel.co.uk.
Price Dorms: 1x3, 1x4, 1x5, 2x6. £19.50, £20.50 at weekends, £21.50 at bank holiday weekends. Hostel also available for sole use, £475 per night.
Facilities Kitchen. On-site parking. Games/common room. Garden. Lockers.
Open Open year-round. Check in: 4pm. Check out: 10am.
Getting there Driving, follow the A591 (Keswick road) past the turn-off for Grasmere, and be prepared to make a right turn just after the *Travellers' Rest* pub. The bus between Ambleside and Keswick runs to Grasmere, and also stops on the A591 near the hostel.

Grasmere Independent Hostel knocks most Lakeland hostels into a cocked hat

How Foot Lodge

Many come to Grasmere on the Wordsworth trail – the poet is buried in the village churchyard, next to his wife and sister – and there's a constant stream of visitors to Dove Cottage, just outside the village, which was the Wordsworth family home from 1799 to 1808. Tucked just behind here is *How Foot Lodge*, a cared-for Victorian villa with a classy selection of rooms at prices that stand out in otherwise high-end Grasmere. All have garden and distant lake or fell views, and while standard rooms are more than satisfactory (king-sized beds, decent bathrooms, old fireplaces and antique armchairs) there are two guest rooms in particular that are usually first to fill. One lovely, light bedroom has French windows opening on to its own private sun lounge – corkscrew and wine glasses provided for that sun-over-the-yardarm drink – or choose a more contemporary style and stay in the handsome suite, with its dark-wood and leather furniture and separate lounge. Grasmere and its restaurants are just five minutes' walk away, though the hosts' *Villa Colombina* tea-room-cum-Italian-restaurant is right next door.

How Foot Lodge, Town End, Grasmere, Cumbria, LA22 9SQ ☎015394 35366, Ⓦhowfoot.co.uk.
Price 4 en-suite doubles £72, sun-lounge room and suite £78. Breakfast included.
Facilities Internet. On-site parking. Games/common room. Garden. TVs in rooms.
Open Closed Christmas week. Check in: 2pm. Check out: 10am.
Getting there Take the A591 to Keswick; the B&B is on the right, just before the turn for Grasmere village, right by Dove Cottage. The bus between Ambleside and Keswick runs to Grasmere, passing Dove Cottage and How Foot Lodge (ask for Dove Cottage).

Ann Tysons

HAWKSHEAD

If you're looking for picturesque in the heart of the Lake District, Hawkshead wins every time. Set midway between Ambleside and Coniston, the tranquil village is a well-known halt on the Wordsworth trail, since William attended school here in the 1780s – lodging in the cottage of local woman Ann Tyson, whom Wordsworth later fondly remembered as "my old Dame". It's now a classic village B&B – whitewashed and rose-clad – on a cobbled alley that once went by the glorious name of "Leather, Rag and Putty Street". The oldest part of the building – right next to where William lodged – contains the best room, with wooden roll-top bedframe and up-to-date slate-floored shower-room. Two other rooms have their own entrances opening directly on to the cobbled lane; and there are three more inside the main cottage – "Room 1" adds another twist to Ann Tysons' singular history with its lovely antique carved bed, sourced from art critic and writer John Ruskin's home at nearby Brantwood. All the rooms are thoroughly traditionally furnished, and bathrooms are squeezed into what are already cosy quarters – but you'd hardly expect anything else in a four-hundred-year-old cottage, and a hearty breakfast under gnarled oak beams is the final poetic flourish.

Ann Tysons, Wordsworth Street, Hawkshead, Cumbria, LA22 0PA ☎015394 36405, Ⓦwww.anntysons.co.uk.
Price 6 en-suite doubles £74–78. Breakfast included.
Facilities Internet. On-site parking. TVs in rooms.
Restrictions Dogs allowed.
Open Year-round. Check in: flexible. Check out: 10am.
Getting there Take the B5286 from Ambleside – you can't drive into Hawkshead itself, and will have to use the signposted car park at the edge of the village. Hawkshead is on the #505 bus route between Windermere (for trains from Kendal), Ambleside and Coniston.

182 ▌CUMBRIA AND THE LAKES

Ellergill

With the slate-grey streets of Keswick awash with reasonably priced B&Bs, it takes something special to stand out from the crowd. Owners Robin and Clare Pinkney have kept the best original features of their Victorian terrace but given the house a European feel that feels chic but personal. There's breathtaking lakeland photography in the breakfast room, while art upstairs in rooms and corridors – much of it local – tends towards the abstract. Colours throughout are bold and furnishings contemporary, so instead of the Lake District default-setting of chintz and country pine you get leather headboards and armchairs, and wine-red bedspreads. Space is relatively tight in this light-and-stylish home-from-home, but another tenner gets you one of the bigger "de luxe" rooms. It may be smart, but it's not precious, and outdoor types get a big welcome here. Out of the door and down the street, you can be on the lake (Derwent Water) or up a mountain (on the way to Skiddaw) within twenty minutes. Or it's just a few minutes' walk into Keswick itself for skinny lattes, gourmet sandwiches, lakeside theatre performances and a fast-growing annual mountain festival (🌐keswickmountainfestival. co.uk) that attracts big outdoor-world names from Chris Bonington to Ray Mears.

> **Ellergill, 22 Stanger Street, Keswick, Cumbria, CA12 5JU ☎017687 73347, 🌐ellergill.co.uk.**
> **Price** 5 en-suite doubles: standard £65, deluxe £75. Breakfast included.
> **Facilities** Internet. On-site parking. TVs in rooms.
> **Restrictions** No children under 12.
> **Open** Year-round. Check in: flexible. Check out: 10am.
> **Getting there** Leave the M6 at junction 40 and take the A66 for Keswick. *Ellergill* is 3min walk from Keswick bus station – regular services run here from Kendal, Windermere, Ambleside, Grasmere and Carlisle.

YHA Keswick

When the YHA wants to convince doubters that hostelling has jettisoned its sackcloth-and-ashes image it cites flagship outfits like *YHA Keswick*. The revamp of this former woollen mill – sited by a babbling river in the northern Lakes' biggest town – puts it firmly in the budget hotel category. There's a smart reception desk offering late check-outs for a fiver, a self-service restaurant with river views, and a score of frill-free, value-for-money rooms. Dorms for hikers and travellers are still its stock in trade, but couples can get a good deal here – one room has the only double in the place (with a single bunk above), while another twin room has the luxury of a small flat-screen TV (whatever happened to nights in cleaning your boots?). Families, meanwhile, like the rooms in the eaves on the top floor, overlooking the river, adjacent park and the hills beyond. Furnishings are solid – robust wooden bunks, under-bed lockers – and sparkly clean bathrooms are down the hall. The licensed restaurant serves big breakfasts, plus bistro meals and pizzas for dinner, and you're only a five-minute walk from Keswick town centre.

> **YHA Keswick, Station Road, Keswick, Cumbria, CA12 5LH ☎0845 371 9746, 🌐yha.org.uk.**
> **Price** Rooms and dorms: 1x2, 7x3, 7x4, 2x5, 4x6. Dorms £23.40, double room £56, twin room £54, 4-bed family room £70.
> **Facilities** Internet. Kitchen. Bar. Cafe. Games/common room. Lockers. Breakfast and dinner available.
> **Open** Year-round. Check in: flexible. Check out: 10am.
> **Getting there** Leave the M6 at junction 40 and take the A66 for Keswick. There are regular buses to Keswick from Kendal, Windermere, Ambleside, Grasmere and Carlisle. The hostel is less than 10min walk from Keswick bus station.

From left Walkers on the Coast-to-Coast path; *Kirkby Stephen Hostel* is a soaring former church

Kirkby Stephen Hostel

Walkers on Wainwright's famous long-distance Coast-to-Coast footpath are a familiar sight in the small Eden Valley market town of Kirkby Stephen, which lies just under halfway along the route. Many head straight to church the minute they arrive in town – Kirkby Stephen's idiosyncratic hostel (formerly the YHA, now independent) is housed in the town's 1902 Methodist chapel. It's fantastically atmospheric – the soaring main hall of the church survives intact, complete with pews, panels, carved ceiling roses, stained glass and an upper gallery that's now a secluded lounge. Bunk rooms are in the old Sunday School building and are all fairly spacious, with high ceilings and adjoining washrooms. There are also two sought-after twin rooms, both with stained-glass windows of their own, one of which is fully en suite, the other with shower and sink in the room and loo down the hall. Walkers and cyclists are the main clientele, so fixtures and fittings throughout are on the frill-free and functional side, but it's a really welcoming place to fall into at the end of a tough day on the trail. There's a simple kitchen for self-caterers, and a fair few pubs along the main street serve bar meals. Meanwhile, mornings see bright and early starts for most, with hikers sent on their way after a big fry-up, eaten on church pews – prayers for a day without rain are optional.

Kirkby Stephen Hostel, Market Street, Kirkby Stephen, Cumbria, CA17 4QQ ☎017683 71793, ⓦkirkbystephen hostel.co.uk.
Price Dorms: 2x2, 2x4, 3x6, 1x8, £19.
Facilities Internet. Kitchen. Games/common room. Lockers. Breakfast available.
Restrictions Dogs allowed.
Open Year-round, though often group bookings only for winter weekends. Check in: 5pm. Check out: 10am.
Getting there Kirkby Stephen is on the A685, 5 miles south of Brough (A66). Kirkby Stephen is on the Settle-to-Carlisle Railway (connecting services from Leeds), and there are buses from Kendal and Penrith most days.

Coachman's Quarters

If ghost-ridden Muncaster Castle is one of Cumbria's great hidden treasures, with its beautiful grounds, wild herons and swooping owls, then an even more in-the-know secret is the fact that you can stay the night. Not, to be strictly accurate, in the castle itself, but in one of ten quality B&B rooms set around the cobbled courtyard of the old coaching quarters, with direct access to castle and gardens. The agreeable, country-pine rooms are of hotel standard – telephones, wi-fi, hairdriers and decent bathrooms – but it's the extras on top that make it a real bargain. There's a large, fully equipped modern kitchen, plus dining room and lounge, under the exposed stone and original beams of the old haylofts, while guests get a free day's entry to the castle grounds and activities, saving you another £10 each.

A footpath leads the mile and a half to the owners' hotel and restaurant, the Pennington, in nearby coastal Ravenglass (starting point of the Ravenglass and Eskdale steam railway), though it's hard to beat a glass of wine on the manicured castle lawn once the last visitors have left. The strange hooting heard at night? They say it's from the Owl Centre, which backs on to the guest accommodation, but our money is on the Muncaster ghosts.

Coachman's Quarters, Muncaster Castle, Ravenglass, Cumbria, CA18 1RQ ☎01229 717614, ⓦmuncaster.co.uk.
Price 8 en-suite doubles £80, 2 family rooms £110. Breakfast included.
Facilities Internet. Kitchen. On-site parking. Café. Games/common room. Garden. TVs in rooms. Lunch and dinner available.
Restrictions Good disabled access.
Open Year-round. Check in: 3pm. Check out: 11am.
Getting there Muncaster Castle is on the A595, a mile from Ravenglass, though there's a separate (signposted) entrance for *Coachman's Quarters*, half a mile past the main entrance, on the right. The nearest train station is Ravenglass, on the Cumbrian coast line, with connnections from Barrow in Furness or Carlisle – ask at the castle about arranging a taxi pick-up.

Clockwise from left A red-tailed hawk at Muncaster Castle; two of *Coachman's Quarters'* agreeable rooms

Idiosyncratic, off-road *Skiddaw House* is England's most remote hostel

Skiddaw House

It might be tough to reach and low on luxuries, but that's all part of the charm at England's highest and most remote hostel, 1550ft up in the Lake District's northern fells. The former shooting lodge and shepherds' shelter is a magnificent base for some stupendous high lakeland walks, starting with the good hour or so that it takes to get here in the first place, along a rugged footpath that forms part of the long-distance Cumbria Way. That's right – there's no road, and no mains electricity, central heating or phone reception either, but these are all plus-points for the hikers and outdoor types who love rustic, off-grid *Skiddaw House* for its isolated idiosyncracy.

Furniture and fittings have seen a lot of wear and tear over the years, but there's a warming wood-burner and well-equipped kitchen, a single solar-heated shower, fresh linen on every bed, and – charmingly – hot-water bottles ranged along the bunk-room windowsills. A simple, help-yourself, toast, eggs and cereal breakfast is available, but everything else needs to be carried in (and out again), including dinner, if you don't want to rely on the very basic shop supplies (tins and packets, no fresh produce). But as dusk falls, and dishes are squared away, out come the maps to plan for the next day's walk from this rough-but- regal mountain diamond.

Skiddaw House, Bassenthwaite, Cumbria, CA12 4QX ☎07747 174293, ⓦskiddawhouse.co.uk.
Price Dorms: 1x4, 2x5, 1x8 (single-sex, unless dorm occupied by a family/group) £17.
Facilities Kitchen. Shop. Games/common room. Breakfast available.
Open Closed Nov 1 to 28 Feb. Check in: 5pm. Check out: 10am.
Getting there No vehicle access – minimum 3.5 mile (1hr-plus) walk required. Park at Latrigg car park, near Keswick, and follow the Cumbria Way footpath directly to the hostel. Proper hiking gear recommended – check the weather forecast before setting out.

Rookhow

The secluded, ivy-covered Quaker meeting house at Rookhow in the southern Lakes has stood in its quiet glade since 1725, backed by a magical private twelve acres of mature trees and leafy paths. The meeting house is still in regular use, but there's overnight accommodation open to all in the adjacent lofty stone building that once served as the stables. Outdoor families and groups used to mucking about are going to have a high old time here, whether playing woodland hide-and-seek, splashing in the river or heading further afield on Lake District days out. It's all pretty bucolic, in a Famous Five kind of way, and if facilities are fairly limited (BYO sleeping bag, no TV, phone service or internet) the deep rural charm certainly isn't. Multi-bed sleeping areas are simple and straightforward (think basic pine bunk-beds, bare walls and thin curtains), and shower and loos are shared, but a soaring open-plan lounge and fully equipped kitchen has old oak beams, a wood-burning stove and plenty of space for get-togethers. Nights are on the quiet side, though the nearest pub is only a couple of miles away in Satterthwaite, but toasting marshmallows around a woodland fire is more the *Rookhow* way.

> **Rookhow, Rusland, Ulverston, Cumbria, LA12 8LA** ☎01229 860231, ⓦrookhowcentre.co.uk.
> **Price** Dorms: 1x9, 1x8, £14. Whole property can be rented for £160. Camping available on request.
> **Facilities** Kitchen. On-site parking. Games/common room. Garden. Lockers.
> **Restrictions** Bed linen required (or hire a duvet for £5).
> **Open** Open year-round. Check in: flexible. Check out: 10am.
> **Getting there** *Rookhow* is on a minor country lane, 2 miles south of Satterthwaite hamlet – check website for exact directions (don't rely on SatNav).

Burnthwaite Farm

There are more farmhouse B&Bs in Cumbria than you can shake a shepherd's crook at, but few as good value as the magnificently sited *Burnthwaite Farm* in remote Wasdale. Set under brooding peaks, the last building in the valley is a classic white-painted cottage on National Trust land, with a scintillating view from the farmyard down to the lake at Wast Water. It's a working sheep farm offering old-school B&B, from swirling floral carpets to sparsely furnished white rooms, but there's real lived-in character in a property that dates back to the sixteenth century. The rooms all have up-close-and-personal views of Lingmell, the adjacent mountain, while a big farmhouse breakfast is served in the rustic dining room and lounge, which is warmed by a wood-burner in winter. Half a mile back down the track is the famous Wasdale Head inn, with a walkers' bar full of outdoor types wolfing down hearty meals, and a mile beyond that is Wast Water itself – England's deepest lake, with awesome 1700ft screes tumbling to its eastern shore. It's a stunning location, well worth the long drive from anywhere to reach it.

> **Burnthwaite Farm, Wasdale Head, Gosforth, Cumbria, CA20 1EX** ☎019467 26242, ⓦburnthwaitefarm.co.uk.
> **Price** 2 en-suite doubles £68, 4 doubles with shared bathroom £58. Breakfast included. Self-catering accommodation (sleeps 4) also available, from £375/week.
> **Facilities** On-site parking. Games/common room. Dinner available.
> **Open** Open year-round. Check in: 2pm. Check out: 11am.
> **Getting there** From Gosforth, just off the A595, follow the signs to Wasdale Head (10 miles). The road up Wast Water lake side is single-track; at the public parking area, a few hundred yards before *Wasdale Head Inn*, bear right along the unsurfaced single-track lane to the farm (fine for cars).

CUMBRIA AND THE LAKES ▌ 187

Rainors Farm

WASDALE

There are those mornings, even on holiday, when getting out of bed seems like too much effort. If brewing up a cuppa and throwing open the curtains is all you're good for, at least at *Rainors Farm* you don't have to do anything else to enjoy the glorious rural surroundings. Propped up in bed, you get gorgeous, sweeping views of fields, valley and fells – though you will eventually have to get dressed if you want breakfast, since they draw the line at room service. There's an updated country feel at the white-painted eighteenth-century farmhouse – door and windows are trimmed in burgundy, a colour that's repeated on bedspreads in the two B&B rooms, which also feature antique fireplaces and stripped pine doors. There's a double bed and single bed in each room, and enough

Rainors Farm, Wasdale Road, Gosforth, Cumbria, CA20 1ER ☎019467 25934, Ⓦrainorsfarm.co.uk.
Price 2 en-suite doubles £65. Available as a triple rooom (£90), or family room (from £80). Yurts from £340 for 3 nights, cottage suite from £250 for 3 nights. Breakfast included.
Facilities Internet. On-site parking. Games/common room. Garden. TVs in rooms.
Restrictions Dogs allowed.
Open Open year-round. Check in: 4pm. Check out: 10am.
Getting there *Rainors Farm* is 1.5 miles east of Gosforth (off the A595), on the Wasdale road; the sign is on the right.

space to add a z-bed, so friends and families get a good deal here, while a stylish, self-catering cottage suite in the main house and two bucolic yurts in the grounds offer more flexible accommodation. You're ten minutes' drive from Wast Water and the high mountains, and the largely unknown Cumbrian coast is ten minutes in the other direction, with miles of unspoiled beach and wildlife-rich estuarine dunes to explore. Two pubs on the green at nearby Nether Wasdale, a couple of miles away, offer good bar meals and local ales – the *Strands Inn* even has its own brewery.

Clockwise from top left Yurts at *Rainors Farm*; the farmhouse; nearby Wast Water

The Archway

If you're a tourist board best-breakfast award winner, you make sure that people know – and at *The Archway* guest house, the trophy sits right on the mantelpiece. Owners Jennifer and Stephen Taylor are passionate about starting the day right, whether it's omelettes, pancakes, marinated fruits and home-made muesli, smoked haddock or bread from the local bakery – only the Lancashire black pudding isn't regionally sourced, but as they're both originally from Bury, that seems fair enough. Stephen's the chef and partner at the local seafood restaurant, while Jennifer runs the traditional slate-built lakeland B&B in a genuinely enthusiastic and welcoming manner, with the smell of freshly baked cakes wafting up the stairs most afternoons and home-made biscuits placed by the bed. Two front-facing rooms, with brass bedsteads and light, fair-sized bathrooms, have distant hill views (a little sketch in each room picks out the peaks you can see, from the Old Man of Coniston to the Langdale Pikes); the two at the rear are slightly smaller and cheaper. Windermere itself is a handy gateway – it's the only place in the Lake District National Park you can reach by train, with the lake and its cruise boats; the nearby towns of Ambleside and Grasmere are a short bus ride away.

The Archway, 13 College Road, Windermere, Cumbria, LA23 1BU ☎015394 45613, ⊛the-archway.com.
Price 4 en-suite doubles; front-facing £66, rear-facing £62. Breakfast included.
Facilities Internet. On-site parking. TVs in rooms.
Open Closed for 2 weeks in Dec – dates vary. Check in: flexible. Check out: 11am.
Getting there For Windermere town, take the A591 from Kendal. *The Archway* is a 5min walk from Windermere train station – there are regular branch-line services from Oxenholme (west coast main line) via Kendal.

Derby Arms

With most of the Lake District's historic inns pricing themselves out of the budget market – over £100 a night is now common – it falls to some of the spruced-up newcomers to provide a better deal. The *Derby Arms* is a case in point, tucked away off the main road in a less-visited part of the southern Lakes, but still close to Kendal, Grange-over-Sands, Cartmel and the lower reaches of Windermere. It's leased from the local community trust – part of the pub serves as the village shop – and the style is traditional with a twist. The opened-out, stripped-floor bar has carved wooden seats, open fires, Turkish rugs and antique prints but serves a modish bistro menu, including organic beef from the inn's own herd and good local ales. The half-dozen small but stylish rooms are very much in the same vein, mixing antique furniture and modern art with up-to-date bathrooms. Three (west-facing) rooms are judged superior by virtue of their countryside views, but to be honest there's little difference in outlook – you won't feel hard done by in east-facing "Room 7", for example, with its Victorian brass bedstead and cast-iron roll-top bath, and you'll have saved yourself £20.

Derby Arms, Witherslack, Cumbria, LA11 6RH ☎015395 52207, ⊛ainscoughs.co.uk.
Price 3 east-facing en-suite doubles £65, 3 west-facing en-suite doubles £85. Breakfast included.
Facilities Internet. On-site parking. Bar. Shop. TVs in rooms. Lunch and dinner available.
Open Closed Christmas Eve and Christmas Day. Check in: flexible. Check out: 11am.
Getting there Witherslack is just off the A590, 5 miles northeast of Grange-over-Sands.

NORTHEAST ENGLAND

England's northeast is border country – a long coastline with the North Sea to the east, Scotland to the north, and to the west, away from the conurbations of Durham and Newcastle, an ever wilder land of dales, hills and forests, much of it contained within the vast Northumberland National Park. It's a region of long, slow drives – at least off the main north–south A1 – and long, slow walks, whether you're touring the famous "coast and castles" route or following the line of Hadrian's Wall. Big towns are few and far between; Newcastle and Durham aside, only Hexham, Alnwick and Berwick-upon-Tweed really cut the mustard, and you need to plan ahead for accommodation. There's no real shortage of places to stay – it's just that you're likely to find yourself with a longer journey, or a more remote location, than you had perhaps envisaged.

Newcastle and Durham themselves stand apart. The former – basically the capital of the northeast, and its one essential urban destination – has plenty of budget chain hotels and hostels. Magnificent Durham and its medieval cathedral is more refined and, as an ancient university town (in England, only Oxford and Cambridge are older), can offer atmospheric budget lodgings in its various colleges.

Elsewhere in County Durham and Northumberland, it's pretty much as you might expect; rural and farmhouse B&Bs, hostels and bunkhouses form the mainstay of the budget-stay trade, and prices are reasonable. Some areas are particularly well served; the opening of the long-distance Hadrian's Wall Path, for example, means there is plenty of judiciously sited accommodation along the way, aimed squarely at hikers and bikers. It's a similar story in certain sections of the Durham Dales, Northumberland National Park and the Northumberland coast, where local operators have an eye firmly on the family and backpacker market and have tailored their prices accordingly. There is always good-value accommodation to hand, whether you're looking to tramp golden Northumberland sands, wildlife-watch in Kielder Forest Park or explore the remains of Roman walls and forts.

The YHA also has a big presence in the region, and while many of the hostels are traditional outdoorsy properties – often in glorious locations – two brand new sites (in Alnwick and Berwick-upon-Tweed) are among the most up to date in the British hostelling network. Basically budget hotels with a hostel label, they're a viable choice for couples, families or touring backpackers.

NORTHEAST ENGLAND

NAME	LOCATION	PAGE		REAL BARGAIN	TREAT YOURSELF	FAMILY-FRIENDLY	GREAT RURAL LOCATION	OUTDOOR ACTIVITIES	GREAT FOOD AND DRINK	DORMS	PUBLIC TRANSPORT
Bamburgh Hall Farm	Bamburgh	194	❷				✓		✓		✓
Barrowburn	Harbottle	198	❸	✓		✓	✓	✓		✓	
Dowfold House	Crook	196	⓬		✓						
Euro Hostel Newcastle	Newcastle upon Tyne	202	❾						✓	✓	✓
Houghton North Farm	Heddon-on-the-Wall	200	❽				✓	✓		✓	
Old Repeater Station	Chollerford	195	❼				✓	✓		✓	
Simonburn	Simonburn	203	❻	✓			✓				
St Chad's College	Durham	197	⓫						✓		✓
Tomlinson's	Rothbury	203	❺		✓		✓	✓	✓	✓	
YHA Alnwick	Alnwick	194	❹			✓				✓	✓
YHA Berwick	Berwick-upon-Tweed	195	❶		✓	✓			✓	✓	✓
YHA Edmundbyers	Edmundbyers	197	❿	✓			✓	✓		✓	
YHA Langdon Beck	Middleton-in-Teesdale	201	⓭				✓	✓		✓	

Clockwise from top left *Simonburn* (see p.203); *YHA Edmundbyers* (see p.197); *Tomlinson's* (see p.203) **Previous page** Bamburgh Castle

Berwick-upon-Tweed ①

Holy Island
(Lindisfarne)

Bamburgh ②
Seahouses
Beadnell

Embleton
Craster

③
④ Alnwick

NORTHUMBERLAND
NATIONAL PARK
⑤

NORTHUMBERLAND
Morpeth
Ashington

Blyth

⑥
⑦
Hexham

⑧
Newcastle-
upon-Tyne
Tynemouth
South
Shields
⑨ Gateshead

Sunderland
Washington

⑩
Consett
Chester-
le-Street

Durham ⑪
Peterlee

⑫
Hartlepool

COUNTY DURHAM
Bishop
Auckland
Newton
Aycliffe

Redcar

⑬
Stockton-
on-Tees

Barnard
Castle
Darlington
Middlesbrough

YHA Alnwick

The Queen opened the northeast's newest hostel in June 2011, and the black velvet chair she sat on gets pride of place in the lobby. It's a sweet touch, but people in the medieval market town of Alnwick can be just as proud of the actual hostel, which is a terrific conversion of the former court house, police station and sergeant's house. The adjacent buildings have been connected in a high-quality refurbishment that retains many of the original features while adding up-to-the-minute hostel comforts. For a start, all the high-ceilinged rooms are en suite, with smart painted metal bunks (double beds in a couple), plus matching carpets, walls and curtains in blue, lilac and mauve, and shiny white bathrooms. There's also a self-catering kitchen and cafeteria-style dining room, and the locally sourced food – from Craster kippers to the home-made raisin griddle cakes known as "Singing Hinnies" – is great. Families have plenty of scope here in four-, five- and six-bed rooms, and kids will appreciate the games room, where there's pool, table football, a TV and Wii. Alnwick itself keeps everyone occupied during the day, with its famous castle (doubling as Hogwarts in two of the Harry Potter films), an amazing contemporary garden and one of England's biggest secondhand bookshops.

YHA Alnwick, 34–38 Green Batt, Alnwick, Northumberland, NE66 1TU ☎01665 660 800, 🖰alnwickyouthhostel.co.uk.
Price Dorms: 57 beds in 15 en-suite rooms, sleeping 1–6 (single-sex, unless occupied by couple/family/group) £22.50; two-bed private room £47, four-bed family room £81.
Facilities Internet. Kitchen. Bar. Games/common room. Lockers. Breakfast and dinner available.
Open Year-round. Check in: 4pm. Check out: 10am.
Getting there The hostel is a 5min walk from Alnwick bus station; regular services run from Newcastle, 35 miles away.

Bamburgh Hall Farm

The directions alone – 500 yards from the castle, next to the village church, opposite the green – have a distinct appeal and gracious *Bamburgh Hall Farm* doesn't disappoint. Built in 1697, the handsome property has a flower-filled English country garden and distant sea views from the upper floors. This is old-fashioned B&B at its best, with two spacious en-suite guest rooms full of period and rustic family furnishings, and a traditional drawing room downstairs with a TV (there aren't any in the rooms) and open fire. There are also two large rooms in the attic, sharing a bathroom, which gives families their own, more secluded space. Despite the elegant look and period nature of the house, there's an informal feel throughout, starting with the chickens wandering the grounds and continuing with the assurance that no one minds you trailing in a bit of sand. This is just as well, as the golden strands of nearby Bamburgh beach, one of the northeast's finest natural attractions, are irresistible; equally appealing is dramatic Bamburgh Castle, a good view of which you get from the attic rooms.

Bamburgh Hall Farm, Bamburgh, Northumberland, NE69 7AB ☎01668 214230, 🖰bamburghhallfarm.com.
Price 2 en-suite doubles and 2 doubles sharing private bathroom, £90 for one-night stay, £70 thereafter. Breakfast included.
Facilities On-site parking. Games/common room. Garden.
Open Year-round. Check in: flexible. Check out: flexible.
Getting there Bamburgh is 20 miles south of Berwick-upon-Tweed, or 17 miles north of Alnwick (take A1 from either); there are regular buses from both towns, stopping on the village green, very near the farm.

YHA Berwick

Berwick-upon-Tweed's two-hundred-year-old riverside grain warehouse suffered a calamitous fire in 1815, which explains the famous leaning facade. It's a landmark building in this handsome border town, and has been redeveloped as a rather spiffy new hostel which is budget hotel in all but name. The funky, ground-floor bistro-bar-cum-atrium is all polished concrete, girders, beams and exposed stone, with the industrial-chic look continuing all the way up to an attic-style top floor, which combines modern lounge, dining room and kitchen with rooftop views of town. Boxy rooms are steely-grey and blue, with keycard doors, simple furniture, lighting consoles above each bed and an en-suite wetroom shower and toilet. Seagulls wheel above the River Tweed outside (it's about the only noise you'll hear), while cheery staff play world music and take turns at the espresso machine. If there's lots to like here, there's more in town, where an hour's walk around the preserved walls takes you past elegant Georgian mansions, well-tended gardens and historic bridges.

> **YHA Berwick, Dewars Lane Granary, Dewars Lane, Berwick-upon-Tweed, Northumberland, TD15 1HJ** ☎0845 371 9676, 🌐yha.org.uk.
>
> **Price** Dorms: 55 beds in 13 rooms sleeping 2–6 (single-sex, unless occupied by couple/family/group) £21.40; two-bed room £43, four-bed family room £73.
>
> **Facilities** Internet. Kitchen. Bar. Café. Shop. Games/common room. Lockers. Breakfast, lunch and dinner available.
>
> **Open** Year-round. Check in: 2pm. Check out: 10am.
>
> **Getting there** The hostel is a 15min walk from Berwick train station.

Old Repeater Station

For a quirky Northumberland budget stay, there's not much that beats spending the night in an old telephone exchange virtually on top of Hadrian's Wall. To be fair, the fixtures and fittings are long gone and the stone building has had a complete refit, but it certainly makes the most of its isolated location, amid windswept moors near the visible line of the Roman wall. Downstairs are two compact, frill-free bunk rooms, plus an en-suite single, while upstairs in the converted attic it's two en-suite B&B rooms. The upstairs rooms are well worth the extra money, with laminate floors, pine beds, smart earth-toned bathrooms and sweeping views across the moors. Downstairs is also home to a light-filled, open-plan, lounge and dining room where breakfast is served: – continental for bunk-dwellers (upgrade for £5), full English for B&B guests. *The Old Repeater Station* is also an ad hoc café – walkers sometimes stop by for drinks and snacks – so you can usually get something to eat during the day. Overnighters, meanwhile, also have the use of a kitchen and can buy a local Wylam or Allendale beer to sip at a picnic bench outside, watching the sun set over what was once the northern limit of the Roman empire.

> **Old Repeater Station, Military Road, Grindon, Northumberland, NE47 6NQ** ☎01434 688668, 🌐hadrians-wall-bedandbreakfast.co.uk.
>
> **Price** Rooms: 2 doubles £60, single £45; all en suite. Dorms: 1x2 and 1x4 with shared bathroom £22.50, or £27.50 for sole use of two-bed bunk room. Breakfast included.
>
> **Facilities** Internet. Kitchen. On-site parking. Café. Shop. Games/common room. Garden. TVs in rooms.
>
> **Open** Closed Nov–March (open by arrangement only during this period). Check in: 3pm. Check out: 10am.
>
> **Getting there** The B&B is 7 miles west of Chollerford on the B6318. The Hadrian's Wall Bus (Easter–Oct), between Newcastle and Carlisle via the Roman sites, stops nearby.

Dowfold House

People travel a long way to sample the award-winning *Dowfold House* breakfast – perhaps the supreme irony, given that Jill and Rupert Richardson are passionate about local sourcing and low food miles. They take the start of the day very seriously here – an eight-page booklet, no less, details ingredients and suppliers, whether it's home-baked bread, apple compôte from their Bramley apple tree, hedgerow blackberries, garden-fruit jam or sausages and bacon from a local farm. Everything else is done just right too at the Richardson's elegant Victorian home, which sits on a panoramic terrace overlooking the small town of Crook, with sweeping views of Weardale and the North Pennines beyond. In good weather, you're greeted with tea and home-made biscuits on the patio, before being shown to one of three charming rooms, known as Red, Pink or Green after the predominant shading. Room facilities are superior – eco-toiletries, hairdryers, hot-water bottles, radios – and breakfast is on polished tables and fine china. This part of County Durham was once synonymous with coal- and lead-mining, and the genteel house was originally the local mine manager's residence. Twenty miles away, you can explore the harsher conditions endured by the workers at the fascinating Killhope Lead Mining Museum, while *Dowfold House* is also only nine miles from the shops and sights of historic Durham itself.

Dowfold House, Low Jobs Hill, Crook, County Durham, DL15 9AB ☎01388 762473, Ⓦdowfoldhouse.co.uk.
Price 3 en-suite doubles £75 first night and £70 thereafter. Breakfast included.
Facilities Internet. On-site parking. Games/common room. Garden. TVs in rooms.
Open Year-round. Two-night minimum stay required if starting on a Sat night. Check in: 5pm. Check out: 11am.
Getting there Dowfold House is 9 miles southwest of Durham, off the A690 road.

Bucolic views and bountiful breakfasts await at *Dowfold House*

St Chad's College

DURHAM

The students at *St Chad's College* live in an enviable location, on a narrow cobbled street beneath the mighty rose window of Durham Cathedral – and when they go home for the holidays their unoccupied rooms are available to B&B guests, making a great base for a tour of this most harmonious of English cathedral cities. Rooms are spread across seven adjacent brick houses with Georgian facades and contain a warren of variously shaped singles, twins and doubles. The style is clean and neutral, with cream walls, hard-wearing carpets and IKEA-style student furniture. Not all are en suite, and not all have any kind of view, though some rooms are very spacious, while others are particularly lovely – such as the cheery single and twin in the main building that overlook a manicured garden; these rooms are the only ones available year round. Breakfast is served under chandeliers in the grand student dining hall, with the cereals laid out reverently on the High Table, and there's a bar in the glass-roofed courtyard. One caveat: overnight parking, although included, is a drive away and then a walk back into the otherwise traffic-restricted old town.

> St Chad's College, 18 North Bailey, Durham, County Durham, DH1 3RH
> ☎0191 334 3358, ⓦwww.dur.ac.uk /stchads.conference.
> **Price** 120 rooms: 56 singles £29, 18 twins & 10 doubles £52; all with shared bathrooms. 25 singles £37.50, 26 twins & 11 doubles £72; all en suite. Discounted YHA price applies to shared-bathroom price only. Breakfast included.
> **Facilities** Bar. Games/common room. Garden.
> **Open** During Christmas and New Year, Easter and summer university vacations only, though 2 rooms available year-round; otherwise, closed during term. Check in: 1pm. Check out: 10am.
> **Getting there** *St Chad's College* is a 20min walk from Durham train station.

YHA Edmundbyers

EDMUNDBYERS

The rush to modernize hostels and upgrade facilities hasn't yet reached every corner of the country, and a good thing too. Among the holdouts is *Edmundbyers*, a classic example of an old-school hostel with simple facilities in a fine location. Set in a sixteenth-century inn in a tiny moorland village between Weardale and Hadrian's Wall, it's been a youth hostel since 1936, making it one of the YHA's earliest properties. Accommodation is a tight squeeze in ancient rooms with low ceilings and black-painted beams, and only one ground-floor room has its own private shower and loo. But the wonderfully cosy lounge speaks of centuries of conviviality, with its well-worn stone-flagged floor, big open fire and deep, red armchairs. It's self-catering only, with a fully equipped kitchen, basic dining area and a tin-and-packet shop-counter. Check-in, check-out and curfew are all fairly strictly observed, but that hasn't stopped generations of walkers and cyclists from enjoying the *Edmundbyers* ambience. With any luck, it'll still be going strong a century from now.

> YHA Edmundbyers, Low House, Edmundbyers, Consett, County Durham, DH8 9NL ☎0845 371 9633, ⓦyha.org .uk.
> **Price** Dorms: 1x3, 1x4, 2x5 & 2x6 (all single-sex, unless occupied by couple/family/group) £19.40.
> **Facilities** Kitchen. Shop. Games/common room. Garden.
> **Restrictions** Curfew 11pm.
> **Open** April–Oct; Nov–March groups only. Check in: 5pm. Check out: 10am.
> **Getting there** Buses (Mon–Sat) run to Edmundbyers from nearby Consett, 6 miles to the east; the nearest train station is at Hexham, 13 miles north.

Barrowburn

HARBOTTLE

The sixteen-mile journey into the upper Coquet valley in the Northumberland National Park is one of those that has "remote" and "end-of-the-line" stamped all over it. The narrow road twists and turns between the rolling green slopes and heather-clad moors of the Cheviot hills, emerging in a wide clearing by the farm at *Barrowburn*, which is set in one of England's most dramatic rural locations.

That anyone lives here at all seems extraordinary, though the owners farm nine hundred sheep from the property, and run a welcoming tea room. That there was once a school here is scarcely credible, yet *Barrowburn*'s small stone Camping Barn was precisely that; built in 1879 and last used as a school in 1970, it lies a couple of hundred yards away from the farmhouse and is now set up as a "stone tent", with a wooden-floored balcony for bring-your-own camping mats and sleeping bags, a bit of furniture, a kitchen with four-ring gas burner and hot water, a cold-water washroom and a multi-fuel (wood and coal) stove for heat.

Barrowburn, Harbottle, Northumberland, NE65 7BP ☎01669 621176, ⓦbarrowburn.com.
Price 2 twins with shared bathroom £80; includes breakfast and dinner. Deer Hut (sleeps up to 6) £60 per night, including fuel. Camping Barn (sleeps up to 17) £80 per night, including fuel, or £10/person for fewer than 8.
Facilities Kitchen. On-site parking. Café. Shop. Garden.
Restrictions Bed linen required.
Open Year-round. Check in: 4pm. Check out: 10am.
Getting there The farm is 16 miles northwest of Rothbury in the Northumberland National Park. It's in the Otterburn Ranges military training area, but there's open access to *Barrowburn* by road; hikers should heed the signs and red flags in other areas that warn of training exercises.

If this sounds too hardcore, the alternative choice stands immediately adjacent in the shape of the heavily weathered, green-painted wooden lodge that was once the teacher's house but is now known as the Deer Hut. This is also available by the night and while still fairly basically furnished is a whole lot more comfortable, with two made-up twin bedrooms, a proper hot-water bathroom, small kitchen with full-sized oven, plus convector heater and an open coal fire.

Failing this, there's even a third grade of accommodation in the shape of two straightforward B&B rooms in the farmhouse itself, offering a simple bed for the night for weary walkers, a thumping big breakfast and a home-cooked dinner.

The views everywhere – naturally – are magnificent. Scotland is just a few miles behind you – with the route of the Pennine Way snaking off over the border – while on walks through the

Coquet valley you'll spot otters, skylarks, buzzards, deer, red squirrels and the ever-present white-faced Cheviot sheep.

The farmhouse tearoom has a big local reputation for its home-made cakes, scones and biscuits, and can rustle up a bowl of soup and a bacon sandwich. From the tables outside it's a joy to listen to the gushing river and watch the clouds scud by, with the occasional floor show provided by zooming attack jets and army manoeuvres in the nearby military training area. There's certainly never a dull moment in England's very own "Big Sky" country.

Clockwise from top left Walkers make their way through the Cheviot Hills, the Pennine Way snakes past *Barrowburn* on its way to Scotland; one of the two farmhouse B&B bedrooms; the gateway to *Barrowburn*'s rural idyll

Houghton North Farm

There are 84 miles of the Hadrian's Wall Path to cover – you've only done the first fifteen by the time you get to Jeff and Paula Laws' classy bunkhouse, but somehow the rest doesn't seem so daunting after a night of backpacker pampering. The Laws family has farmed here for over a century, but it's the growing popularity of "walking the wall" that provided the impetus to convert the old pigsties into decidedly un-piggy overnight accommodation. Three four-bed dorms and one twin sit under high ceilings and sky-lights, all with terracotta tiled floors and burnished wood doors, and sharing immaculate separate men's and women's washrooms. There are also two crisply furnished en-suite family rooms, the largest of which throws more personal comforts your way – bedside tables, a small TV, and pictures and mirrors on the wall. The rooms are ranged around a sunny, flower-filled courtyard with barbecue area, off which there's also a bright lounge with help-me-out-of-here sofas and a wood burner. A spick-and-span self-catering kitchen, drying room and laundry deals with wet and hungry walkers, though the nearest pub is only a ten-minute walk away and local take-out places will deliver to the bunkhouse. And the wall walk? Well, you're back on the path in ten minutes, completely refreshed, with just 69 miles to go.

Houghton North Farm, Heddon-on-the-Wall, Northumberland, NE15 0EZ
☎01661 854364,
🌐hadrianswallaccommodation.com.
Price Dorms: 1x3, 1x5, both en suite; 1x2, 3x4, both with shared bathroom; all beds £25. Sole use of rooms available: 2 in four-bed room £58, family of 4 (children under 10) in five-bed room £90. Breakfast included.
Facilities Internet. Kitchen. On-site parking. Games/common room. Garden. Lockers.
Restrictions No children under 5.
Open Closed Christmas and New Year; also groups (ie sole-use) only from November until February. Check in: flexible. Check out: 10am.
Getting there The farm is 9 miles west of Newcastle, off the A69. Bus #684 (Newcastle–Hexham) and #685 (Newcastle–Carlisle) both stop around 50yds from the gate.

Beautiful countryside and a powerful sense of history make the Hadrian's Wall Path a must-do walk

Langdon Beck village is just up the road from the eponymous youth hostel, where many walkers end up soothing their tired muscles after a day spent tramping the nearby Pennine Way

YHA Langdon Beck

MIDDLETON-IN-TEESDALE

There aren't many houses in the wild upper reaches of Teesdale, but if you're not sure which is the *Langdon Beck* hostel, look for the wind turbine. It – and the fact that you park your car by the reed-bed water-system – says much about the nature of what is probably England's greenest hostel. Hot water and electricity is provided, in large part, by solar and wind power, rainwater is harvested for the toilets, there's a toasty wood-burner in the lounge and an organic garden outside. There's also plenty of light and a modern feel inside the stone-built house, which has sweeping views across the North Pennine escarpment; it's only quarter of a mile off the Pennine Way, so long-distance walkers form a large part of the clientele.

YHA Langdon Beck, Forest in Teesdale, Barnard Castle, County Durham, DL12 0XN
☎0845 371 9028, ⊛yha.org.uk.
Price Dorms: 2x2, 4x4, 1x5 & 1x8 (all single-sex unless occupied by couple/family/group) £19.40. Two-bed private room £47, four-bed family room £63.
Facilities Kitchen. On-site parking. Bar. Games/common room. Garden. Lockers. Breakfast and dinner available.
Open Year-round. Check in: 5pm. Check out: 10am.
Getting there The hostel is about 16 miles northwest of Barnard Castle, on the B6277, six miles from Middleton in Teesdale.

Smart dorm-rooms (including one twin) have painted metal bunks, good carpets and cheery curtains. The one en-suite room, meanwhile, is great for families, with five beds and a spacious disabled-access bathroom. New tables and chairs in the lounge and matching crockery and glasses in the kitchen show an evident care for comfort and attention to detail. Pooped-out walkers will welcome the good-value bistro meals and licensed bar, or the nearest pub is just ten minutes' away.

Euro Hostel Newcastle

Old prejudices might die hard in places – Newcastle upon Tyne as a vibrant city-break destination? – but there's no question that northeastern England's major city is now a stylish cultural centre with a legendary nightlife to boot. Spanking new *Euro Hostel Newcastle* runs with the times, pitching itself firmly at the leisure and weekend market (there's a good-time designer bar on the premises) while offering flexible – and flexibly priced – en-suite accommodation that can cater for single travellers just as easily as large families. Rooms are sleek, budget-chic – key-card doors, earth tones, wall-mounted freeview TV, and space-pod-style shower and loo – with the bulk containing a double bed, a bunk above and two other bunks. The cheapest beds are in eight- and ten-person en-suite backpacker dorms. Although the included breakfast is only cereal-tea-and-toast continental, you can pay for a cafeteria-style fry-up in the bar, and there's also a self-catering kitchen. It's worth remembering that Friday and Saturday night in Newcastle is party night and although the soundproofing is good, both from the late-opening bar and in the rooms themselves, there will be a fair amount of coming and going and some bleary eyes over breakfast. It's less full-on during the week, when guests are more likely to be families, tourists, business travellers and backpackers.

Euro Hostel Newcastle, 17 Carliol Square, Newcastle upon Tyne, Northumberland, NE1 6UQ ☎0845 490 0371, ⓦeuro-hostels.co.uk/newcastle.
Price 256 beds in 53 rooms, sleeping 2–10 (single-sex, unless occupied by couple/family/group), from £16. Private rooms for 2 adults from £29, family rooms from £50. Continental breakfast included.
Facilities Internet. Kitchen. Bar. Café. TVs in rooms. Breakfast, lunch and dinner available.
Open Year-round. Check in: 3pm. Check out: 11am.
Getting there The hostel is a 15min walk from Newcastle train station.

Newcastle's Swing Bridge (foreground), Tyne Bridge and Gateshead Millennium Bridge

Tomlinson's

Tomlinson's owner, Jackie Sewell, has travelled the world and it shows in her bright and buzzy café and bunkhouse situated right in the heart of the Northumberland National Park's most appealing town. There's the kind of feel and vibe here that is commonplace in countries such as Australia and New Zealand, but harder to find in the UK – a good-looking café downstairs (blonde wood, bright paint, classy bistro meals and real coffee), with contemporary-style bunk accommodation above featuring chunky wood furniture, leather sofas, snazzy tiled shower rooms and a useful little kitchen. The rooms aren't huge, though three out of the five are en suite and will do just fine for big families or small groups. It's very bike-friendly – the huge mountain-bike photos rather give the game away

> **Tomlinson's, Bridge Street, Rothbury, Northumberland, NE65 7SF** ☎**01669 621979,** **🖱tomlinsonsrothbury.co.uk.**
> **Price** Dorms: 1x6, 1x7, 1x8, all en suite; 1x2, 1x5, both with shared bathroom; all beds £20.
> **Facilities** Internet. Kitchen. Café. Games/common room. Tours. Bike rental. Breakfast and lunch available.
> **Open** Year-round. Check in: 3pm. Check out: 10am.
> **Getting there** Rothbury is 31 miles northwest of Newcastle, off the A1. There are regular bus services to the town; *Tomlinson's* is a couple of minutes' walk from the bus stop on the main street.

– with secure storage available, a wash-down area and bike rental direct from the café. The building itself, a converted nineteenth-century schoolhouse, overlooks the babbling River Coquet and makes a good base for exploring one of Northumberland's more individual towns. The long main street still has plenty of proper independent shops, including several traditional butchers, bakers and tearooms, while cycle paths and hiking trails snake out on all sides into the national park.

Simonburn

It's hard not to fall in love with Simonburn, a gem of a village in the bucolic North Tyne Valley, with its ancient church, old memorial cross and green, spreading trees. The perfect place for a traditional tearoom you'd think, and you'd be right – it's also called *Simonburn*, and tucked away at the end of the lane in its own gorgeous cottage garden. Owner Ann Maddison calls it her "piece of heaven", which she shares with guests in the form of three pretty B&B rooms. Facing out over the garden, they are lovely and light, with a style best described as vintage boutique: think creams and fawns, French country furniture, stripped-pine doors, dainty chairs and pattern-stitched bedding. All three share one

> **Simonburn, The Mains, Simonburn, Hexham, Northumberland, NE48 3AW** ☎**01434 681321,** **🖱simonburntearooms .com.**
> **Price** 1 twin and 2 doubles, all with shared bathroom £60, or £40 for single occupancy. Breakast included.
> **Facilities** Internet. Café. Shop. Garden. TVs in rooms. Lunch and dinner available.
> **Open** Year-round. Check in: 3pm. Check out: 10am.
> **Getting there** Simonburn is 9 miles north of Hexham; turn off the A6079 at Chollerford.

equally elegant bathroom, and bathrobes are provided in each room. The tearoom below is open daily and the garden is an absolute delight, with its swing-chairs, bowers, roses, nesting doves and bumblebees (*Simonburn* has won awards for the variety of bees seen here). There are home-cooked evening meals for guests, and rustic walks right off the property, and while it might seem utterly secluded it's only a twenty-minute drive to Hexham, thirty minutes to the bright lights of the MetroCentre at Gateshead, and 45 minutes to the wilds of Kielder Water and Forest.

THE LOWLANDS

Stretching north from tranquil towns that skirt the English border, the Lowlands covers an undulating swathe of the Scottish mainland. Though it's home to most of Scotland's population, much of the region is surprisingly rural in character: wild rivers crisscross the fertile farming landscape, while verdant green forests and shimmering blue lochs await exploration. History is everywhere – from the deepest mist-filled glens to the highest cliff-top castles – but this is also the heartland of a proud and modern Scotland.

At the centre of it all is Edinburgh, a city as famous for its comedy and culture as it is for its iconic castle. We've picked accommodation both around the bustling, historic Royal Mile and further afield, with options ranging from luxurious yet reasonably priced self-catering tenements to £15-a-bunk hostels. Then there's Glasgow, a gritty city of almost 600,000, where moody cocktail lounges and top-end curry houses now shape the social scene as much as the traditional Scottish boozer. There are run-of-the-mill hostels and guesthouses here, of course, but those visiting the city for the first time can find nuggets of true Scottish heritage at places like the National Piping Centre, which has a museum, a hotel and a restaurant all rolled into one.

In the Lowlands' smaller towns and cities, we've found quirky budget places that act as a perfect antidote to bland international hotel chains. There's the *Station Hotel* in Perth, for example, with its secret passage and rich royal history, and Stirling's *Willy Wallace Hostel*, where the youthful staff make partying part of the experience.

Visitors seeking the wilds tend to skip Scotland's south and, like the midges, head straight up to the Highlands. But away from the major urban centres, the Lowlands has plenty of bucolic appeal. In the area around Loch Lomond, walking, birdwatching and golf are the main attractions, and there's excellent trout fishing to be had at the Lake of Menteith, home to long-established B&Bs. Big, fresh-air adventure is never far away with mountain biking at Perthshire's *Comrie Croft*, a kind of hostel, campsite and farm lodge rolled into one, and horseback riding at Glenmarkie, an equestrian school-cum-health spa set deep in the Angus Glens. Those seeking tranquillity though will fall in love with the remote farmsteads of Lanarkshire and Stirlingshire, where guests can enjoy substantial home-cooked breakfasts and snuggle up to crackling log fires.

THE LOWLANDS

NAME	LOCATION	PAGE		REAL BARGAIN	TREAT YOURSELF	FAMILY-FRIENDLY	GREAT RURAL LOCATION	OUTDOOR ACTIVITIES	GREAT FOOD AND DRINK	DORMS	PUBLIC TRANSPORT
Aberlaw Guest House	Dundee	213	❸			✓					
Belford Hostel	Edinburgh	213	❾	✓					✓	✓	✓
Castle Rock	Edinburgh	214	❿	✓					✓	✓	✓
Comrie Croft	Crieff	212	❺			✓	✓	✓		✓	✓
Cross Keys Hotel	Kelso	219	⓲						✓		✓
Douglas Arms	Castle Douglas	211	⓴		✓				✓		
Elphinstone Hotel	Biggar	210	⓱								✓
Glenmarkie Guest House	Blairgowrie	211	❶				✓	✓			
Inchie Farm	Port of Menteith	220	❻				✓				
The Lairg	Edinburgh	215	⓬		✓				✓		✓
Loch Lomond Hostel	Arden	208	❽				✓	✓		✓	✓
Merryburn Hotel	Birnam	210	❷		✓						✓
New Lanark Youth Hostel	New Lanark	219	⓰	✓			✓	✓	✓	✓	✓
O'Neill Flat	Edinburgh	215	⓫		✓	✓			✓		✓
Piper's Tryst	Glasgow	216	⓮						✓		✓
Rennie Mackintosh Art School Hotel	Glasgow	217	⓯			✓			✓		✓
Rockville Hotel	Edinburgh	216	⓭								✓
Station Hotel	Perth	220	❹								✓
Willy Wallace Hostel	Stirling	221	❼							✓	✓
Wiltonburn Farm	Hawick	218	⓳				✓	✓			

From left *Inchie Farm* (see p.220); *Station Hotel* (see p.220) **Previous page** Edinburgh from Calton Hill

Loch Lomond Hostel

ARDEN

The western edge of Britain's largest lake is well known for its abundant wildlife. For centuries the forests here were prized by hunters, who came in search of deer. These days most visitors are content with walking, rather than shooting, which means you can still hear the occasional clatter of antlers as you wander through the woodland.

Even if you don't, you'll still have the opportunity to come face-to-face with a deer – albeit a stuffed one – at Auchendennan House, which was built on this huge estate in the nineteenth century. Turreted, magical and with glorious views over the loch below, it was once the country home of a hugely wealthy tobacco trader. Now it's a youth hostel, but it still has all the charm and intrigue of a beautiful pseudo-castle. First impressions begin with a single-track road, which winds gently up and away from the main road, before opening out onto a grand, fountain-crowned driveway. Passing under the stone archway, you enter into a wood-panelled entrance room, where a huge tartan rug leads the way to the dimly lit reception desk.

Loch Lomond Hostel, Auchendennan, Arden, Alexandria, Dunbartonshire, G83 8RA ☎01389 850226, ⓦsyha.org.uk.
Price Dorms: 6x6, 4x8, 2x5, 2x4, 1x3 £19.50. Rooms: 4 family rooms (3 with a double and 3 singles; 1 with a double and 2 singles) £115; 1 triple £60; 1 en-suite double and 2 twins, both £50.
Facilities Kitchen. On-site parking. Games/common room. Garden. Tours. Breakfast, lunch and dinner available.
Restrictions Curfew 11pm.
Open May–Nov. Check in: 3pm. Check out: 10am.
Getting there Trains from Glasgow Queen Street stop at Balloch railway station, a 25min walk from the hostel. By road, follow the A82 towards Loch Lomond until you see signs for the hostel.

Much brighter is the main stairway, illuminated by tall, lead-piped windows, which guides guests up past hunting trophies and lofty domed ceilings and into the great hall. It's here you'll find people staring awestruck at the portraits, elaborate plasterwork and carved wooden beams that give the hostel a real feeling of luxury. It's no wonder wedding parties often book the place out. You won't find a honeymoon suite here, though. The actual bedrooms are relatively basic, with high ceilings and standard-issue bunk beds. Some of them have views over the water, while others look out over the grounds of the property. Not that you'll spend a lot of time in the rooms when there's so much to see and do in the area – from playing golf to quad biking. For some visitors a wander down to the loch is quite enough exercise, but if you're feeling especially active you can take on 974m-high Ben Lomond, which rises dramatically in the distance.

A lot of guests self-cater in the sparkly clean kitchen, but if you'd rather not, breakfast and lunch can be provided, and soups, stews and vegetarian dishes are served each evening. The tidy and sociable dining room has enough seats for a healthy mix of families, walkers and backpackers. All of this is a far cry from the old days, when the huge estate attracted Scotland's rich and powerful – including Robert the Bruce, who, when he wasn't busy capturing castles and launching raids against the English, was said to have hunted hereabouts.

From top *Loch Lomond Hostel* overlooks Britain's largest lake; boats moored at nearby Balmaha

Elphinstone Hotel

Midway between the bright lights of Glasgow and the rugged beauty of the Scottish Borders, the sleepy market town of Biggar seldom figures on transient tourists' itineraries. But those who take time to discover its quaint little shops and attractions (there are six museums) usually leave with a smile on their face. The best base for exploring the town is *Elphinstone Hotel*, a wooden-framed coaching inn with a reputation for hearty and wholesome food. It's a little dingy in the restaurant, and the furniture's in need of an update, but a quick browse through the menu is enough to get your stomach rumbling. The range of pies made by the pub's former proprietor has a page to themselves, with everything from haddock to haggis acting as the filling. Stark, step-filled corridors at the back of the building lead the way to the guest rooms, with wine-red carpets and plump white pillows. There are coffee- and tea-making facilities on the sturdy wooden chests of drawers, and larger rooms have their own cosy U-shaped armchairs. Most guests stay for one night, but if plans for a new beer garden out back go ahead the *Elphinstone* could well find itself with visitors wanting to stay a night or two longer.

Elphinstone Hotel, 145 High Street, Biggar, Lanarkshire, ML12 6DL ☎01899 220044, ⓦelphinstonehotel.co.uk.
Price 1 single £48, 4 en-suite doubles £72, 3 en-suite family rooms (1 double and a bunk bed, or 1 single and a pull-out) £85. Breakfast included.
Facilities Internet. On-site parking. Bar. TVs in rooms. Lunch and dinner available.
Open Year-round. Check in: 1pm. Check out: noon.
Getting there Regular buses run to Biggar from Edinburgh and Lanark. If you're travelling from Edinburgh by car, take the A702 south until you reach Biggar.

Merryburn Hotel

The roads around Birnam are lined with guesthouses serving hearty Scottish breakfasts to the crowds of salmon and trout fishermen who visit this part of the country each year, and *Merryburn Hotel* is the prettiest by far. Sitting midway between the train station and the River Tay, it was once an ironmonger's shop and did a booming trade on this busy village thoroughfare. Today, guests are drawn from much further afield – and most are more interested in the arts, music and comedy that takes place across the road at the Birnam Arts & Conference Centre than in angling. Like the downstairs restaurant, the *Merryburn*'s bedrooms feel sophisticated, with cream-coloured duvets and – perhaps with a nod to the building's heritage in mind – dangling candelabras. Many of the building's original features are still proudly intact, from the the cone-shaped turret that overlooks the street to the splendidly high ceilings and tall windows, which help keep the rooms nice and bright; with all this space, light and vintage feel, it seems churlish to complain that not all rooms are en suite. Indeed, it's probably the last thing you'll notice after a night out at a performance or a full day fishing.

Merryburn Hotel, Station Road, Birnam, Perthshire, PH8 0DS ☎01350 727216, ⓦmerryburn.co.uk.
Price 2 en-suite doubles £80, 1 en-suite twin £80, 1 single £40, 1 family room (2 doubles) from £70; shared bathrooms for both. Breakfast included.
Facilities On-site parking. Bar. Garden. Lunch and dinner available.
Open Closed Christmas Day. Check in: 2pm. Check out: 11am.
Getting there The hotel is a couple of minutes' walk from the Birnam and Dunkeld railway station. From nearby Dunkeld, it's a 7min walk along the main road. Turn right when you see the Arts Centre.

Glenmarkie Guest House

Horseriding is what really draws people to *Glenmarkie Guest House*, a bright white farmhouse surrounded by the fragrant pine forests of the Angus Glens. With seventeen horses available groups of eight can ride together, making this a place ideal for and popular with hen parties. But don't let that sway your decision; couples come here, too, and enjoy the delightful spa treatments (including facials, massages and reiki) that are available just as much as a bride-to-be and pals do. There's even a hot tub, and after a good old soak friends can unwind together in a conservatory overlooking a paddock full of horses. High tea is on offer, or you can order a three-course meal complete with coffee and mints. Although the bedrooms aren't huge, they're almost as bright as the conservatory and have glossy white wardrobes, plus views over the rugged hillsides. If you're lucky, you'll catch sight of deer bounding across the land, which might give you an incentive to clamber out from beneath the soft white sheets and go out riding again. Despite the focus on things equine, there are plenty of other group activities well suited to such a remote and beautiful location, including fishing, trekking, cycling and birdwatching.

Glenmarkie Guest House, Glenmarkie, Glenisla, nr Blairgowrie, Perthshire, PH11 8QB ☎01575 582295, ⓦglenmarkie .co.uk.
Price 1 double £56, 1 twin £56, 2 family rooms (1 double, 1 bunk bed) £28 per person; all rooms en suite. Breakfast included.
Facilities Games/common room. Garden. TVs in rooms. Tours. Bike rental. Lunch and dinner available.
Open The riding school is closed Nov–April. Check in: 2pm. Check out: 11am.
Getting there A car is essential. From Blairgowrie, take the A93 north to Lair. Turn right onto the B951 and follow the road until you reach Glenisla. Take the second left after leaving the village and follow the track for three miles.

Douglas Arms

From outside, you might not even realize there are rooms in *Douglas Arms*. Sitting on the corner of a narrow street in the centre of Castle Douglas, and with a tired-looking white-and-green facade, it feels more like a late-night drinking den than anywhere you'd want to lay your head for the evening. Step inside, however, and you'll be greeted by a fresh-feeling family-run hotel complete with its own little gastropub. Pass through the bar area, where you'll see tourists taking on haggis burgers served with fried onions and coleslaw, and grab your key from the dinky little reception desk. All of the luxuriously modern rooms are at the top of the creaking wooden staircase, and from at least half of them you can look out over the town's cosy cafés and galleries. If you want to splash out, there's even a room with its own jacuzzi-bath, studded leather sofa and a four-poster bed draped in flowing white curtains – not bad for a coaching inn that dates back to 1779.

Douglas Arms, 206 King Street, Castle Douglas, Kirkcudbrightshire, DG7 1DB ☎01556 502231, ⓦdouglasarmshotel .com.
Price 4 singles £55, 10 doubles £85, 10 twins £85, 2 family rooms (1 double and 1 or 3 singles) £95; all rooms en suite. Breakfast included.
Facilities Internet. On-site parking. Bar. TVs in rooms. Lunch and dinner available.
Open Year-round. Check in: 2pm. Check out: 11am.
Getting there Regular buses run from Dumfries to Castle Douglas. By car, take the A75 south from Dumfries and then the A713 into the centre of Castle Douglas.

Comrie Croft

Heading west on the A85, rural Perthshire's flat plains are soon replaced by rugged hillsides tumbling down towards shimmering lochs. This is mountain biking and hiking heaven, but to explore these trails properly you'll need more than a day's visit, which means a place to rest for the night. *Comrie Croft* – a kind of farm, hostel and biking centre all rolled into one – is the best base you'll find. You can hire bikes here, of course, and then the choice of accommodation is pretty much up to you. You can camp in the fields behind the main building (or in one of the fire-heated *kåtas*, a type of traditional tent used in parts of Scandinavia), or go for one of the rooms inside. Alternatively, there are bunks in the eco-conscious steading (guests are encouraged to recycle), whose kitchen looks out over a sunny courtyard complete with its own sociable firepit and BBQ area. Families and big groups might prefer the nearby farmhouse, which has sanded wooden floors and views over the hillsides that had you gripping the handlebars of your bike so tightly. The sheets and mattresses feel a little worn, but after a day of cycling and a couple of drinks by the fire you'll probably not notice.

Comrie Croft, Braincroft, nr Crieff, Perthshire, PH7 4JZ ☎01764 670140, Ⓦcomriecroft.com.
Price Steading: 2 en-suite family rooms; 1 with double and bunk £45, 1 with double and 3 singles £63. Dorms: 1x4 (en suite) ▌£16, 3x6 £15, 2x6 (en suite) £17, 1x8 £15. Farmhouse: 2 family rooms, 1 with double and single £40, 1 with double and 3 singles £56; eight-bed dorm £15 per bed; all farmhouse rooms have shared bathrooms. *Kåta* from £13 each (based on 4 sharing).
Facilities Internet. Kitchen. On-site parking. Shop. Games/common room. Garden. Bike rental.
Open Year-round. Check in: call for time. Check out: call for time.
Getting there The hostel is two miles from Comrie and four miles from Crieff, just off the A85. Bus #15 runs from Perth towards Loch Earn seventeen times a day (fewer at weekends); ask the driver to stop at Comrie Croft.

Clockwise from left *Comrie Croft* is a good base for exploring Perthshire's rugged hills; the grounds; relaxing by the hostel's entrance

Aberlaw Guest House

House-proud and enthusiastic are two words that accurately describe Linda Livingstone, who runs *Aberlaw Guest House* with a real eye for detail. Many of the guests have stayed before (there are even some regular business travellers) and they're drawn in by the homely, naturally lit bedrooms and fresh Scottish breakfasts. Meat for the fry-ups comes from the local butcher, while the eggs are delivered from a local farm. The rooms are all en suite, with shiny-bright taps and toothpaste-white toilets. There's free wi-fi, too, and – unusually for a city – it's so quiet that you won't have any worries about getting a decent kip. From the moment you arrive at this spick-and-span home, separated from Dundee's River Tay by a busy main road, you'll find Linda is on hand to offer tips and advice on what to do in the local area. For first-time visitors to the sprawling city this can be a godsend, as it's not always clear where you need to go to find the best places to eat, drink and be merry.

> **Aberlaw Guest House, 230 Broughty Ferry Road, Dundee, DD4 7JP** ☎ **01382 456929,** ⓦ **aberlaw.co.uk.**
> **Price** 2 singles £35, 2 twins £60, 1 double £60, 1 family room £60; all rooms en suite. Under-14s charged at £1 extra per year of age; over-14s pay £30. Breakfast included.
> **Facilities** Internet. On-site parking. TVs in rooms.
> **Open** Year-round. Check in: 5pm. Check out: 10am.
> **Getting there** Aberlaw is on the A92, facing the River Tay. Head out of Dundee towards Broughty Ferry and the B&B is on your left-hand side. If arriving by train, it's a 30-40min walk along the waterfront from Dundee station.

Belford Hostel

Swing open the heavy red door at *Belford Hostel*, a converted Gothic church in Edinburgh's west end, and the first face you'll see is that of Sir Henry Wellwood Moncrieff, once minister of this parish. The surrounding walls are covered by the usual hostel fodder – posters, tourist information leaflets and cheap drinks promos – but Sir Henry's severe visage remains uncovered, staring back from behind the reception desk. The marble sculpture was part of the building's original 1888 design, which remains largely intact, and it's only when you step into the main nave that you'll notice bigger changes. Stark white internal walls have been erected, dividing the floorspace into windowless but comfortable dorm rooms, which have robust metal-framed bunks. Occasionally, you can hear the sound of travellers' voices echoing around the vaulted ceiling; this used to keep people awake, but "roofs" have since been added to the dorms, ensuring a good night's sleep, if not a unique view of the ceiling for those in the topmost bunks. Despite the lack of anything much to look at inside the rooms, you can still spot many of the original stained-glass windows from the corridors. And, rather unexpectedly, a quick hop downstairs reveals a sociable common room with pool table and games machines. It's all very popular with big groups, although stag and hen parties aren't allowed – a rule which Sir Henry himself would probably have approved of.

> **Belford Hostel, 6–8 Douglas Gardens, Edinburgh, EH4 3DA** ☎ **01312 202200,** ⓦ **hoppo.com.**
> **Price** Dorms: 10x6, 3x4, 2x8, 1x10, all from £14 per night. Rooms: 3 doubles and 3 twins (all with shared bathroom) £50; 1 en-suite double £60. Online discounts.
> **Facilities** Internet. Kitchen. Games/common room. Garden. Tours. Breakfast available.
> **Open** Year-round. Check in: 2pm. Check out: 10am.
> **Getting there** The hostel is a 5min walk from Princes Street and a 10-minute walk from Waverley station.

Castle Rock

Locations don't get any better than this. The super-popular *Castle Rock* sits right beneath Scotland's most iconic fortress, Edinburgh Castle, and is within easy staggering distance of the bars of the Royal Mile. Unfortunately this is no secret and, as a result, it's almost always chock-a-block with international backpackers. Unlike some of the Scottish capital's staid hostels, where common rooms are quiet and dreary, the emphasis here is firmly on fun and mingling with other guests. The dorms feel busy and lived-in, with clothes and towels strewn over a mishmash of metal and wooden bunks, and each bed comes with its own secure locker to stow your valuables in. If you book ahead, you can be a bit more picky about where you stay; the best rooms are spacious, with nice high

Castle Rock, 15 Johnston Terrace, Edinburgh, EH1 2PW ☎01312 259666, Ⓦscotlands-top-hostels.com.
Price Dorms: 21x8 to 18-bed dorms £15, 11x4 £73, 2x3 £60. Rooms: 7 doubles and 1 twin, all with shared bathrooms, £45.
Facilities Internet. Kitchen. Games/common room. Tours. Lockers.
Open Year-round. Check in: 2pm. Check out: 10am.
Getting there The hostel is on Johnston Terrace, right at the foot of Edinburgh Castle. Arriving by rail, walk south from Waverly station and turn right onto the Royal Mile. The hostel is a 10min walk ahead, and on the left.

ceilings (note that as this guide went to press, renovations were ongoing and that room layouts may vary from what's listed here). In the dining area, there's a table that seats up to ten people at a time. And at the far side of the building you'll find a washed-out-looking movie lounge complete with big, saggy sofas. Whenever the nearby pubs start seeming a little pricey, guests hang out by the hostel's pool table, or in the internet room, which has high-backed chairs carved out of jagged pieces of wood. The *piéce de rèsistance* is most surely the beautiful lounge and reading area, with ornate baroque-style armchairs and an inky-black baby grand piano. However, it seems like the aquarium might have attracted a little unwanted attention in the past – there's a big sign on the front reminding guests not to feed the fish.

Clockwise from left Edinburgh's Princes Street, as seen from Calton Hill; standing sentinel over Scotland's capital, the castle is far and away the city's most popular attraction; the lounge at *Castle Rock*

The Lairg

Luxury doesn't usually come cheap in the Scottish capital – especially if you're anywhere near the city centre. So the *Lairg*, an old Georgian town house in the West End, occupies something of a niche. It feels luxurious, but does without all the usual trappings of a top-end hotel; there's no restaurant for evening meals, and your bags certainly won't be picked up by a porter. The reception area is warm and inviting (albeit a little dark once the heavy, painted door has swung shut behind you), with carpets so deep you'll feel as if your feet are sinking into them. Wander deeper into the building and you'll find the too-small breakfast room, where bottle-green floor-to-ceiling curtains frame the big bay window. It's strangely sumptuous, but nothing compared to the bedrooms upstairs. In the best of these you'll find rococo-style double beds set against vivid sapphire-coloured wall coverings, vanity mirrors in silver frames and street-facing windows which allow light to flood in, while others have a firm, four-poster bed, or a fancy feature fireplace. Either way, if you can manage to ignore the sometimes surly service, it's unlikely you'll be left wanting.

> **The Lairg, 11 Coates Gardens, Edinburgh, EH12 5LG ☎01313 371050.**
> **Price** 3 singles £65, 12 doubles £70, 10 family/twin rooms (3 singles, or 1 double and 1 single) £90; all rooms en suite. Breakfast included.
> **Facilities** Internet. TVs in rooms. Breakfast available.
> **Open** Year-round. Check in: 2pm. Check out: 11am.
> **Getting there** The hotel is a 2min walk away from Haymarket station, and it's less than a mile on foot to Edinburgh Castle.

O'Neill Flat

It's been said the tenements lining Edinburgh's Royal Mile were some of the world's first skyscrapers. They still seem high today, but back in the seventeenth century, when most of them were built, they must have appeared huge. One of the few not to have had a kilt shop or pub shoe-horned in at ground level in this most touristy part of the city is Gladstone's Land, just a stone's throw from the castle and once the home of a wealthy merchant. Most of the plot is taken up by a tourist attraction showing what life was like here almost four hundred years ago, but follow the vertiginous turnpike staircase up through the front of the building to the top two floors and you'll enter a slick self-catering flat with superb views over the city's rooftops to Fife. It's relatively new, so you get an ultra-modern kitchen, an expansive sitting room (accented by a tasteful tartan rug, of course) with a flatscreen TV in the corner and more excellent views, this time over the Royal Mile. On the second floor there's a double and twin room, both with crisp white bed sheets and soft beige carpets, and a shared bathroom with shower. Most of the decor is unremarkable, but reminders of the building's past are evident, namely the original wooden shutters and some painted stonework dating back to 1617.

> **O'Neill Flat, Gladstone's Land, 477B Lawnmarket, Edinburgh, EH1 2NT ☎08444 932100, ⏁nts.org.uk/holidays.**
> **Price** The whole flat can be rented for short breaks (Fri–Mon or Mon–Fri) or for an entire week for £400; prices rise considerably during the Edinburgh Festival. Check the website for discount offers.
> **Facilities** Kitchen.
> **Open** Year-round. Minimum stay one week. Check in: 4pm. Check out: 11am.
> **Getting there** *Gladstone's Land* is at the top end of the Royal Mile, close to Edinburgh Castle. Trains into Edinburgh stop at Waverley station, a 5min walk away. Buses #27, #45, #42, #41 and #2 stop on George IV Bridge, a 3min walk from the flat.

Rockville Hotel

If the prices don't put you off staying in central Edinburgh, the lively nightlife might. *Rockville Hotel*, built onto the wave-lapped rocks of Portobello's seafront, is an excellent alternative for those who want a quiet night's rest. It's family-run, the ocean views are captivating and it's still only a 25-minute bus ride into the city centre. The coastline hereabouts was famed for its salt panning industry in the 1870s, and has endured the wearing action of twice-daily tides since long before then. This geological process has been a boon to guests dining in the bright and airy ground floor conservatory, which is just a few feet from the water. Similarly inspiring views can be had from some of the first-floor guest rooms, which have chandeliers dangling over black-and-white bedspreads. The showers are refreshingly powerful, and binoculars (hung by the window for guests who like to birdwatch) are a nice little addition, although you're best skipping the smaller rooms, built into the roof, which don't have views. Looking up at the lofty ceiling after a glass of whisky in the downstairs bar, you'll be glad you went the extra mile for some peace and quiet.

> **Rockville Hotel, 2 Joppa Pans, Edinburgh, EH15 2HF ☎01316 695418, Ⓦrockvillehotel.co.uk.**
> **Price** 1 single £50, 1 twin £70, 2 doubles £70, 2 family rooms (both with 1 single and 1 double) £75; all rooms en suite. Breakfast included.
> **Facilities** Internet. On-site parking. Bar. Lunch and dinner available.
> **Open** Year-round. Check in: 2pm. Check out: 11am.
> **Getting there** Bus #26 runs from Princes Street in the city centre to the layby on Musselburgh Road. The hotel is 100yd away along the seafront.

Pipers' Tryst

The haunting drone of bagpipes fills the air at Scotland's National Piping Centre, a quirky and free-entry tourist attraction just across from Glasgow's Theatre Royal. Inside the curio-filled gallery, which has a fascinating range of pipes on display, visitors have the chance to learn about every aspect of the instrument – from its key role in the clans' military conflicts, to the way in which reeds are fed by a constant flow of air, a process that gives the pipes their uniquely nagging sound. For some, five minutes in here is enough, but others get swept away by the music and end up swilling Scotch and local cider in the intimate bar next door. If you end up joining them, you could do much worse than checking yourself into one of the eight subtly Scottish rooms upstairs, decorated with tartan chairs and curtains. They feel modern, with clean white sheets and enough space to spread your belongings out, but they still have some of the trappings of old-fashioned British hotels. There are trouser presses by the beds, for example, and every room has its own coffee- and tea-making facilities – nice little extras that are seldom seen in most of today's budget city hotels. The breakfast that's included with the room rate isn't up to much, with only basics such as toast and cereals included, but you can pay extra if you need a fry-up to get over the previous night's indulgence.

> **Pipers' Tryst, 30–34 McPhater Street, Glasgow, G4 0HW ☎01413 530220, Ⓦthepipingcentre.co.uk.**
> **Price** 1 en-suite double and 7 en-suite twins, all £65. Single occupancy £50, or £75 for 3 sharing. Breakfast included.
> **Facilities** Internet. Bar. TVs in rooms. Breakfast, lunch and dinner available.
> **Open** Year-round. Check in: 2pm. Check out: 11am.
> **Getting there** The hotel is a 5min walk from Cowcaddens subway station, right in the city centre. Glasgow Queen Street station is 15min to the south.

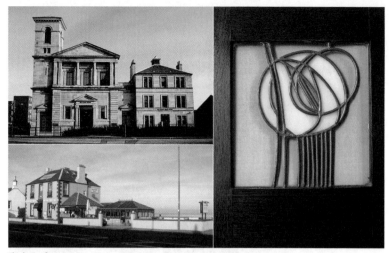

Clockwise from top *Pipers' Tryst* and the National Piping Centre; signature Rennie Mackintosh styling, on show at House for an Art Lover in Glasgow's Bellahouston Park; *Rockville Hotel* is a cosy escape from central Edinburgh's bustle

Rennie Mackintosh Art School Hotel

GLASGOW

The cheekily named *Rennie Mackintosh Art School Hotel* doesn't actually have anything to do with the Glasgow School of Art, a two-minute walk away on Renfrew Street, or indeed the famous architect it shares its name with. Still, this place has carved itself a bit of niche by offering tourists the chance to surround themselves with some of the shapes, colours and ideas that made Glasgow's own design icon famous the world over. When you clamber up steep stairs and enter the doorway, marked by three chunky pillars, you'll notice how skinny and cramped the hallway feels; it's certainly not the kind of design Mackintosh would have come up with. The rooms are similarly uninspiring; while totally comfortable, with wooden bedsteads and pillows like giant marshmallows, they're not quite in keeping with the overall feel of the place. However, when you wander around other parts of the building, which once housed two rich Glaswegian families, you'll pick up traces of the Art Nouveau style Mackintosh helped to popularize in Britain. An elegant white metal bannister runs up the side of the staircase, which twists gracefully up towards an impressive stained-glass skylight, and on the ground floor you'll find a pair of strikingly spindly occasional chairs and a well-stocked bookcase – perfect for those rainy evenings in.

> Rennie Mackintosh Art School Hotel, 218–220 Renfrew Street, Glasgow, G3 6TX ☎01413 339992, ⓦrennie mackintoshartschoolhotel.co.uk.
> **Price** 11 singles £35, 2 doubles £68, 10 family rooms (1 double, 2 singles) £80; all rooms en suite. Breakfast included.
> **Facilities** Internet. TVs in rooms.
> **Open** Year-round. Check in: noon. Check out: 10am.
> **Getting there** The hotel is a couple of minutes' walk from the Glasgow School of Art. From the airport, take bus #500 to the corner of Blythswood and Bothwell streets; from there, the hotel is a 10min walk away.

Clockwise from top There's no shortage of peace and quiet at pleasantly isolated *Wiltonburn Farm*; Kelso's *Cross Keys Hotel* has been playing host to guests since 1769; the old mill workers' house at *New Lanark Youth Hostel*

Wiltonburn Farm

HAWICK

About halfway up the mile-long track to *Wiltonburn Farm*, your mobile signal will drop out, signifying that you've made it to the middle of nowhere. There's nothing you can do about it, so you might as well forget the outside world and just start relaxing. It's easy to do, too. Birdsong fills the air. A steam trickles gently past the side of the track on its way down towards Hawick, a charming little riverside town. And all around you, there are sheep and cows chomping happily on the grass. By the time you've reached the farmhouse itself – a gorgeous, 200-year-old structure with high ceilings, wide doorways and deep Victorian bathtubs – you'll be feeling suitably de-stressed. The three rooms here are large, spotlessly clean and oozing traditional charm, with pictures of rural landscapes hanging from the painted walls and gorgeous hillside views spilling in through the large windows. And if, like many visitors, you trotted up to the farm on horseback or have a dog with you, don't worry – both creatures can rest easy in the stable outside.

Wiltonburn Farm, Hawick, Roxburghshire, TD9 7LL ☎01450 372414, Ⓦwiltonburnfarm.co.uk.
Price 2 doubles with separate, private bathrooms £65, 1 en-suite family room (1 double, 2 twins) £85. Breakfast included.
Facilities Internet. On-site parking. Shop. Garden. TVs in rooms.
Open Year-round, except at Christmas; call for exact dates. Check in: 4pm. Check out: 10am.
Getting there The farm is a mile and a half from Hawick. Walking or driving, take the A7 south from Hawick towards Carlisle for one mile, and follow the brown signs for Wiltonburn Country Cashmeres.

Cross Keys Hotel

From rooms high up at the front of *Cross Keys Hotel*, which overlooks one of Scotland's prettiest cobbled squares, you can just about make out the crumbling remnants of Kelso's medieval abbey, built in 1128. Over time, the town became more popular with craftsmen than monks, and in 1769 the old Cross Keys coaching inn was rebuilt as a proper hotel. Now, with flowers filling its window boxes and an elegant Italianate balustrade running along the top of its symmetrical roof, it continues to lord it over the town's main meeting place. Inside, the rooms have dark wooden furniture, and the beds are dressed in deep shades of gold. As you'd expect from a building this old, rooms come in different shapes and sizes, but, as a rule, those on the first floor are biggest. Back downstairs, there's a popular ground-floor restaurant with a fun mix of Scottish specialities and Italian classics. In the mornings it's worth trying the lightly spiced haggis, which attracts praise from the locals and confused looks from tourists.

Cross Keys Hotel, 36–37 The Square, Kelso, Roxburghshire, TD5 7HL ☎01573 223303, ⓦcross-keys-hotel.co.uk.
Price 12 en-suite doubles £80, 1 family room (1 double, 1 single) £90. Children sharing rooms with parents charged £15 each. Breakfast included.
Facilities On-site parking. Bar. TVs in rooms. Tour. Bike rental. Lunch and dinner available.
Open Year-round, except at Christmas and one week in early Jan; call for exact dates. Check in: 4pm. Check out: 11am.
Getting there Bus #51 from Edinburgh stops at Kelso Wood Market, just across from the hotel. Travelling by car, leave the A68 at Bonjedward and follow the A698 towards Kelso.

New Lanark Youth Hostel

The Unesco World Heritage-listed village of New Lanark occupies a spectacular location by the River Clyde. Founded in 1786 as a cotton-producing settlement, it eventually fell under the control of businessman Robert Owen, who believed in a better world for working people. His utopian settlement remains virtually unchanged – visually, at least – from those giddy days, and it's splendidly isolated. Most visitors come to see the village itself, a collection of stone-built terraced houses centred around a series of pretty watermills, but a small population of rare peregrine falcons has helped to make it a popular base for twitchers, too. The cheapest accommodation option in town (the only other choice is a pricey hotel) is an old millworkers' house, which also happens to be one of the SYHA's best-kept properties. The en-suite dorm rooms are immaculately maintained and equipped with modern bunks, while groups can take advantage of the hostel's catering service and order three-course meals throughout the week, including local dishes such as slow poached Scottish cod; self-caterers, however, are limited to a rather small, separate kitchen.

New Lanark Youth Hostel, Wee Row, New Lanark, Lanarkshire, ML11 9DJ ☎01555 666710, ⓦsyha.org.uk.
Price Rooms: 1 en-suite double, 3 en-suite twins, all £39. Dorms: 2x6, 7x4, 2x3, all en suite, all £16.75. 1 five-bed family unit £94.
Facilities Internet. Kitchen. On-site parking. Bar. Games/common room. Breakfast, lunch and dinner available.
Open Early April to late Oct; call for exact dates. Check in: 3pm. Check out: 10am.
Getting there Public buses run from Glasgow to Lanark station. From there, take the minibus (2 per hour) to New Lanark. Arriving by car, go past the car park at the top of the hill and drive right down to the hostel.

Station Hotel

In the golden age of rail, there was only one way for the monarch to get around. Even so, journeys could be arduous. So when Queen Victoria made the trip from London to Balmoral, she often stopped at Perth, an important transport hub at the time. Instead of stepping outside (one did not like to get rained on) she'd slip straight from the station and into the city's landmark hotel. Today, the passage that joins the two buildings is still there, but it's stacked with supplies for the hotel's extensive and ongoing renovations. After years of neglect, new owners have finally taken over and the establishment is recapturing some of its former charm. The grand wooden staircase leads to airy double rooms with soft and cosy beds, in which you should have no problem drifting off to sleep. Otherwise, the rooms feel stark and a little outdated (those bulky TVs!), and the floors remain a little creaky; whether this is meant as a charming anachronism or simply hasn't been ticked off the renovation schedule yet remains to be seen. Nevertheless, if you're in Perthshire to play golf, go hillwalking or, like Queen Victoria, are just on your way to the Highlands, the *Station Hotel* is quirky enough to warrant a night or two.

> **Station Hotel, 1 Leonard Street, Perth, Perthshire, PH2 8HE ☎01738 624141, ⓦperthstationhotel.com.**
> **Price** 5 singles £39–59, 30 doubles and 28 twins £49–79, 5 family rooms (all with 1 double and 1 or 2 singles) £79–109; all rooms en suite. Prices increase as week progresses; £10–30 supplement applies at busy times. Continental breakfast included.
> **Facilities** Internet. On-site parking. Bar. Games/common room. Garden.
> **Open** Year-round. Check in: noon. Check out: 11am.
> **Getting there** The hotel is next to Perth station. Free parking is available at the back of the hotel.

Inchie Farm

You won't find TVs in the rooms of this 250-year-old farmstead on the edge of the Lake of Menteith, so don't plan on catching up on your soaps. *Inchie Farm* is much more about enjoying the great outdoors. With the Trossachs National Park and Ben Lomond practically on the doorstep the farm makes an ideal stay for walkers and cyclists, while less adventurous visitors should get a kick out of owner Norma Erskine's cows, who often wander up the field to the farmhouse to suss out the guests. Norma has been offering B&B accommodation in this house for 30 years and certainly knows what she's doing, especially when it comes to breakfast. Your day starts with a stomach-stretching meal, which includes everything from porridge to eggs that were laid on the farm. Of course, after stuffing yourself you may just feel the need to head back to the somewhat dated-looking rooms (think flowery curtains and patterned duvet covers), both of which face south, allowing views of the surrounding hills to flood in; do your best to ignore the delicious homemade shortbread placed next to the coffee- and tea-making facilities. Better still, get a move on and take a gentle stroll down to the nearby lakeshore and ease into another day of exploring the stunning surrounding countryside.

> **Inchie Farm, Port of Menteith, nr Stirling, FK8 3JZ ☎01877 385233, ⓦinchiefarm.co.uk.**
> **Price** 1 en-suite double, 1 twin with private bathroom, both £56. Solo visitors pay £35 per night. Breakfast included.
> **Facilities** Internet. On-site parking. Garden.
> **Open** Year-round. Check in: flexible. Check out: flexible.
> **Getting there** The farm is on the B8034, a mile south of Port of Menteith; turn right when you see the big grey barn.

Clockwise from top Green and serene at *Inchie Farm*; *Willy Wallace Hostel*'s cheery common room; *Willy Wallace's* dorms follow the common room's lead, and are decorated with lively splashes of colour

Willy Wallace Hostel

STIRLING

Vibrant, cheery and a big hit with backpackers, Stirling's only independent hostel does a good job of giving budget travellers a colourful place to mix and mingle. So instead of the usual drab dorms, guests are greeted by airy, street-facing shared rooms with brightly painted walls and window frames. The bunks are painted blue, and daubed with the names of film stars, which means you could end up spending the night with anyone from Ewan McGregor to Mel Gibson, who played Willy Wallace himself in *Braveheart*. The film wasn't actually shot in Stirling, so most visitors make do with a wander up to the castle instead. The best thing about the hostel is its small but sociable common room, which does a good job of bringing everyone together. There's a free Wii for everyone to use, plus a film library that's heaving with DVDs and videos. The kitchen isn't too sparkly, though, and it's so small you might find yourself shoulder to shoulder with other visitors when it comes around to dinnertime; depending on your temperament, that means you're either in for a good laugh or it's a case of too many cooks spoiling the fun. If you don't fancy staying in, note there is a good selection of bars, cafés and restaurants to try out on nearby Barnton Street.

Willy Wallace Hostel, 77 Murray Place, Stirling, FK8 1AU ☎01786 446773, ⓦwillywallacehostel.com.
Price Dorms: 1x18 (mixed; best for groups), 1x12 (mixed), 1x10 (mixed), 1x8 (female-only), all £12–16. Rooms: 1 double £38, 1 twin (bunk beds) £36, 1 family room (1 double, 1 sofabed) £42. All dorms and rooms have shared bathrooms.
Facilities Internet. Kitchen. Games/common room. Tours.
Open Year-round. Check in: flexible. Check out: 10am.
Getting there The hostel is a 2min walk away from Stirling's railway station on Murray Place. Cross Goosecroft Road, follow Station Road to Murray Place, and the hostel is on your right-hand side.

THE HIGHLANDS AND ISLANDS

Lochs, whisky, mountains and monsters: whatever springs to mind when you think about Scotland, the chances are you'll find it here. Nature abounds – deer, grouse and red squirrels populate the hills and forests, single-track roads are far more common than motorways and Neolithic stone circles stand silhouetted against the sea.

From Perthshire's plunging glens to the towering sea stacks of Orkney, the Highlands and Islands are stupendously beautiful. And for those who love outdoor activities, the options are seemingly limitless. Near Killin's tempestuous waterfalls there are ancient clan burial grounds waiting to be explored. Elsewhere, armed with the right gear, you could spend an entire weekend kayaking through lochs or along the coast, or fly-fishing in one of the spectacular salmon-filled streams near Ullapool. Some walkers dedicate their life to bagging Munros (mountains over 3000ft high) like Ben Nevis, Britain's highest, which is often cloaked in grey clouds.

Unfortunately rain, the bane of the British holiday, is never in short supply. Indeed, Dalness, in Inverness-shire, bears the cross of being the wettest place in the country. But even with the often gloomy skies and infamous clouds of midges, people keep coming back. After all, it was rain that helped to shape these craggy landscapes,

giving them a misty, almost magical appeal, and there are some fantastic budget places to stay here. You can sleep in a converted railway carriage for less than a one-way trip on the Heathrow Express, enjoy fantastic loch views from an eco-friendly bunkhouse, spend the night in a glitzy Airstream trailer in the wild northwest, or cross a wobbly footbridge to an unofficial micro-nation in Wester Ross.

There's lots of traditional accommodation too – especially in cities like Inverness and Aberdeen – and our selection across the chapter features a fairly equal mix of B&Bs and hostels. The places we've listed in the south, around Perthshire and Argyll, are often easily accessible from Edinburgh and Glasgow. As you push north past the Great Glen and the mighty Cairngorms, the roads get slower and the rail network thinner, but the landscape becomes ever more enthralling, with perhaps the most exhilarating views in Britain. The Scottish Islands have some splendidly isolated places to stay, and are accessible via ferries, flights or – in the case of Skye – a bridge from the mainland. Here, it's gazing out across the vast and swirling seas that feels most rewarding, with wind-beaten bunkhouses and bothies putting you just steps from the crowd-free beaches.

THE HIGHLANDS AND ISLANDS

NAME	LOCATION	PAGE		REAL BARGAIN	TREAT YOURSELF	FAMILY-FRIENDLY	GREAT RURAL LOCATION	OUTDOOR ACTIVITIES	GREAT FOOD AND DRINK	DORMS	PUBLIC TRANSPORT
Aird Hill	Gairloch	230	15		✓	✓	✓	✓			
Am Bothan	Harris	232	12				✓	✓		✓	
Badrallach	Dundonnel	227	13		✓		✓	✓			
Barn Westray	Orkney	240	1	✓		✓					✓
Bazpacker's Hostel	Inverness	234	19							✓	✓
Bellavista	Orkney	241	3	✓							
Ben Nevis Inn	Fort William	229	25				✓	✓	✓		
Birsay Hostel	Orkney	242	2				✓	✓	✓		
Braemore Square Country House	Ullapool	249	14				✓	✓			
Broadford Backpackers Hostel	Skye	246	22							✓	✓
Brown's Hostel	Orkney	243	4	✓						✓	✓
Bunrannaoch House	Kinloch Rannoch	236	27				✓		✓		
Butler's Guest House	Aberdeen	226	23						✓		✓
The Ceilidh Place	Ullapool	249	10						✓	✓	✓
Culdees Bunkhouse	Fearnan	228	30				✓	✓	✓		
Dervaig Bunkrooms	Mull	238	29	✓			✓		✓	✓	
Dry Island	Gairloch	231	16			✓	✓	✓			
Falls of Dochart Inn	Killin	236	32		✓		✓	✓			
Galson Farm	Lewis	237	7	✓			✓			✓	
John O'Groats Hostel	John O'Groats	235	6					✓		✓	✓
Leumadair Guest House	Lewis	237	8				✓		✓		
Loch Ness Backpackers Lodge	Drumnadrochit	227	21	✓		✓	✓	✓		✓	
Loch Tummel Inn	Strathtummel	248	26		✓		✓	✓			
Ness Bank Guest House	Inverness	235	20						✓		✓
Orca Hotel	Orkney	243	5						✓		✓
Rua Reidh Lighthouse	Gairloch	231	11			✓	✓	✓		✓	
Sleeperzzz	Pittentrail	244	9	✓		✓			✓	✓	✓
Stein Inn	Skye	246	18				✓	✓			
Strumhor	Oban	239	31	✓							✓
Tobermory Hostel	Mull	238	28	✓					✓	✓	✓
Uig Hostel	Skye	247	17				✓	✓	✓	✓	✓
Woodend Chalet Holidays	Royal Deeside	245	24			✓	✓	✓			

Previous page Marram grass and beach near Luskentyre, Harris

Butler's Guest House

ABERDEEN

If you're planning a weekend amid the galleries and theatres, striking Victorian architecture and oil money of the Granite City, you could easily kiss goodbye to £100 a night. But look closely and there are still cheaper, family-run B&Bs in the centre that offer the kind of service that's hard to find at big chain hotels. One of the best is *Butler's* – an elegant stone-built town house on a quiet street that's edged by wrought-iron railings – which has a fantastic selection of different-sized rooms, some with en-suite bathrooms and some with shared facilities. The interiors are flowery, with large stretches of pink and green running through the building, but it's all so well cared for by the friendly owners that it feels classic rather than old-fashioned. This is helped by the fact that the bedrooms are nice and airy, with free wi-fi, fluffy bathrobes and TVs. Breakfast is a big deal at *Butler's* and although fruit, cereals and drinks are included in the room rate, it's worth paying the £5 supplement for the cooked breakfast. In addition to all the usuals, you can try local specialities such as the Aberdeen brose – porridge mixed with whisky and honey.

Butler's Guest House, 122 Crown Street, Aberdeen, Aberdeenshire, AB11 6HJ ☎01224 212411, ⓦbutlersguesthouse. com.
Price En-suite rooms: 5 singles £57.50, 3 doubles £65, 3 twins £65, 2 family rooms with either a double or a single, or three singles £32.50 per adult (25 percent discount for children 2–12). Rooms with shared bathroom: 5 singles £40, 1 double £55. LIght breakfast included.
Facilities Internet. Garden. TVs in rooms.
Open Year-round. Check in: noon. Check out: 11am.
Getting there *Butler's Guest House* is on Crown Street, a 5min walk from Aberdeen Station. To reach the hotel, exit the station onto College Street and then head west up Marywell Street. Take the second right, and the guesthouse will be on the right-hand side.

Aberdeen's Castlegate, with the Mercat Cross and the grandiose facade of the Town House in the background

Loch Ness Backpackers Lodge

If you're looking for an inexpensive and sociable base for Nessie spotting, you'd be hard pressed to do any better than this friendly hostel a few minutes' walk from the famed loch's shores. Sure, the six- and seven-bed dorms in either the charmingly rustic old farmhouse or adjacent barn can feel quite cramped. But there is a bar – something very few places at the budget end of the market can offer – and the toasty-warm lounge area is the ideal place to rest up after a day of horseriding, mountain biking or fishing. There are two self-catering kitchens, too, giving you more space to eat on the cheap. Other extras include a massage service provided by a local specialist, a great outdoor BBQ area, and a huge map, hand-drawn in chalk, that describes what's on offer in the surrounding villages. The hostel also offers family rooms with a mixture of double and single beds, and there's even a private double room, although it's frequently booked out. There's no guarantee you'll spot any monsters though – except for the huge green Nessie painted on the outside wall.

Loch Ness Backpackers Lodge, Coiltie Farmhouse, East Lewiston, Drumnadrochit, Inverness-shire, IV63 6UJ ☎01456 450807, ⓦlochness -backpackers.com.

Price Dorms: 3x6, 2x7, both £17 per person. Rooms: 2 family rooms £70 (1 with 1 double and 2 singles, and 1 with 1 double and 3 singles; discounts available for those with children), 1 double £38. All dorms and rooms have shared bathrooms. Third night free in winter (late Oct–April).

Facilities Internet. Kitchen. On-site parking. Bar. Games/common room. Garden.

Open Open year-round. Check in: flexible. Check out: 10am.

Getting there The hostel is in East Lewiston, just off the A82. From Inverness, take bus #19 to Drumnadrochit; ask the driver to drop you at Lewiston.

Badrallach

The area south of Loch Broom is a wild, wet and handsome place. Even in the middle of summer, campers can expect to get drenched a couple of times. No surprise then that Badrallach's most luxurious "outdoor" option – a gleaming silver Airstream trailer – is usually booked up for months in advance. According to welcoming owners Mick and Ali Stott, who offer everything from tent pitches to bothy accommodation in this remote Highland valley, it's one of only a handful available for rent in Britain. The sofas are real leather and the sinks ceramic; then of course there's the bed – a proper double, surrounded on three sides by windows that overlook the steep slopes of the Scoraig Peninsula. There's also a complete kitchen, unless you'd prefer to pop over to the Stotts' spectacular glass-and-timber eco-house for your meals. Those who do without the trailer can set up a tent or stay in the simple, £6-a-night bothy or the Stotts' cottage – built inside a reclaimed stone building and lit by gas lamps.

Badrallach, Croft 9, Badrallach, Dundonnel, Ross-shire, IV23 2QP ☎01854 633281, ⓦbadrallach.com.

Price "Airstream" (double) £40 per person (£20 for under-16s). "Caravan" (double) £45. "Bothy" £6. Cottage (sleeps 4) £340 per week.

Facilities Kitchen facilities. On-site parking. Garden. Breakfast and dinner available.

Open Year-round. Minimum stay in cottage one week in high season, 3 days in low season. Check in: call for time. Check out: call for time.

Getting there Badrallach is 30 miles from Ullapool. Follow the A835 south from Ullapool for 12 miles, then turn right onto the A832. When you reach Dundonnell House, veer right and follow the track for 4.5 miles. Take a left at the junction, and the site is on your left.

Loch Tay forms a lovely backdrop to eco-friendly *Culdees Bunkhouse*

Culdees Bunkhouse

FEARNAN

Plenty of places claim to be green. There aren't many, however, that can be working as hard for the planet as *Culdees Bunkhouse*, on the edge of majestic Loch Tay, where eco-conscious bunk rooms cling to the emerald hillside. A charitable project, *Culdees'* aim is to educate people about environmental issues and eventually become a fully self-sufficient eco-village.

The 124-acre site is still very much a work in progress, but the location is undeniably fantastic, with big moody skies reflected in the mirror-smooth loch. Guests stay in either the stone-built bunkhouse, which has shared bathrooms and pine bunk beds, or in the attached farmhouse which has private rooms. Either way, you'll find rooms that are simple but cheery. There are two spacious kitchens, plus a peaceful sitting room with a vast collection of books, videos and DVDs. Artistic types will love the music room, with two pianos, guitars and bongos.

The entire place feels rustic, tatty even, but with twelve Munros within walking distance, it's easy to enjoy the great outdoors. In the garden there's a meditation yurt, a dusty barn where visitors can chatter around a bonfire, and an impressive collection of edible plants and vegetables. Meeting people is easy too, with guests often teaming up to cook meals or play music together. You can even take reiki lessons – perfect for those days when rainy weather keeps you inside.

Culdees Bunkhouse, Boreland Farm, Fearnan, nr Aberfeldy, Perthshire, PH15 2PG ☎01887 830519, ⓦculdeesbunkhouse.co.uk.
Price Bunkhouse dorms: 4x4 £17 per person; whole bunkhouse rental £272 per night. Farmhouse rooms: 1 double £43, 3 family rooms (each with 1 double and 2 singles) £23 for adults, and £12 for children. All rooms and dorms share bathrooms.
Facilities Internet. Kitchen. On-site parking. Games/common room. Garden.
Open Year-round. Check in: 4pm. Check out: 11am.
Getting there The A827 runs southwest from the A9, heading through Aberfeldy, reaching Fearnan after a further 10 miles; take the second right and then the first left. An infrequent bus service (#91) runs from Aberfeldy to Fearnan on Mon, Thurs and Fri.

Ben Nevis Inn

Fort William, the self-proclaimed "outdoor capital of the UK", welcomes thousands of visitors each year. They come to gawp at the scenery, scale Ben Nevis (4409ft) and complete the epic West Highland Way, which snakes almost as far south as Glasgow. Most people choose to spend the night in the rather functional town, where dozens of snug B&Bs provide beds for weary heads. But if you just want to get into the hills, get back down, and then relax with a warm cuppa as you enjoy uninterrupted views back up towards Ben Nevis, you could stay in this bunkhouse, tucked away at the foot of the mountain in wild Glen Nevis. You'll be kipping in a basic dorm with space for 24, but the place has all the essentials, including its own kitchen and a small drying room. The downside to being so close to the mountain is that you're a forty-minute walk from town, although the inn does have a pub (closed Mon–Wed between Oct and April). The dishes aren't cheap, but there's a fantastic selection on offer, from fresh Mallaig haddock to Highland sirloin steaks. Time it right and you might even catch one of the bands that come here to play folk to the families, couples and ale-swilling ramblers that share the cosy bar area.

Ben Nevis Inn, Claggan, Achintee, Fort William, Inverness-shire, PH33 6TE
☎01397 701227, ✆ben-nevis-inn.co.uk.
Price 1x24 dorm, split into 3 eight-bed sections. £15.50.
Facilities Kitchen. Bar. Garden. Breakfast, lunch and dinner available.
Open Open year-round. Check in: noon. Check out: 10am.
Getting there From Fort William's centre and railway station, take the A82 towards Inverness. Turn right onto Claggan Road, then take the first right. Follow the road for a mile and the hostel is on your right. A taxi ride from town should take 10min, or you could walk in 40min.

Clockwise from left Mountain views from *Ben Nevis Inn*; the inn's simple interior; relaxing in the sunshine

THE HIGHLANDS AND ISLANDS ▌229

Tranquil *Aird Hill* has two comfortable B&B rooms and is a good base for hikes in the Torridon Hills

Aird Hill

GAIRLOCH

Few B&Bs feel as welcoming and relaxed as *Aird Hill*, a cutesy whitewashed farmhouse that sits atop a grassy hill overlooking the remote fishing village of Badachro. It's the tranquility that draws people to this isolated part of the Western Highlands, but the hospitality that makes them stay. Aird Hill is very much a home, so you might see kids' toys lying around the sociable living room, but care has been taken to make sure guests can have their own space when they want it, and the two hotel-quality rooms, which have big mirrors, crisp bed linen and solid wooden floors – using timber reclaimed from an old chocolate factory – sit next to each other in a quiet part of the house.

Owners Vanessa and Gordon Quinn escaped the rat race to live here, and are passionate about using local ingredients – the bread is made on site, the eggs are laid on site, and the bacon comes from the couple's own pigs. After breakfast in the sunny conservatory, you can request a map and a packed lunch before heading off for hikes up the dramatic Torridon Hills or shorter walks to the Fairy Lochs. If you fancy splashing out, check into Little Aird Hill, a lovely self-catering cabin with its own log-burning stove – perfect for those long winter nights.

Aird Hill, Badachro, Gairloch, Ross-shire, IV21 2AB ☎01445 741282, Ⓦairdhill .com.

Price 1 en-suite twin room £80, 1 en-suite double £80. Breakfast included. Discounts for stays of 2 nights or more. 1 self-catering cabin with double bed £450/week.

Facilities Internet. Kitchen. On-site parking. Garden. TVs in rooms. Lunch available.

Open Year-round. Minimum stay 1 week in self-catering cabin. Check in: 4pm. Check out: flexible.

Getting there From Gairloch, follow the A832 south along the coast until just after Kerrysdale. Turn right onto the B8056 and follow the road for 4 miles. Drive through Badachro, and then take the first turning on your right. *Aird Hill* is 300 yards along the track, on your left.

Dry Island

"Welcome to Islonia," says the sign on the floating bridge. "Beyond this point...Islonian passports and customs laws apply." As owners Ian and Jess McWhinney admit, it's all a bit of fun, but they really did have the tiny island of Islonia listed on an online database of micro-nations, and if you pre-book accommodation here (advisable) you'll receive your very own "passport" in the post. Before becoming a citizen, you'll have to choose between the island's two self-catering apartments. On the ground floor of the owner's house is the "Old Curing Station", which has a flowery lounge-dining area and views across the mountains. Then there's the delightfully tranquil "Creel Cabin", out on its own among the trees, with a private deck facing a secluded corner of Loch Gairloch; if you keep a sharp eye, you might just spot seals gliding among the white fishing boats which dot the calm, blue waters. Both apartments have their own kitchens, which you'll need after a day of fishing off Ian's boat (you can eat what you catch). After dark, consider strolling to the lochside village of Badachro to sample the local and lively inn's tasty real ales.

Dry Island, Badachro, Gairloch, Ross-shire, IV21 2AB ☎01445 741263, ⓦdryisland.co.uk.
Price "Old Curing Station" £395 per week, "Creel Cabin" £450 per week. No short breaks in high season; off-peak cost for short breaks £50 per apartment per night. Call ahead for exact dates.
Facilities Internet. Kitchen. On-site parking. Garden. TVs in rooms. Tours on offer. Breakfast available.
Open Year-round. Check in: flexible. Check out: flexible.
Getting there From Gairloch, follow the A832 south along the coast until just after Kerrysdale. Turn right onto the B8056 and follow the road for four miles. Drive through Badachro, and then take the first turn on the right; the car park for Dry Island is on the right after 500 yards.

Rua Reidh Lighthouse

The first thing you should know about *Rua Reidh Lighthouse*, anchored on a craggy stretch of shoreline in Scotland's far northwest, is that you can't actually sleep in the tower. But since 1989 – three years after an automatic system put the lighthouse keepers out of a job – it's been possible to stay in the adjoining house, a far more comfortable option. The choice, then, is between a good mix of double, twin and family rooms, or even a bunk room; most of these have high ceilings and allow bags of light to flood in, which helps to make up for the dated decor. There's also a sitting room with a supply of books, board games, a log-burning fire, plus views across to Skye and the Western Isles – perfect for those days when it's too blustery to venture outside. In fine weather, though, there's plenty of space for exploring – the lighthouse is three miles from its nearest neighbour and 12 miles from the nearest village. With sharks, whales and dolphins frequently spotted in these waters, and the free visitors' centre has a powerful telescope that lets you scan the horizon for signs of life. The owners also run guided tours along the seashore.

Rua Reidh Lighthouse, Melvaig, Gairloch, Ross-shire, IV21 2EA ☎01445 771263, ⓦruareidh.co.uk.
Price 1 en-suite twin £48, 1 twin with shared bathroom £38, 1 en-suite double £42, 3 family rooms: 1 en suite sleeps 4 £50, 1 en suite sleeps 3 £52, 1 with shared bathroom sleeps 4 £45. 1x6 dorm £13.50. Self-catering flat that sleeps 5 £595 per week. Breakfast (served Easter–Oct) £6.50.
Facilities Kitchen. On-site parking. Games/common room. Garden. Dinner available.
Open Year-round. Viewing room open summer only. 2 night minimum in the flat. Check in: 4pm. Check out: 10am.
Getting there A car is essential. From Gairloch, follow signs to Melvaig. After 10 miles join the private road leading to the lighthouse (3 miles). The track is very narrow on the edge of steep drops, and there are often sheep in the road.

Am Bothan

If you're partial to a bit of luxury, spending the night in a bunkhouse can mean letting your standards drop. You won't have any such worries at Am Bothan, a privately owned hostel on the windswept Isle of Harris, which has some of the cosiest, cleanest dorms anywhere in Scotland. Housed in a lobster-red building by the sea, the tall and spacious rooms here are flooded with daylight, and the wooden bunks are carefully padded out with warm blue duvets. Harris is a damp and sometimes frozen place, so these – and the central heating that warms the brightly painted rooms – could be a real friend come bedtime.

Before turning in for the night, guests usually mingle in the communal sitting room – a hip, open-plan space with Harris-Tweed sofas positioned around a sizzling-hot peat-burning stove. Here, among the countless nautical-themed curios – including splintered driftwood, bundles of rope and a rowing boat that hangs from the ceiling – you'll find people reading, playing music or eating meals prepared in the big adjoining kitchen. Settling down for meals at the huge wooden dining table, made from great slabs of polished timber, guests can take in views of Loch Steisebhat, a sapphire-coloured basin that spills into the Sound of Harris.

Hilly Harris offers reasonable hiking and some stunning (and usually bracing) beaches, but for people who make the trip out to this remote and weather-beaten place, it's these stretches of water that hold the greatest allure. Owner Ruari Beaton, himself a keen sailor, runs powerboat trips out into the sound and, depending on the season, there's the chance to see puffins, seals and even whales. The most popular tour is to the Shiants, a group of islands 5 miles east of Lewis, where a population of black rats runs riot. No one is certain how they got here, but given the treacherous state of the waters that surround the islands, there's every chance they came ashore with a shipwreck.

Am Bothan, Ferry Road, Leverburgh, Harris, HS5 3UA ☎01859 520251, Ⓦambothan.com.
Price Dorms: 3x4,1x6 £20.
Facilities Internet. Kitchen. On-site parking. Games/common room. Garden.
Open Year-round. Check in: noon. Check out: flexible.
Getting there Ferries (Ⓦcalmac.co.uk) connect Ullapool with Stornorway, and Uig (on Skye) with Tarbert – the A859 connects Leverburgh with both §Stornoway and Tarbert. Hebridean bus #W10, which has several departures a day, covers the route – ask the driver to stop when you see the bunkhouse. Car ferries from North Uist dock at Leverburgh Pier, a few hundred yards west of the hostel. Just follow Ferry Road east and Am Bothan will be on your right-hand side.

Stories from the sea can often be overheard from up on the internal balcony, the hostel's best architectural feature, which overlooks the entire common room. Up here, funky futons are laid out on the floor, making it a great place to unwind with a cockle-warming dram or two. If you're lucky enough to be sleeping in the attached dorm, you can simply swing open the adjacent door – featuring its own cheeky porthole – and lay your head down to rest.

Clockwise from top Looking out to Leverburgh and Northton – Ceapabhal hill is in the background; *Am Bothan*'s spick and span dorms; white sand and sheep at Luskentyre Beach, northwest Harris; the snug bunk house

Bazpackers Hostel

Some visitors to Inverness might argue the claims of the SYHA, which has gorgeous pine-coloured bunk beds and fresh blue sheets. But it sits on the edge of the city, a twenty-minute walk from the centre, and if you're only making a short trip, whether en route to the rest of the Highlands or to check out Inverness's galleries, museums and cathedral, small, welcoming Bazpackers is a better bet. This converted Victorian town house is just two minutes' walk from the castle, and ten minutes from the shops and restaurants of Church Street. There are some compromises – the two six-bed dorms aren't as fresh or spacious as those at the city's other hostels, and the private rooms look dated. But Bazpackers is small and friendly, providing plenty of opportunities to meet other guests, especially when it comes to meal times in the well-stocked kitchen. It's also comfortable and reasonably quiet, and you won't be paying a lot to

Bazpackers Hostel, 4 Culduthel Road, Inverness, Inverness-shire, IV2 4AB
☎01463 717663, ⓦbazpackershostel.co.uk.
Price 3 doubles £44, 2 twins £44. Dorms: 2x4 £17 (1 female-only), 2x6 £15. Self-catering apartment £80 (sleeps 4).
Facilities Internet. Kitchen. Games/common room. Garden. Lockers.
Open Year round. Check in: flexible. Check out: 10am.
Getting there From Inverness train station, turn left onto Academy Street, take a slight right onto Inglis Street, and then head right onto High Street. After 100 yards, turn left onto Castle Street, which becomes Culduthel Road: the hostel will be on your right. There's free parking 5min walk away – staff can advise.

stay here – a single bed in one of the dorms costs £15 regardless of the time of year. Dorm beds have their own lamps, some rooms have views out over the castle, and the sociable lounge downstairs has a lovely feature fireplace. A self-catering apartment with its own kitchen and private bathroom is available next door.

Inverness, seen from the west bank of the River Ness, looking towards the city centre and *Bazpackers Hostel*

Ness Bank Guest House

On the banks of the River Ness, this family-run guesthouse boasts all the extras you'd expect from a mid-range hotel. Every room at the nineteenth-century *Ness Bank Guest House* is a double, complete with a flatscreen TV, DVD player and iPod dock, and guests get free access to wi-fi. The pastel coloured walls, curtains and bed sheets may take a bit of getting used to but there are nice touches, such as the hospitality tray stuffed with Fairtrade tea bags and the detailed information packs on Inverness and the surrounding area pieced together by owners David and Judith Milne. Ceilings are high, and even if you go for one of the smaller rooms at the back of the house (only two out of the five rooms face the river), you'll still have plenty of room to unpack, put the kettle on and get yourself ready for a trip up to Inverness Castle, a five-minute walk away. If you're headed off further afield on a day-trip from Inverness, make sure to fuel up before you go with one of *Ness Bank*'s can't-miss breakfasts, freshly made with local ingredients, including eggs from the local farm, served in a cheery-bright dining room overlooking the water.

Ness Bank Guest House, 7 Ness Bank, Inverness, Inverness-shire, IV2 4SF ☎01463 232939, Ⓦnessbankguesthouse.co.uk.
Price 5 doubles: 2 en suite, 1 of which has an extra single bed; 1 with private bathroom; 2 with shared bathrooms. Rooms £60–80, depending on facilities and location within house. Breakfast included.
Facilities Internet. Garden. TVs in rooms.
Open Year round. Check in: 4pm. Check out: 10am.
Getting there The guesthouse in on Ness Bank, right by the riverfront, about a 10min walk from Inverness Station. Leave the station, heading southwest toward the river, then follow Castle Road southeast until it joins Ness Bank; the guesthouse is on the left.

John O'Groats Youth Hostel

To most visitors, John O' Groats comes as a bit of a disappointment. Bar a few tacky souvenir shops, there's not much else of any substance to keep you in the town. In fact, you're more likely to enjoy your time in the area if you head directly for the rather misleadingly named *John O'Groats Youth Hostel*, which is three miles from the actual village. For starters, it's less expensive an accommodation option than most central places and it has the cosy feel of a small private house. The other big advantage, as you'll see on the approach, is that it has superb views over the Pentland Firth. Inside, brushed-steel bunks make the dorms feel surprisingly modern but it's the spacious twin rooms that are the real prize. Downstairs you'll find a roomy kitchen with private cubby holes for guests to store their food in. The lounge has a good selection of board games, while its soft green and beige sofas are the ideal place to sink into after a solid day of outdoor activity.

John O'Groats Youth Hostel, Canisbay, nr Wick, Caithness, KW1 4YH ☎01955 611761, Ⓦsyha.org.uk.
Price 2 twins. Dorms: 1x3, 1x4, 2x6 all £21.50 per person for adults and £16.75 for under-16s.
Facilities Kitchen. On-site parking. Games/common room. Garden.
Open Closed mid-September to mid-April. Reception closed between 10am and 5pm (no admission to hostel between those times). Check in: 5pm. Check out: 10am.
Getting there Stagecoach bus #X99 from Inverness to Thurso and Wick drops passengers right outside the hostel. By car, follow the A9 from Inverness towards Wick, then take the A99 to John O'Groats. Leave John O'Groats on the A836 and follow signs towards Canisbay. The hostel is well signposted.

Falls of Dochart Inn

The heart-warming image of a crackling log fire gets taken to a new level at the *Falls of Dochart Inn*, home to what must be one of the biggest inglenooks in Scotland. When the weather's bad, the temptation is to grab a glass of single malt and relax as Gaelic music is piped over the sound of lively chit chat, and look across the road to the eponymous falls themselves. If this all sounds a mite sedate, rest assured that this mountainous chunk of central Scotland is in fact quite wild, with more walking trails, lookout points and fishing spots nearby than you could ever hope for. Accommodation comes in the form of either a one-bed self-catering cottage tucked behind the inn, complete with its own kitchen and sitting room, or rooms above the bar. The latter are sleek and uncluttered spaces with views of the falls, and the best of them have four-poster beds, roll-top baths and luxurious hardwood floors. There's underfloor heating in the slate-tiled bathrooms and – this being an establishment that's fully aware of just how good its location is – there aren't any TVs to disturb your slice of wild Highland peace.

Falls of Dochart Inn, Gray Street, Killin, Perthshire, FK21 8SL ☎**01567 820270,** 🌐**falls-of-dochart-inn.co.uk.**
Price 7 doubles £80, 2 family rooms sleeping four £120. Cottage with 1 double £95 per night. Breakfast included.
Facilities Internet. On-site parking. Bar. Café. Garden. Lunch and dinner available.
Open Year-round. Check in: 2pm. Check out: 11am.
Getting there The Falls of Dochart are at the southwestern edge of Loch Tay, along the A827. Cross the falls using the single-track bridge and the pub is on the left-hand side.

Bunrannoch House

Bunrannoch House, a former hunting lodge and now atmospheric guesthouse in HIghland Perthshire, is a little tricky to find, given that it is surrounded by steep peaks, including the iconic Schiehallion (3553ft). Walkers and fly fishermen leave their boots and waders downstairs before heading up the original Victorian-era staircase to the guest rooms. Here, the splashes of floral decor feel dated, but the beds have soft white sheets and the walls of the building are thick enough that you won't have to worry about being woken by other guests. The best room for love birds is the en suite with an impressive four-poster bed, while the two big family rooms are ideal for couples with kids.

For those with a taste for Scottish cuisine, there's no better place to base yourself. The traditional air of the guesthouse continues in the kitchen; owner Ben Henderson shoots and butchers the venison that makes it onto the tables at the hotel's tiny licensed restaurant. Almost everything is locally sourced – from the wild salmon to the freshly caught pike – and there are plenty of vegetarian options.

Bunrannoch House, Kinloch Rannoch, Strathtummel, Perthshire, PH16 5QB ☎**01882 632407,** 🌐**bunrannoch.co.uk.**
Price 6 en-suite doubles, 1 en-suite family room (1 double and 2 single beds). £45 per person including breakfast, £72 per person including breakfast and dinner. Breakfast-only rates not available Fri & Sat in high season.
Facilities Internet. On-site parking. Bar. Games/common room. Garden. Lunch available.
Open Year-round. Check in: 2pm. Check out: 11am.
Getting there Kinloch Rannoch is off the A9, 21 miles west of Pitlochry – follow the B019 and B846. From the village's main square, head left over the bridge, drive past the country store and leave the village. Take the first right (after around half a mile) and the house is 50yd away on your left.

Galson Farm

On the wild and windy west coast of the Isle of Lewis, Galson is a working crofting village with views stretching far out into the swirling Atlantic Ocean. There's an edge-of-the-universe feel to the place, without a supermarket in sight, and you're more likely to hear Gaelic being spoken than English. For people from the city it's this feeling of isolation, with opportunities for whale- and-birdwatching right on your doorstep, that makes this remote location so appealing. At the centre of the village is *Galson Farm*, a tumbledown collection of stone buildings which house the local post office and two excellent places to stay. There's either an eighteenth-century farmhouse, which has two spacious and picture-filled guest lounges, plus a handful of guest rooms with plush carpets and sofas, or the back-to-basics bunkhouse, with its own simple shower rooms and nice pine bunks with storage drawers underneath, plus a kitchen for self-catering. For those without food, owners Hazel and David Roberts can provide meals, from breakfasts of sizzling bacon and eggs to lavish three-course evening meals.

Galson Farm Guesthouse, Galson, Isle of Lewis, HS2 0SH ☎01851 850492, ⓦgalsonfarm.co.uk.
Price 1 bunkhouse up to 8 beds and shared bathroom £15 per person. 1 large double £96, 1 double £84 and 2 twins £80, all en suite. Breakfast included. Group discounts available.
FacilitiesKitchen. On-site parking. Games/common room. Garden. TVs in rooms. Lockers. Lunch and dinner available.
Open Year round. Check in: flexible. Check out: flexible.
Getting there Caledonian MacBrayne ferries (ⓦcalmac.co.uk) run between Ullapool and Stornoway. Bus #W1 runs from Stornoway to South Galson every one to two hours (except Sundays). You'll be dropped on the A857; Galson Farm is towards the sea, a 5min walk away.

Leumadair Guest House

Most visitors to the Isle of Lewis swing through the small crofting village of Callanish, on the island's west coast, to visit the 4500-year-old Callanish Stones that jut out from the landscape like a mouthful of broken teeth. *Leumadair*, a working croft with views of the stones from many of its windows, is owned by the MacLeod family and is as popular for its evening meals as it is for its family-friendly accommodation. Surrounded by fields full of farm animals, the house itself is no beauty, but the four en-suite rooms have been purpose built and are well appointed. The twin room, with carpets featuring the MacLeod's own tartan, even has a bathroom adapted for wheelchair users – a rarity in these parts. Both family rooms have a double bed and a set of bunks, and there's a separate double for couples who want their own space. Stornoway, fifteen miles to the east, has plenty of places to eat, but when you can pack away three delicious courses plus tea or coffee for £20 before snuggling up in your bed, there's little reason to go exploring.

Leumadair Guest House, 7a Callanish, Callanish, Isle of Lewis, HS2 9DY ☎01851 621706, ⓦwww.leumadair.co.uk.
Price 1 twin, 1 double, 2 family rooms, all en suite, adults £35 per night, children 5–11 £10, children 12–15 £20. Breakfast included.
Facilities Internet. On-site parking. Garden. Dinner available.
Open Closed Christmas Eve and Christmas Day. Check in: 4pm. Check out: 10am.
Getting there Caledonian MacBrayne ferries (ⓦcalmac.co.uk) run between Ullapool and Stornoway on the Isle of Lewis. From Stornoway, take the A858 west towards Callanish, leaving the main road just before the village. Take the first right; the guesthouse is on your left-hand side after the church.

Dervaig Bunkrooms

When forward-thinking councillors drew up plans for a new community centre in Dervaig, a delightfully isolated village on the northwestern side of the Isle of Mull, they allocated a little extra space for visitors. The result is that those who now want to stay in one of the quieter parts of the island, where golden eagles soar high above the misty lochs, now have somewhere cheap to stay. There are two dorm rooms in the village hall, each with its own en-suite bathroom and solid wooden bunks. Guests can also make use of the village hall's kitchen, which is shared with the local "lunch club" and other community groups. Of course, there are often events on in the main hall itself, but whether it's a yoga class or a ceilidh, guests staying at the bunkrooms can usually join in. From the bunkrooms, it's 200 yards downhill to the *Bellachroy Inn*, the island's oldest pub, and you're within strolling distance of Loch Cuin, where otters and waders can be spotted in the water. Best of all, you're only a nine-mile drive from Ulva Ferry, where small boats run wildlife-spotting trips to Staffa, Iona and the Treshnish Isles.

Dervaig Bunkrooms, Dervaig Village Hall, Dervaig, Mull, PA75 6QN ☎01688 400491, Ⓦdervaigbunkroomsmull.co.uk. Price Dorms: 1x4, 1x6, both £15, both en suite. £1.50 heating supplement Nov–March. Entire bunkhouse rental £120.
Facilities Kitchen. On-site parking. Garden.
Open Year round. Check in: call for time. Check out: call for time.
Getting there Caledonian MacBrayne ferries (Ⓦcalmac.co.uk) run between Oban and Craignure on the Isle of Mull. Follow the A848 north until you reach Tobermory. Then take the B8073 from Tobermory to Dervaig. On entering the village, the bunkhouse is the large building on the right, opposite the bus station. Bus #494 to Dervaig leaves from outside Tobermory's post office several times a day (30min).

Tobermory Hostel

Tobermoray has been placed firmly on the map since its brightly coloured houses that skirt the waterfront became the home of TV's *Balamory* – the popular children's show. So if the idea of going to a remote Scottish island at first doesn't appeal to your little ones, tell them they get to stay in one of the show's big red houses. Even though the inside of the hostel is rather stark (and nothing like the programme) there are things to keep younger children entertained, including a TV room and a nature garden designed to attract wildlife. The dorms can be rented as individual rooms and those at the front of the building have views over the picture-postcard harbour. Unlike many hostels, the kitchen here is roomy, bright and very clean, so you won't be knocking shoulders while preparing dinner after a hard day of dolphin-spotting or *Balamory* tourism. There's plenty for adults to enjoy in and around Tobermory, too, from castles and country houses to charming tearooms – the only trouble is finding the time to see it all.

Tobermory Hostel, Main Street, Tobermory, Mull, PA75 6NU ☎01688 302481, Ⓦsyha.org.uk. Price Dorms: 3x6, 1x5, 3x4, 1x3 with shared bathrooms. Adults £20.75, under-15s £16.75. Small breakfasts (£3.75) and packed lunches (£5.50) available.
Facilities Internet. Kitchen. Games/common room. Garden.
Open Closed Oct–April. Check in: 5pm. Check out: 10am.
Getting there Caledonian MacBrayne ferries (Ⓦcalmac.co.uk) run between Oban and Craignure on the Isle of Mull. Minibuses are on hand to pick up passengers at Craignure and drive them into Tobermory. The hostel is on the waterfront.

Strumhor

The vast majority of visitors to Scotland's west coast dash past the mainland's seaside resorts and head straight across to the Hebrides instead. Connel, which lacks the fishing-port charm of nearby Oban, feels especially forgotten about. But there's more than one reason to visit this peaceful coastal town – including the spectacular, blood-red sunsets and some first-class sea kayaking – and it has some great-value places to stay. Strumhor, right by the town's loch-spanning cantilevered bridge, is the best by a long chalk.

Rooms are spacious, modern and brightly lit, and you'll find homely treats, such as KitKats and crumbly chocolate biscuits, next to the bedside tea-making facilities. Although the single rooms upstairs share a bathroom, that's more than made up for by the powerful shower, puffy-white duvets and in-room handbasins. Downstairs, the en-suite doubles have tall ceilings and are equipped with gleaming white bathtubs. Breakfast is a hotel-like affair, with an excellent little buffet table and made-to-order specials – try the blueberry pancakes drizzled in maple syrup. With a full belly, you'll be ready to take to the water with the owner's popular sea kayaking school. If you don't have a great deal of time here but still fancy a splash about, ask for a lesson on the tidal Falls of Lora, which are just across the road from the B&B.

Strumhor, Connel, Oban, Argyll, PA37 1PJ
☎01631 710167, ⍵strumhor.co.uk.
Price 2 singles with shared bathroom £28, 2 en-suite doubles £60. Breakfast included.
Facilities Internet available. Dinner available. On-site parking available. Breakfast available. Bar. Games or common room. Garden. TVs in rooms.
Restrictions No children under 6.
Open Open year-round. Check in: 4pm. Check out: 10am.
Getting there Strumhor is five miles north of Oban on the A85. Follow the road until you see the big metal bridge; the B&B is on the right, up a slip road. Connel Ferry rail station, served by West Highland Line trains, is a 12min walk away.

Clockwise from left *Tobermory Hostel* sits on the town's bright, iconic seafront; *Strumhor* is in peaceful Connel; one of *Strumhor*'s en-suite doubles

THE HIGHLANDS AND ISLANDS ▌239

The rooms at *Barn Westray* are a snug base for spotting sea birds and exploring Neolithic sites

Barn Westray

ORKNEY

Reaching the tiny Orkney island of Westray isn't exactly easy – you'll need to fly, or take at least two ferries from the Scottish mainland – so for people considering a trip the obvious question is: is it worth the journey? The simple answer is yes, thanks to the thriving island's varied landscapes and the warm family welcome you'll receive on arrival at this quaint coastal hostel, which has spectacular ocean views from every room. This is a hushed, peaceful place and, aside from a tiny heritage centre, there's little to see or do in the seafront village of Pierowall. But if you like your tranquility, it's an excellent base for a weekend of spotting sea birds or mooching around Westray's Neolithic sites. The large and spotlessly clean self-catering kitchen here is more like something you'd find at a country house than a hostel, and the small rooms are kept toasty-warm by individual panel heaters. After eating fish and chips at nearby *Pierowall Hotel*, most guests head upstairs to a long, brightly lit lounge area, which runs almost the entire length of the converted nineteenth-century barn. There's a TV and a well-stocked bookcase to explore, or you could just crash out on one of the sofas.

Barn Westray, The Barn, Chalmersquoy, Pierowall, Westray, Orkney, KW17 2BZ
☏ 01857 677214, ⓦ thebarnwestray .co.uk.
Price 3 twins with shared bathroom (1 with good disabled access) £32, 1 en-suite family room (1 double, 2 twin beds £50), 1 family room with shared bathroom (1 double, 1 single bed) £40. Whole barn rental: £150.
Facilities Kitchen. On-site parking. Games/ common room. Garden. Lockers.
Open Year-round. Check in: flexible. Check out: flexible.
Getting there Ferries (ⓦ orkneyferries. co.uk) run from Kirkwall on Orkney Mainland to Rapness, 7 miles from Pierowall and accessible via minibus. You can also fly to the island (ⓦ loganair.co.uk).

Bellavista

Just beyond the residential sprawl that surrounds Kirkwall harbour, a pebbledash house offers a cheap alternative to some of the town's more central B&Bs. It doesn't look great from the outside, but don't let that fool you; this is a bright and surprisingly modern place to stay if you want to explore the eastern half of Orkney Mainland, with its pebble-speckled beaches and its relics of world wars and Neolithic settlement. Run by a friendly mother-and-daughter team, its decent-sized rooms have sturdy wooden furniture and fresh, hotel-quality bed linen, while the tastefully papered walls feature art by a relative of the owners, and in the sparkly clean en-suite bathrooms you'll find little bonuses like power showers and heated towel rails. Some rooms even have a view of the surprisingly serene seafront, where jagged grey rocks lead down towards the water, although you might have to crane your neck to see it. Guests have access to a communal fridge and a microwave, so it's easy to fix a snack without taking the fifteen-minute walk along the seafront into the town centre, which has pubs, takeaways and a couple of decent hotel restaurants. Breakfast is a tasty affair, offering everything from Orkney cheese to home-made coleslaw, and the big lawn out back is ideal for kids who need to let off some steam.

Bellavista, Carness Road, Kirkwall, Orkney, KW15 1UE ☎01856 872306, ⓦbellavistaorkney.co.uk.
Price 3 en-suite doubles and 2 en-suite twins £60, 1 en-suite double £80, 1 en-suite single and 1 single room with private bathroom £35. Breakfast included (£5 reduction per person for guests who do not want breakfast).
Facilities Internet. Kitchen. On-site parking. Games or common room. Garden. TVs in rooms.
Open Year-round. Check in: 2pm. Check out: 10am.
Getting there The B&B is a mile northwest of Kirkwall town centre. If arriving into Kirkwall by ferry, turn left and follow the waterfront road for just over a mile. When you see the junction, stay left, and then take the first right. Kirkwall Airport is 4 miles southeast of the ferry terminal.

Bellavista offers seafront views on the outskirts of Kirkwall

Birsay Hostel

Apart from visiting the island's ghostly stone circles and Skara Brae, a Neolithic house that's older than the Great Pyramid, the main reason to stay on Orkney Mainland is to get up close with nature. Wherever you stay, there's a chance of spotting some weird and wonderful birdlife, but at plain and simple *Birsay Hostel*, in the northwest of the island, the odds are higher than usual. Sometimes sea birds swoop low over the grassy camping area out back, and it's only a 3-mile walk across to Marwick Head, a protected colony that's alive with the squawks of guillemots, razorbills and puffins. Bounded by low stone walls, the hostel itself is not nearly as old-fashioned as its moss-covered exterior suggests. The shared bathrooms feel fresh, and although the actual dorm rooms are quite tight, pastel-coloured walls and sky-blue bedsheets help brighten the mood. The six-bed dorm downstairs has dual-aspect windows, and is just across from the hostel's "study", where a vending machine dishes out mint humbugs and the like, useful snacks if you're exploring the sandy beaches to the west. For proper self-cooked meals, the huge dining area stuffed with info on local wildlife is just the ticket. There aren't many places to eat within walking distance, so there's every chance you'll get to mingle over dinner.

Birsay Hostel, Birsay Outdoor Centre, Birsay, Orkney, KW17 2LY ☎01856 873535, ⓦsyha.org.uk.
Price Dorms: 1x2, 2x4, 1x6, 1x12. £16.50.
Facilities Kitchen. On-site parking. Games / common room. Garden.
Open Open year-round. Check in: 6pm. Check out: 10am.
Getting there From Kirkwall, take the A965 towards Stromness for 8 miles. Join the A986 and then, at the village of Twatt, join the A967. Pass through Birsay and the hostel is on your left, just past the community centre. Stagecoach bus #6 from Kirkwall runs twice a day Mon–Fri, passing the hostel on the way to Birsay Palace.

Grand Marwick Head, 3 miles from *Birsay Hostel* and home to guillemots, razorbills and puffins

Brown's Hostel

Stromness isn't the biggest town on Orkney Mainland but, perched on a steep slope leading down to the inky sea, it certainly is a looker. The gables of the grey, stonebuilt houses face outwards along the harbour, which flourished in the eighteenth century thanks to the North American fur trade. Today tourism is the big money-spinner, and it's hard to find rooms in the centre for less than £50. One notable exception is *Brown's*, a family-run hostel right on the main street, which offers bargain rooms to a friendly mix of backpackers, business types and budget-conscious couples. Even in summer, you can get a bed here for £16. Perhaps inevitably, the place is a little rough around the edges, with shared bathrooms and a real mish-mash of old-fashioned furniture in the smallish rooms, but while solo travellers might feel cramped sharing a triple with strangers, the single rooms aren't much more expensive. And all the essentials are here, from free wi-fi and a well-equipped kitchen to – most important of all – that fine harbourside location.

Brown's Hostel, 45/47 Victoria Street, Stromness, Orkney, KW16 3BS ☏01856 850661, Ⓦbrownsorkney.com.
Price 2 singles, 3 doubles, 3 family rooms (sleeping 3), 1 triple dorm, from £16 per person. All share bathrooms. Special rates and discounts for groups.
Facilities Internet. Kitchen. Games/common room.
Open Year-round. Check in: call for time. Check out: call for time.
Getting there Ferries (Ⓦnorthlinkferries .co.uk) from Scabster, on the Scottish mainland, dock 5min walk north of the hostel. Walk down Ferry Rd, which turns onto Victoria St, keeping the sea on your left. You'll see the hostel on your right, just after the fountain. The hostel is on a narrow street, with limited parking nearby, but there are some free spots on the other side of the ferry terminal on North End Rd and Ferry Rd.

Orca Hotel

Stromness, the second-biggest town on Orkney Mainland, is a much more attractive base for exploring the island's stonce circles and neolithic villages than the capital, Kirkwall. The town has range of accommodation options, but *Orca Hotel* is your best bet. The pluses here are the en-suite bathroom and the in-room tea- and coffee-making facilities; the not-so-cutting-edge interior design – pink bed-side lamps and dated furniture – may be a bit harder to appreciate. Despite the decor, it's clear *Orca* is well looked after, as evidenced by its bright and cheery breakfast room, which feels much more up to date That's the other big advantage *Orca* has over a youth hostel: breakfast is included. It's worth stocking up on food in the morning, before exploring Stromness and its museum, which is stuffed with exhibits on the islands' natural history. There's a bistro underneath the hotel serving good-quality evening meals, and a clutch of decent pubs can be found just along the street.

Orca Hotel, 76 Victoria Street, Stromness, Orkney, KW16 3BS ☏01856 850447, Ⓦorcahotel.com.
Price 2 twins £52, 1 double £50, 1 triple £59, 2 family rooms £66; all rooms en suite. Breakfast included.
Facilities Bar. Games/common room. TVs in rooms. Dinner available.
Open Year round. Check in: call for time. Check out: call for time.
Getting there Ferries (Ⓦnorthlinkferries .co.uk) connect Kirkwall with Aberdeen and Lerwick; a separate route runs from Scrabster to Stromness. Ferries from Scrabster dock at Stromness Orkney Ferry Terminal, a 5min walk north of the hostel. Follow Ferry Road south for two minutes, then head right until you reach Victoria Street; the hostel is on the left, around 50m after the fountain.

Sleeperzzz

The railway journey between Wick and Inverness is one of Britain's finest, hugging Scotland's east coast for miles as it travels south towards the gaping Dornoch Firth. In all, the trip is more than four hours long and it's best when savoured, so tourists and railway buffs alike often choose to break the journey into two shorter legs. The quirkiest place to stay en route by far is *Sleeperzzz*, which has its own special train carriages available for rent and is just steps from Rogart station in Pittentrail.

You won't get rocked to sleep here – the hostel's old Network SouthEast carriages are on a raised siding wrapped by fragrant flowerbeds – but apart from the odd passing train the place is tranquil, so you shouldn't have any problems chugging off to the land of nod. Each "dorm" has a set of wooden bunk beds and a row of three original train seats, and there are teeny-tiny kitchens built into compartments at the end of each carriage. The beds are comfy enough for a night or two, but the authentic train interiors, complete with under-seat heaters and dark-blue upholstery, might not be to everyone's taste.

Sleeperzzz, Rogart rail station, Pittentrail, Sutherland, IV28 3XA ☎01408 641343, 🖥sleeperzzz.com.
Price 2 carriages that each sleep 8 across 4 two-bed compartments, plus a thrid carriage with 1 twin and 1 double. Showman's wagon that sleeps 2, plus a big red bus that can sleep up to 3. Adults £15, under-12s £10. Shared bathrooms throughout. Guests arriving by bike or public transport get a 10 percent discount.
Facilities Kitchen. On-site parking. Games/common room. Garden. Bike hire.
Open Year-round. Check in: flexible. Check out: 10am.
Getting there The hostel is just behind Rogart rail station, on the Far North Line, in the village of Pittentrail. Arriving by car from points north and south, take the A9 to the Mound, then follow the A839 until you reach Pittentrail. The train station is well signposted.

The best way to pass the time while waiting for the next morning's train to arrive is to rent a bike (for free) from the hostel and head out to explore the great trails that crisscross the surrounding countryside. Then, on the way back, you can stop at nearby *Pittentrail Inn*, which does a great line in tasty evening meals – just make sure you don't doze off for the second half of your journey.

Sleeperzzz's converted railway carriages are set among fragrant flowerbeds

Clockwise from left *Woodend Chalet Holidays*' playground in winter; there are red squirrels in the surrounding forests; one of the relaxed resort's chalets

Woodend Chalet Holidays

ROYAL DEESIDE

Holidaying with their family in Scotland and Europe, Ursula and Adrian George found that self-catering accommodation was often lacking in some way, whether it was the missing kitchen utensils or the silly rules about needing to bring your own bed linen. They decided they could do it better, and the result is *Woodend Chalet Holidays*, a small, family-oriented alternative to big outdoor holiday resorts such as Center Parcs. The chalets are surrounded by woodland and instead of a resort-style giant tropical swimming pool, the main attraction is the attractive grassy area at the centre of the site, which gives kids a safe and secluded place to play. There's also a games room that's stuffed with toys and a library full of books for little ones. Bikes are free to rent, as are cots, highchairs and booster seats.

While the kids get a kick out of exploring the forest (there's a good chance of spotting roe deer and red squirrels) parents can unwind in the well-equipped chalets, which feel like real houses with large bathtubs, leather sofas and proper double beds. The decor is more pleasingly functional than flash – but there are chalets to suit most families, from one-bed affairs to "luxury" units that sleep six, complete with wood-burning stoves and their own covered deck areas. Banchory, three miles away, has some decent, family friendly inns.

Woodend Chalet Holidays, Banchory, Royal Deeside, Aberdeenshire, AB31 4DB ☎01339 882562, Ⓦwoodendchalets .co.uk.
Price Prices based on 3-night stays: 2 one-bedroom chalets £240, 3 two-bedroom (1 double, 2 singles) chalets £240, 2 larger two-bedroom (1 double, 1 bunkbed) chalets £285, 2 "luxury" three-bedroom (1 double, 2 singles, 1 bunkbed) chalets £465. Five- and 7-night stays also availlable; no 3 or 5-night stays from July 2 to September 24 and Christmas & New Year.
Facilities Kitchen. On-site parking. Games/ common room. Garden. Bike hire.
Open Year-round. 3 night minimum stay usually applies for all the chalets. Call ahead to see if exceptions will be made. Check in: 4pm. Check out: 10am.
Getting there From Banchory, head west along the A93 until the road forks, then head right. Pass through East Mains, and you'll reach another fork. Turn left and then simply follow the road. The entrance is immediately after the bridge, on the right-hand side.

The Broadford Backpackers Hostel

These days, hostel standards are so high that you're as likely to be sharing with a family as a big group of backpackers. There are still lively places about, like this friendly, independently owned hostel in a former care home on the Isle of Skye that's a useful base for exploring the south of the island, including the grand, iconic Cuillin mountains. Don't start imagining big raves – the village of Broadford is a sleepy place best known for its serpentarium – but there's a cool, sociable vibe at this hostel, and guests of all ages are encouraged to get to know each other. In the garden there's a fire pit, where backpacker-tour groups usually spend the evenings chatting and sinking beers, and, if it's wet, people stay inside in the funky dining area or head upstairs to the sitting room, which has a TV and a couple of long brown couches. Rooms come in a useful range of shapes and sizes: there are private doubles, twin rooms and triples, plus a couple of six-bed dorms lit up by big skylights. Luxurious this place ain't, but it does have a bathtub, hot showers and a drying room, all of which are handy if you've spent the day outdoors.

The Broadford Backpackers Hostel, High Road, Broadford, Isle of Skye, IV49 9AA ☎01471 820333, ⊕www.broadford -backpackers.com.
Price 1 en-suite twin £47, 2 twins £47, 3 doubles £43.75, 2 family rooms (1 double and 1 single bed) £75. Dorms: 2x6 £18.75.
Facilities Internet. Kitchen. On-site parking. Games/common room. Garden.
Open Year-round. Check in: 11am. Check out: 10am.
Getting there After crossing the Skye Bridge, turn right and follow the A87 west towards Broadford. Pass through the village, taking the second right after the petrol station. The hostel is on your left before you reach the hospital. Stagecoach bus #66X from Portree stops at the hospital.

Stein Inn

SKYE

At any one time, there are around 130 different whiskeys (and a decent selection of cask ales) behind the wood-panelled bar of cosy, whitewashed *Stein Inn*, on Skye's northwest coast. During the winter the place is kept warm by a smoky peat fire, while in summer patrons step outside to watch the sun set slowly over glistening Loch Bay. People come for more than just a dram and idle chatter, of course; much like the rest of Skye, the area on *Stein*'s doorstep is a walkers' paradise, and there are dozens of routes to explore, including a 21.5km loop around the heather-strewn Waternish Peninsula. The rooms may be low-ceilinged in places, but all overlook the bay and are individually styled, from the cheery yellow walls and framed prints in "Ardmore" to the more muted tones and patterend throw rugs of "Lochbay". Mobile phones don't work inside the inn's thick stone walls – fitting for an eighteenth-century building – and there's nary a TV in sight, so you'll have to browse the small downstairs library if you fancy a quiet night in.

Stein Inn, Waternish, Isle of Skye, Inverness-shire, IV55 8GA ☎01470 592362, ⊕steininn.co.uk.
Price 1 en-suite single £47.50, 4 en-suite doubles (two of which can be used as twins or family rooms) £36–53 per person, depending on size of room. Breakfast included.
Facilities On-site parking. Bar. Games/ common room. Garden. Lunch and dinner available.
Open Closed Christmas Day and New Year's Day. Check in: 4pm. Check out: 11am.
Getting there A car is essential. From Portree, take the A87 towards Uig for five miles. Turn left onto the A850 heading towards Dunvegan, and then, after 14 miles, turn right onto the B886. Drive through Waternish and at the end of the road take a left at the T-junction. Head down the hill towards the water and the inn is on your left.

 THE HIGHLANDS AND ISLANDS

Eighteenth-century *Stein Inn*, home to peat fires, cask ales and plenty of hikers

Uig Hostel

SKYE

For a village of less than four hundred people, Uig gets its fair share of visitors. Many are just passing through, waiting for one of the daily ferries to the Outer Hebrides, but you can be sure the people removing muddy footwear outside the entrance to *Uig Hostel*, set high on a hill overlooking the bay, are less concerned about what lies over the water than what awaits them in the surrounding countryside. Although not ideally sited for early morning ferry departures (it's a 45min walk to the pier) the hostel is a good budget bet, especiallly for walkers. Nearby is the enchanting Fairy Glen, famous for its rocky towers and tufts of grass sprouting from cone-shaped contours in the landscape, while further afield the picturesque circular walk following the cliffs to Staffin beach (where dinsosaur footprints were unearthed in the 1990s) is also popular. The hostel used to be a maternity hospital and still feels quite clinical, but there are plenty of spacious "waiting areas" for guests to relax in, including a brightly lit sitting room. Rooms are a decent size and can be hired as private units – perfect for families travelling together. Come bedtime, you'll spend the night tucked up in a modern steel bunk bed, with clean sheets and thick duvets keeping you warm until it's time to begin the next day's adventure.

Uig Hostel, Uig, Isle of Skye, Inverness-shire, IV51 9YD ⓣ01470 542746, ⓦsyha.org.uk.

Price Dorms: 2x3, 1x8, 2x6, 1x4, 1x7, 1x5, all £17.50, under-15s £15.50. Adults who are not a member of SYHA or IYHF are required to pay £2 extra per person per night to cover a temporary membership pass.

Facilities Internet. Kitchen. On-site parking. Games/common room. Garden.

Restrictions Curfew 11.30pm.

Open Closed mid-Oct to April. Check in: 5pm. Check out: 10am.

Getting there The hostel is on the A87, half a mile south from the centre of Uig. From the pier, turn right and follow the main road for 1.5 miles, passing the church and the Uig Hotel on the way; the hostel is signposted, and at the top of a steep driveway on the left-hand side of the road. Buses travelling in either direction will stop at the hostel; ask the driver.

Loch Tummel Inn

Twisting high above the banks of Loch Tummel, the drive from Pitlochry to Kinloch Rannoch is one of Scotland's finest. And, if you're not too busy craning your neck to take in views of the mountains tumbling down towards the water, you might just spot *Loch Tummel Inn*. Built from chunky stone blocks and with pretty wooden picnic benches overlooking the water, it's a welcome detour for those en route from Inverness to Blair Castle, nearly 50 miles south.

When you step inside, running your eyes along a bar that's chock-a-bloc with real ales, it's hard to believe that this place was messy and neglected before the current owners took over. After some serious refurbishments, it's now home to some of Scotland's most charming loch-side rooms. Each one is spacious and uniquely cosy, with antique furniture and spectacular country views complemented by modern beds, which can be zipped and linked together to suit guests' needs. The pick of the bunch by far is Room 4, which has a beautiful feature fireplace next to its roll-top bath. Whichever one you opt for, you can enjoy classy pub grub such as country pate and steamed mussels in the bar, or make use of the two intimate guest lounges, where evenings are spent sipping whisky and getting lost in good books. Don't worry if you didn't bring your own; there are plenty in the hotel to choose from.

Loch Tummel Inn, Queens View, Strathtummel, Perthshire, PH16 5RP
☎01882 634272, 🌐lochtummelinn. co.uk,

Price 6 en-suite doubles £80. Families can use double rooms, but must pay a £12.50 supplement for each child. Breakfast included.

Facilities Internet. On-site parking. Bar. Games/common room. Garden. Lunch and dinner available.

Open Open year-round. Check in: 3pm. Check out: 10am.

Getting there The inn is 10 miles west of Pitlochry on the B8019. Go past the Queens View viewpoint and after three miles you'll see the inn on the right.

Loch Tummel Inn looks out over the gorgeous loch of the same name

Braemore Square Country House

It's the small things that make places special, and *Braemore Square Country House*, a stone-built former staging post near Loch Broom, has extras by the dozen. The two guest lounges leave plenty of space for lazing in front of the TV or stretching out with the newspapers that appear each morning. Walls dotted with photos of the owners and their family lead to a kitchen for guests and, as there is a washing machine here too, the only time you really need to make the trip into Ullapool, 10 miles away, is for extra food supplies. In the B&B rooms upstairs, chandeliers dangle over the tartan bedspreads and light carpets, adding a touch of elegance to the three otherwise quite plain B&B rooms. One of the strange features of this nineteenth-century house is its up-and-over staircase, which means you have to go upstairs to get from one side of the ground floor to the other. Any inconvenience is soon forgotten about once

Braemore Square Country House, nr Ullapool, Loch Broom, Wester Ross, Ross-shire, IV23 2RX ☎01854 655357, ⓦwww.braemoresquare.com.
Price 2 en-suite doubles £70, 1 family room (sleeps 3) with private bathroom £35 per person. Breakfast included. Also 3 self-catering apartments from £335 per week.
Facilities Internet. Kitchen. On-site parking. Games /common room. Garden. TVs in rooms.
Open Year-round. Self-catering apartments generally let Sat–Sun. Check in: 4pm. Check out: 9am.
Getting there The B&B is 10 miles south of Ullapool on the A835. As you travel along the road from Ullapool, look out for a large stone building on your right-hand side.

you reach the breakfast room, where tasty Scottish grub is made to order. There are 1.5 miles of trout and salmon fishing within the B&B's grounds, which means anglers needn't actually leave, and the Victorian suspension bridge at Corrieshalloch Gorge is just a mile's walk away.

The Ceilidh Place

In Ullapool, an appealing town on the shores of Loch Broom that acts as a gateway to the Outer Hebrides to the west and the free-standing peaks and stunning coast of Assynt to the north, *Ceilidh Place* has something of a reputation. Not just for its home-made soups and salads, which are delicious and very reasonably priced, but for its cool cultural vibe. The main building houses a great bookshop and a handful of pricey hotel rooms, each with its own hand-picked selection of tomes, while the clubhouse across the street is home to an intimate little live music venue. It's a fantastic place to hear proper Scottish folk music – new and old – and, rather conveniently (especially after a couple of sherbets), there are cheap beds to be had in the bunkhouse upstairs. Don't expect anything too cosy – the mattresses are a bit on the skinny side and the walls are painted a stark shade of white – but if you're just looking for somewhere to rest before

The Ceilidh Place, 14 West Argyle Street, Ullapool, Ross-shire, IV26 2TY ☎01854 612103, ⓦtheceilidhplace.com.
Price Dorms: 4x2, 3x4, 4x4, all £17, all with shared bathrooms. En-suite doubles in the main building start from £68 in the high season.
Facilities Internet. On-site parking. Bar. Shop. Games/common room. Garden. Breakfast, lunch and dinner available.
Open Closed for 2 weeks in early Jan. Check in: call for time. Check out: call for time.
Getting there Ullapool is at the end of the A835 from Inverness. *The Ceilidh Place* is 3min walk from the harbour, where buses from Inverness, Dingwall and Garve stop. Head left down West Shore Street, then turn right onto West Lane and you'll see the guesthouse.

taking the boat to Stornoway, or scrambling up dramatic mountains such as Suilven (2398ft) and Stac Poliadh (2000ft), you could do much worse.

SMALL PRINT AND INDEX

Rough Guide credits

Editor: James Smart
Design and layout: Diana Jarvis
Cartography: Stuart James
Picture editor: Jess Carter
Proofreader: Susannah Wight
Contributing editors: Charlie Melville, Harry Wilson
Managing editor: Kathryn Lane
Project manager: Nicole Newman
DK digital media team: Lakshmi Rao, Jasmine Kshetrimayum, Ravi Yadav, Pallavi Pandit, Pallavi Sherring
Production: Rebecca Short

Cover design: Scott Stickland
Marketing, Publicity & roughguides.com: Liz Statham
Design director: Scott Stickland
Travel publisher: Joanna Kirby
Digital travel publisher: Peter Buckley
Reference director: Andrew Lockett
Operations coordinator: Becky Doyle
Operations assistant: Johanna Wurm
Publishing director (Travel): Clare Currie
Commercial manager: Gino Magnotta
Managing director: John Duhigg

Acknowledgements

Thanks to our five fine writers, who trooped around Britain in weather fair and foul and dealt with perplexing XML forms and countless queries, and to the establishments they visited. Thanks too to Ally Thompson, who first proposed the guide, Mani Ramaswamy, who was closely involved with the book's set-up, Rob Mitchell, who provided invaluable picture assistance, and Tracy Smith, who worked on early layouts. Edward Aves was a great help with maps and tickboxes, Emma Dodd made vital last-minute checks, Jo Wurm, Lorna North and Becky Doyle all provided much-needed help with templates and Sonal Modha and Marisa Renzillo took in corrections when the going got tough.

Publishing information

This first edition published April 2012 by
Rough Guides Ltd,
80 Strand, London WC2R 0RL
11, Community Centre, Panchsheel Park,
New Delhi 110017, India
Distributed by the Penguin Group
Penguin Books Ltd,
80 Strand, London WC2R 0RL
Penguin Group (USA)
375 Hudson Street, NY 10014, USA
Penguin Group (Australia)
250 Camberwell Road, Camberwell,
Victoria 3124, Australia
Penguin Group (NZ)
67 Apollo Drive, Mairangi Bay, Auckland 1310,
New Zealand
Rough Guides is represented in Canada by Tourmaline
Editions Inc. 662 King Street West, Suite 304, Toronto,
Ontario M5V 1M7

Printed in Singapore by Toppan Security Printing Pte. Ltd.
© Jules Brown, Samantha Cook, Helena Smith, James
Stewart, Steve Vickers 2012
Maps © Rough Guides

256pp includes index
A catalogue record for this book is available from the
British Library
ISBN: 978-1-40539-102-3
The publishers and authors have done their best to ensure the accuracy and currency of all the information in
**The Rough Guide to The Best Places to Stay in Britain
on a Budget**, however, they can accept no responsibility
for any loss, injury, or inconvenience sustained by any
traveller as a result of information or advice contained
in the guide.
1 3 5 7 9 8 6 4 2

Picture credits

Images not listed below were supplied courtesy of the
establishments reviewed.
(Key: t-top; b-bottom; c-centre; l-left; r-right)
Front cover Courtesy of YHA Pwll Deri, in South Wales
Back cover (r) © Arcaid Images/Alamy
Introduction p.2–3 © Peter Barritt/Alamy; p.5 (b) © John
Morrison/Alamy
London p.8–9 © Pawel Libera Images/Alamy; p.10 (tl &
r) © Rough Guides; p.15 (br) © Rough Guides; p.17 (t) ©
Rough Guides; p.20 (r) © Rough Guides
East Anglia p.22–23 © Rough Guides; p.26 © Rough
Guides; p.27 (r) © Rough Guides; p.29 (b) © Rough
Guides; p.31 © Rough Guides
Southeast p.36–37 © Peter Lewis/Corbis; p.38 (tr & bl)
© Rough Guides; p.42 (t & br) © Rough Guides; p.45 (tr &
bl) © Greg Ward; p.48 (tl, br & tr) © Greg Ward; p.48 (bl)
© Rough Guides
Southwest p.52–53 © Guy Edwardes/Getty; p.57 (l) ©
Helena Smith; p.61 (bl) © Helena Smith; p.75 (l) © Kevin
Britland/Alamy; p.75 (b) © Ashley Cooper/Corbis
Midlands p.76–77 © Brian Lawrence/Getty; p.88 (l) ©
Ocean/Corbis
South Wales p.96–98 © Chris Warren/Corbis; p.107 (cl)
© Nic Cleave Photography/Alamy; p.111 © Liquid Light/
Alamy
North Wales p.118–119 © Realimage/Alamy ; p.127 ©
Richard Klune/Corbis; p.132 © Jeff Morgan 07/Alamy;

p.133 (t) © Peter Adams/Alamy; p.133 (bl) © Jeff Morgan
09/Alamy; p.133 (br) © Michael Austen/Alamy; p.133 (cr
& cl) © James Stewart
Northwest England p.136–137 © Alan Novelli/Alamy;
p.138 (tl) © Rough Guides; p.140 (r) © Helena Smith;
p.143 (l) © Nick Scott/Alamy; p.144 © Helena Smith;
p.146 © Helena Smith; p.147 (tl) © Paul Melling/Alamy;
p.147 (tr) © PBstock/Alamy; p.147 (b) © Joe Cornish/
Arcaid Images/Alamy; p.147 (c) © Helena Smith; p.149
(l) © Jon Sparks/Alamy; p.149 (tr) © Mar Photographics/
Alamy
Yorkshire p.150–151 © Superstock; p.159 (bc & br) ©
Rough Guides; p.166 (br) © Rough Guides
Cumbria p.170–171 © Chris Hepburn/Getty; p.184 (l) ©
Rob Hadley/Alamy; p.185 (l) © Annie Griffiths Belt/Getty;
p.188 (bl) © Craig Joiner/age fotostock/Superstock
The Northeast p.190–191 © Brian Lawrence/Getty;
p.199 (l) © Dave Porter/Alamy; p.199 (tr) © David Taylor
Photography/Alamy; p.200 © Dave Porter/Getty; p.201 ©
Graham Uney/Alamy; p.202 © Islandstock/Alamy
The Lowlands p.204–205 © Douglas Pearson/Corbis;
p.209 (t & b) © DK; p.214 (l & tr) © DK; p.217 (r) © DK
The Highlands and Islands p.222–223 © Patrick
Dieudonne/Getty; p.226 © Ian Dagnall/Alamy; p.234 ©
Joel Santos/Corbis; p.242 © Mark Ferguson/Alamy; p.245
(tr) © Clearview/Alamy; p.248 © nagelestock.com/Alamy
Small print and index p.250 © Rough Guides

Opposite The beach at Winterton-on-Sea, Norfolk

Index

Maps are marked in grey

THE SWISS ARMY KNIFE OF CAMPERVANS

LIKE A GOOD CAR TO DRIVE WITH MORE
USEFUL FEATURES THAN A CAMPERVAN

OPTIMUS PRIME

For Travellers' Adventures

FROM £20 A DAY!

xplore the UK and Europe's outer space!

 SPACESHIP FEATURES:

rge double bed | attachable back awning for 30% more space and ventilation | unlimited
leage | standard insurance and breakdown cover in UK and Europe | fridge | cooker and
oking equipment | water supply | seat-belted seating for 3-4 | DVD/CD player and ipod
nnector | self-charging dual battery system | access to unique Space Stations for travel
vice, local deals and DVD exchange! Pick up and drop off from London depot.

ACESHIPS ARE ALSO AVAILABLE IN AUSTRALIA AND NEW ZEALAND!

BOOK NOW!

call: +44 (0) 208 573 2300
From Australia call 1300 139 091
From New Zealand call 0800 772237
email: info@spaceshipsrentals.co.uk
or visit www.spaceshipsrentals.co.uk